Ruled Reading and Biblical Criticism

Journal of Theological Interpretation Supplements

MURRAY RAE

University of Otago, New Zealand

Editor-in-Chief

Ruled Reading and Biblical Criticism

MATTHEW T. BELL

University Park, Pennsylvania
EISENBRAUNS
2019

Printed in the United States of America

www.eisenbrauns.org

Library of Congress Cataloging-in-Publication Data
Names: Bell, Matthew T., 1977– author.
Title: Ruled reading and Biblical criticism / Matthew T. Bell.
Other titles: Journal of theological interpretation supplements.
Description: University Park, Pennsylvania : Eisenbrauns, [2019] |
Series: Journal of theological interpretation supplements series | Includes
bibliographical references and index.
Summary: "Examines how the gulf in interpretive priorities between ancient
and modern readers has been exaggerated, and argues that careful study of early
Christian reading practices suggests possibilities for re-contextualizing 'ruled
reading' for a postmodern setting"—Provided by publisher.
Identifiers: LCCN 2019029687 | ISBN 9781575069951 (paperback)
Subjects: LCSH: Bible—Hermeneutics. | Bible—Reading.
Classification: LCC BS476.B444 2019 | DDC 220.601—dc23
LC record available at https://lccn.loc.gov/2019029687

For Tim and for Ruth;

as Tim might say it, "Memory eternal!"

Contents

Acknowledgments

This project would not have been possible without the prayers, hospitality, encouragement, advice, and sometimes correction of several people for whom I cannot sufficiently be grateful. This book's first incarnation was as a Ph.D. dissertation. In the labyrinthine paths of the past that led me up to that time of postgraduate study various persons—too many to name in their total number—stand tall in my memory as road-markers and guiding lights, notably my mother Heather Rose, father Norman Creighton, pastor Michael Milano, and professors Janyce Wiebe, Scott Sunquist, Andrew Purves, Edith Humphrey, and Dale Allison. Doctoral study then commenced; gracious supervision was provided by two professors in Theology and Religion at Durham, Carol Harrison overseeing the writing of the first two chapters and Walter Moberly the concluding two. Each read draft after draft, always supplying the balance of encouragement and recalibrated direction due at the next step. The lessons learned from them overflow what I can represent in the course of this dissertation and, indeed, in any career I presently imagine.

Friends, too, have come alongside in the process. Especially during the first year of study, and then afterward, diligent prayer and timely friendship was extended by several denizens of Durham and by fellow graduate students in Ustinov College; among these, special thanks are due to Kathleen Johnson, Chris Nielsen and Nathan Paylor for their company and strategically applied interruptions and to the Ustinov Bible Study for its spiritual support. From that Bible study I am particularly grateful to Ben, Jo, Zultan, and Manush. After returning to the United States to study and write from a distance the intellectual and spiritual friendship of Tim Becker and, later, the House of St. Michael community which he led, was, for me, a fairly clear case of iron sharpening iron. Around this time, Alyssa Lynn agreed to be my wife, having surely no idea of the challenges of taking a young husband through the end of a Ph.D. To her and to our daughter, Theresa Joy, I am inestimably indebted—for patience, for love, for fun and laughter. Those early years of marriage and closing years of study saw adventure and misadventure, including the birth of one and the loss of two others while yet unborn, Irene and Bede, to whom I dedicated the finished dissertation. Finally, as dissertation writing began to end and transition to publication in JTI Supplements began, two longsuffering sources of spiritual encouragement joined the Church triumphant: my grandmother, Ruth, and my friend, the afore-mentioned Tim Becker. To them and to my Lord, who comforts me in their passing until the resurrection of the just, I dedicate this published volume.

A final note of gratitude cannot be omitted. Flaws in grammar and mechanics are nigh impossible to see when you have stared at a project for going on five years. Connie Licata, English literature and grammar teacher extraordinaire, took off a month's weekends to spot and correct mine—at the beginning of term time at that! I will never forget the Oxford comma, nor my proclivity to overuse scare-quotes, because of her patient and careful reading.

Introduction

Well Noah was a righteous man
  Livin' in a world gone wrong
God looked down and saw the mess
  And he had to confess . . .
    – "Noah"[1]

I think that there is a certain schizophrenic aspect to my own relation to the Bible. . . . I think there are these two very different sides to my relation to the Bible: one, my professional life; the other, a more private concern, interest and fascination with the Bible.
  – **Frank Moore Cross, in interview with** *Biblical Archaeology Review*[2]

The two quotes above, though manifestly unrelated historically and in what I might term their "plain sense," nonetheless involve, however indirectly, a thread of common themes. The first lines are from a children's song about Noah designed to mediate what Paul Ricoeur famously termed a "first naïvete" experience of scripture.[3] In that sense, it is what is commonly called a "noncritical" or "precritical" reading of scripture—reading that involves an attitude and stance that the academic guild associates with premodern readers, and, sometimes, with the act of devotion. The second quote could not be further from children's song in terms of genre. It comes from an interview of the noted Old Testament scholar Frank Moore Cross and the celebrated Jewish author and activist Elie Wiesel, conducted by Hershel Shanks of the *Biblical Archaeology Review*. Shanks has just asked each of the luminaries in turn how he relates to the Bible. Wiesel unambiguously describes his hermeneutic in terms of wonder, beauty, devotion, passion, and he understands Cross to be the same, whatever the Old Testament scholar may think of himself. Cross, however, demurs, at least at first. His is a split personality with a critical, scientific side and an uncritical, devoted one. Shanks interrogates this dichotomy to which Cross is surrendered

---

1. Georgian Banov and Mark Pendergrass, "Noah" (Sparrow Song, 1980).

2. Frank Moore Cross, "Contrasting Insights of Biblical Giants: BAR Interviews Elie Wiesel and Frank Moore Cross," *Biblical Archaeology Review* (August 2004): 28–36.

3. Paul Ricoeur, *Symbolism of Evil* (New York: Beacon, 1967).

1

and that Wiesel denies, and, in the process, a world is evoked that Wiesel admires openly, but which Cross keeps respectfully on the shelf—"the history of interpretation"—Rashi, the Talmud, and (for Cross) the early Church Fathers.

To Cross's self-professed schizophrenia there has arguably been a corresponding division, perhaps originally religious but later methodological, in the religious studies academy and allied fields. At issue is not simply whether to adduce or acknowledge the positions of past interpreters as a historical matter; on the merits of doing that there is no disagreement. Sections entitled "the history of interpretation" are standard fare in commentaries and exegetical research papers. Rather, the controversy has to do with the *stance* of the interpreter. How much cognitive distance should she maintain between her critical analysis of the text and other factors at play in the courtyard of her personality—ideological, devotional, and existential? How is that distance responsibly to be bridged, acknowledging with realism all the core elements, particularly when the text in question (and engagement of it) possesses religious or theological significance to at least the majority of its readers? The great, ugly ditch acknowledged by many in this regard is not, it seems, solely a gulf between the Bible's world and ours or even between those seminal interpreters from the crucial period of canon formation (with their immediate intellectual heirs) and modernity.[4] It is also, in a significant way raised by Cross, a chasm in the mental geography of the modern and postmodern biblical interpreter—even and especially the critical one.

I open this book with these paragraphs and with the paragraphs that immediately follow because the body of this book substantially concerns what at least certain streams flowing out of the premodern world think scripture *is* and, following from that, aspects of *how* scripture ought to be read. As illustrated by the conversation between Cross and Wiesel (mediated by Shanks), that premodern outlook is one to which many denizens of our age, modern and postmodern, feel awkwardly related. Before outlining this book and stating its thesis, we should spare some space to set the stage and acknowledge some of the ways in which that awkwardness has been experienced over the last century and a half.

---

4. Often acknowledged as the first person explicitly to name the "ditch" is Gotthold Ephraim Lessing in his essay entitled, in English translation, "On the Proof of the Spirit and of Power" (Henry Chadwick, ed. and trans., *Lessing's Theological Writings* [Stanford: Stanford University Press, 1956], 51–56). Lessing's concerns in the original essay are more philosophical than literary: he worries over whether and how the contingent facts of history might guide the intellect towards the ostensibly necessary truths of reason, his sense being that they cannot.

Navigating the Chasm

The Scandal of "Precritical" Exegesis

One scholar often echoed in relation to navigating Lessing's chasm is the nineteenth-century English divine, Benjamin Jowett, famously one of the modern voices who intoned the mantra that the Bible should be interpreted "like any other book."[5] Recent scholarship has (to my eye, sufficiently) acquitted him of the charge of implying the anti-theological or caustically anti-doctrinal attitude sometimes heard in the refrain.[6] Nonetheless, his rhetoric on the relationship between doctrine and exegesis does sound a distinct note:

> The office of the interpreter is not to add another [meaning], but to recover [the] original one; the meaning, that is, of the words as they first struck on the ears or flashed before the eyes of those who heard and read them. He has to transfer himself to another age; to imagine he is a disciple of Christ or Paul; to disengage himself from all that follows. The history of Christendom is nothing to him. . . . All the afterthoughts of theology are nothing to him; they are not the true lights which light him in difficult places.[7]

This has consequences for appreciating (or not) those whose legacy doctrine is: premodern interpreters. It turns out that what they were doing was, in significant ways, unrelated to interpreting the Bible, however much they believed their activity was scripturally regulated and occasioned. First, their methods have been outgrown:

> Is it admitted that the Scripture has one and only one true meaning? Or are we to follow the fathers into mystical and allegorical explanations? Or with the majority of modern interpreters to confine ourselves to the double senses of prophecy, and the symbolism of the Gospel in the law? In either case, we

---

5. Benjamin Jowett, "On the Interpretation of Scripture," in *Essays and Reviews* (London: John W. Parker and Son, 1860), 331–434.

6. R.R. Reno reads Jowett as a proponent of a caustically anti-doctrine species of historical criticism, at least in the sense that Reno understands doctrine; see Reno's general editor's preface to the Brazos Theological Commentary on the Bible series in his contribution to it, the volume on *Genesis* (Grand Rapids, MI: Brazos Press, 2010), 9–14. While not dismissive of Reno's objections to Jowett, I find James Barr's arguments that Jowett is not straightforwardly calling for historical criticism (in Reno's sense) to be persuasive; see Barr, "Jowett and the 'Original Meaning' of Scripture," *Religious Studies* 18.4 (December 1982): 433–37. Another reader who seems to agree with Barr (albeit while also calling for Jowett's axiom to be retired) is R.W.L. Moberly; see his "'Interpret the Bible Like Any Other Book'? Requiem for an Axiom," in *Journal of Theological Interpretation* 4.1 (2010): 91–110.

7. Jowett, *On the Interpretation of Scripture*, 338.

assume what can never be proved, and an instrument is introduced of such subtlety and pliability as to make the Scriptures
mean anything—'Gallus in campanili,' as the Waldenses described it; 'the weathercock on the church tower,' which is
turned hither and thither by every wind of doctrine. That the
present age has grown out of the mystical methods of the
early fathers is a part of its intellectual state.[8]

Second, as already stated, their accomplishments really are not examples
of the activity for which Jowett would reserve the term interpretation:

It may be thought another ungracious aspect of the preceding
remarks, that they cast a slight upon the interpreters of Scripture in former ages. The early Fathers, the Roman Catholic
mystical writers, the Swiss and German Reformers, the Non-
conformist divines, have qualities for which we look in vain
among ourselves; they throw an intensity of light upon the
page of Scripture which we nowhere find in modern commentaries. But it is not the light of interpretation. They have a
faith which seems indeed to have grown dim nowadays, but
that faith is not drawn from the study of Scripture; it is the
element in which their own mind moves which overflows on
the meaning of the text. The words of Scripture suggest to
them their own thoughts or feelings. They are preachers, or
in the New Testament sense of the word, prophets rather than
interpreters. There is nothing in such a view derogatory to the
saints and doctors of former ages.[9]

Jowett's essay proved provocative in its own setting, and, though time may
have muted his volume, he can still provoke today, both inside and outside the
fields wherein biblical interpretation is (variously) practiced, biblical studies included. After all, Jowett was neither a biblical scholar nor typical, either for his
own day or for ours. We should also note that, whatever their (de)merits, it is
likely unhelpful not to empathize with Jowett's main concerns, whether one
sympathizes with his theological views or not. In the totality of his argument,
the immediate problem he sees is a cacophonous babel of divergent and incompatible interpretations. That din arose from what Jowett perceived to be a dys-

---

8. Ibid., 369.

9. Ibid., 377–78. Jowett's opinions echoed in his larger context—sometimes in arguably more strident forms as in the case of his friend F.W. Farrar, who dedicated his *History
of Interpretation* (London: Macmillan and Co., 1886) to Jowett and who said that the history
of interpretation was largely "a history of errors" (8). Less directly related but perhaps
interesting in the ways he might have influenced Jowett's setting and outlook was Jowett's predecessor (by a couple centuries), Benedict Spinoza, whose understanding of
the inspiration of the biblical prophets seems suggestively cognate to Jowett's understanding of religious genius; see Spinoza's *Tractatus Theologico-Politicus*, esp. chapters 1
("Of Prophecy") and 2 ("Of Prophets").

functional ecclesial culture that mistook inspiration (of a sort) for interpretation (also, of a sort). That we have to qualify the terms *inspiration* and *interpretation* in this context underscores, however, that Jowett's word would not be the last.

Approaching Premodern Interpretation from a Very Different Angle

If we now cross the Tiber in our exploration of the land abutting Lessing's ditch, we may discover Henri de Lubac—a complex, voluminous writer. He also is only questionably a voice in the debate that includes Jowett, as de Lubac's object, though related, is primarily the significance of the history of interpretation for Roman Catholic theology and only secondarily biblical interpretation in late modernity. Further, he stands tall in a veritable forest of related voices, including among others his student Hans Urs von Balthasar. For all these reasons, any treatment we give de Lubac *et alii* must be focused, partial, and brief. Still, the issues he raised and the role he has come to play, whether he intended to do so or not, in debates over the enduring vitality of premodern interpretation seem as important as a mountain range on the horizon.

A small handful of features adjacent to our topic stand out immediately. 1) The spiritual senses of medieval exegesis, rooted in patristic accomplishments and formulations, were and remain enduringly vital to believers, not least in relation to the communal act of worship. 2) The intellectual trajectory that produced biblical criticism so defines the modern period that it is impossible and counterproductive to ignore interpretation in its modern mode and simply return to or repristinate the older procedure. 3) As a corollary, or perhaps better, a presupposition of the second point: the two modes of interpretation, modern and medieval/patristic, are not the same. In pursuing these three points, this school or stream of which de Lubac stands at the head also carefully develops a generally cordial criticism of modernity for its having allowed observation of the second and third points effectively to disable the first.

A cento of quotes from de Lubac and von Balthasar can illustrate these three points. The first point, which we might call the hypothesis of precritical vitality, is visible even on the surface of de Lubac's project. Though his total treatment is massive and overflows the scope of the following paragraph, it nonetheless comes close to a summary of his outlook:

> Now this "complete act" that is ancient Christian exegesis is a very great thing. . . . It sets up an often subtle dialectic of before and after. It defines the relationship between historical reality and spiritual reality, between society and the individual, between time and eternity. It contains . . . a whole theology of history, which is connected with a theology of Scripture. It organizes all of revelation around a concrete center, which is fixed in time and space by the Cross of Jesus Christ. It is itself a complete and completely unified dogmatic and spiritual theology. . . . In brief, this ancient form of Christian exe-

gesis is something quite other than just an ancient form of exegesis. It forms "the thread" of Christian literature and Christian art. It constitutes, in one of its essential aspects, ancient Christian thought. It is the principle form that the Christian synthesis had for a long time been shaped by. At the very least, it is the instrument that permitted this synthesis to be constructed, and today it is one of the devices by which a person can approach it most easily.[10]

This holds despite the fact that exegesis in the modern sense is something quite distinct:

And inasmuch as these commentators [i.e., the ancient ones] were quite often not exegetes in the modern, specialized sense of the word, the examination of their thought that I have undertaken will be less a contribution to the history of exegesis properly speaking than to the history of theology, or rather to the study of Christian thought and spirituality generally.[11]

This difference between modern and ancient "exegesis" makes it in fact impossible to return to the ancient procedure and apply it in the discipline of biblical studies today. In de Lubac's own words, "It is ... quite certain ... that the techniques of the science of biblical studies, not to mention those of theology, can no longer accommodate themselves to this ancient form."[12] Despite this, modernity is not to be excused for what the Jesuit luminary sees as its sneering ignorance, its sloppy misreading, of the ancient mode. Particularly with regard to how it related the Old and New Testaments he protests:

While ... the Christian tradition reiterates ... that "the spiritual sense of the Old Testament is the New Testament," how many expositions of ancient forms of exegesis, how many judgments bearing on these forms do not even allude to the significance of the relationship between the two Testaments on this question!. ... [T]he extent to which this tradition seeks the spirit in the letter is thought to result merely from a Platonic prejudice that makes the body the prison house of the soul. The processes that it uses or the abuses that injure it are described at length and severely judged. But its original principles remain veiled.[13]

This is not (yet?) a criticism of the modern, critical trajectory itself. De Lubac merely remonstrates for the dignity and integrity of the tradition he studies. Although he is not here addressing Jowett, one wonders if the Jesuit would

10. Henri de Lubac, *Medieval Exegesis*, vol. 1 (Grand Rapids, MI: Eerdmans, 1998), xix.
11. Ibid., xiii.
12. Ibid., xix.
13. Ibid., xiv.

take the Anglican to task for completely rejecting the term *interpretation* as applicable to patristic and medieval readers. But, de Lubac was the master of Hans Urs von Balthasar, and the second scholar proceeds from *ressourcement* to critique of criticism, at least in certain of its paradigmatic procedures:

> Only the final result of the historical developments which lie behind a text—a history never to be adequately reconstructed—may be said to be inspired, not the bits and scraps which philological analysis thinks it can tear loose from the finished totality in order, as it were, to steal up to the form from behind in the hope of enticing it to betray its mystery by exposing its development. Does it not make one suspicious when Biblical philology's first move in its search for an 'understanding' of its texts is to dissect their form into sources, psychological motivations, and the sociological effects of the milieu, even before the form has been really contemplated and read for its meaning as form? For we can be sure of one thing: we can never again recapture the living totality of form once it has been dissected and sawed into pieces, no matter how informative the conclusions which this anatomy may bring to light.[14]

Scripture is a *form*—in von Balthasar's heart language a *gestalt*—and approaching such a thing requires that that totality be observed for what it is. Once dissected, the totality, which is more than the sum of its parts, is lost. Biblical philology, as von Balthasar perceives it, dissects first and then presumes it has understood the *gestalt*, but its conclusion is erroneous on methodological grounds. As an aside, the connotation of vivisection audible from our position makes his polemic sound particularly cutting. Perhaps more interesting, and returning us back to Jowett (although not citing him in particular), von Balthasar hints at positive proposals that run counter to the dictum that scripture must be read like any other book:

> Scholars are right in their concern for the different literary genres in Scripture and in paying due regard to the general principles of these genres in their interpretations of the texts. But this activity by no means exhausts the question concerning the particular poetics of Scripture. In fact, this question may really be raised only when the other more general considerations have been concluded, and when for the interpretation of this inspiration—a particular inspiration, even though it is integrated into the general forms of inspiration—the interpreter himself enjoys an inspiration in accordance with the inspiration of his subject, analogous to the way the divine Sophia interprets and praises herself in the Wisdom

---

14. Hans Urs von Balthasar, *Seeing the Form*, vol. 1 of *Glory of the Lord: A Theological Aesthetics* (Edinburgh: T&T Clark, 1982), 31.

books. We must, then, always see clearly where the compe-
tence of the philological and archaeological method really lies
and where it must be complemented and even surpassed by a
special method suited to the uniqueness of its object. The Fathers frequently exhibit this second element, while the first is
often painfully absent; among modern scholars the first element may be found either with or without the second.[15]

A couple of points deserve to be observed just from von Balthasar at this
juncture for purposes of contextualizing the succeeding decades' hermeneutical
controversies. Von Balthasar is concerned 1) for larger, and irreducibly complex
units or structures of meaning and, 2) those units possibly are larger even than
the individual biblical book, indeed larger even than the Bible, for they seem to
include the encounter of the reader with the text in the form being discovered.
Interpreter and interpreted must share a single inspiration. Thus, philological
and literary critical attentiveness will never be enough. Interpreting the scriptures and, *mutatis mutandis*, any *gestalt* demands a radical engagement in which
a method special to the object is discerned in addition to literary criticism's
methods. The Fathers might be faulted for occasionally missing the general hermeneutic, but the moderns should not be congratulated for eschewing the special one.

A Modern Allergy to the Emerging Hermeneutic?
The geography sharply changes with another landmark in the historical
theologian R.P.C. Hanson. His thorough work on Origen of Alexandria—Origen
being arguably the font of the quest for scripture's spiritual senses, as de Lubac
saw him—has become a classic on its subject and was apparently something of
a negative reply to de Lubac (among others).[16] Where the Catholic scholar had
been interested, on a certain level, in defending the ancient Alexandrian's procedure as authentically a mode of interpretation or exegesis, Hanson sees things
quite another way. He appreciates Origen. The ancient Father is a sublime genius—even something of an exemplar for theological method.[17] However, he is
not a great interpreter of the Bible. Reading into the Bible his own thoughts is
his failure; disrespect for history is the cause:

> Why can we not go further? Why can we not call Origen a great
> interpreter of the Bible, in the same sense that Augustine and
> Luther and Westcott and perhaps Barth can be called great in-
> terpreters?

---

15. Ibid., 44.
16. Joseph Trigg's introduction to Westminster John Knox Press's reprinting of Hanson's *Allegory and Event* (Louisville: Westminster John Knox Press, 2002) has a useful summary of the debates with which Hanson was engaging, see esp. x–xiv.
17. Hanson, *Allegory and Event*, 374.

The answer in my opinion lies in the fact that in one important respect Origen's thought remained outside the Bible and never penetrated within it. Of the great interpreters ... it is always evident that their minds were soaked in biblical thought; they give the reader the impression that they are speaking to him from inside the Bible; at least for purposes of exposition, they have successfully put themselves into the minds of the biblical author whom they are interpreting. Origen never quite conveys this impression, and on countless occasions gives the opposite impression, that he is reading into the mind of the biblical author thoughts which are really his own. The critical subject upon which Origen never accepted the biblical viewpoint was the significance of history.[18]

In some respects, Hanson's reading of Origen is more positive than Jowett's of patristic interpretation generally. He even accords Origen some points of similarity to then contemporary biblical scholars he admired, notably Bultmann. However, in crucial respects, Hanson's picture of Origen is far more damning, for "history"—and the connotation of the term in Hanson is perspicaciously modern—is his Achilles' heel, and "history" is of crucial theological centrality.[19] Related to this is Origen's view of inspiration, along which lines Hanson appears to see him as rather an ancient analogue to our day's fundamentalists: "Origen's doctrines of the inspiration and of the inerrancy of the Bible, which had so controlling an influence upon his exegesis, are wholly unacceptable to most modern scholars, and from those who still accept them they demand so much explanation and modification that they disappear almost wholly into the realm of theological fantasy."[20] Hanson reflects almost voluminously on the unacceptable quality of Origen's exegesis arising from these improper theologoumena. The chief fruit of his tree is allegory, which must be dismissed,[21] and the bloom from which that fruit comes, Origen's conception "of the Logos as active in the Old Testament" is a notion that "historical criticism has also made entirely unacceptable."[22]

Given Hanson is primarily targeting but one ancient reader of scripture, it may seem something of a stretch to perceive a pattern of response within the controversy we have been outlining. However, a few key features of his dismissal of Origen evoke a sense of late modern incredulity or allergy to sympathetic

---

18. Ibid., 363.

19. Ibid., 363–64.

20. Ibid., 367.

21. Ibid.

22. Ibid., 367–68. Although Hanson does not explain himself, it seems likely he has the christological referent of Jn. 1:1 in view. As a side note, Hanson's objection here is aimed towards a target larger than Origen—in fact, a target that contains the biblical text itself—as the conviction that the Logos was active in the OT is pervasive in early Christianity, for example Jn. 12:41 where the prophet Isaiah is said to have "seen" Jesus's "glory."

re-engagement with the patristic and medieval project. That allergy involves an intuition about what historical criticism has (ostensibly) once-and-for-all demonstrated. *Inspiration* is a fantasy, especially in the sense of the Logos's perceived activity in the Old Testament, for the Logos was *not* active in the Old Testament. Noting these points of incredulity in Hanson underscores what he means by the terms *history* and *historical criticism*. Assuming Hanson intends the christological referent of Jn. 1:1, the Logos is a transcendent entity. Somehow, then, historical method has weighed in on the activity of at least one transcendent entity, demonstrating that it is starkly absent. The resultant vision is a history from which any possibility of the rationality of the spiritual senses of medieval exegesis and Christ-types of patristic and, indeed, New Testament interpretation of the Old have been excluded. Hanson may well be targeting only Origen, but his aim strikes wide.

Additionally, it seems important to mention that Hanson's wide aim is intrinsically open to critique, even from practitioners of the historical criticism he celebrates, and, indeed, even when those practitioners would likely be sympathetic to his judgments regarding patristic biblical interpretation. For example, however much the biblical scholar John Collins's constructive proposals designedly oppose biblical theologians accounting for matters such as inspiration, in the process he stipulates that this is because biblical theology should be pursued as a species of historical theology where the methods of the latter ostensibly do not enable its practitioners thereby to make assertions (either positive or negative) about the nature and activities of the divine.[23] About such matters, the historical theologian and biblical scholar must remain agnostic. If the biblical critic embraces Collins's proposal on this point, she surely must defer questions of the Logos's activity in the Old Testament either to practitioners of other disciplines or to other occasions when she is wearing a different hat herself— not assert, as Hanson does, that the Logos was inactive in the Old Testament. With historical method thus described, even by an (on balance) anti-confessional scholar (which Collins is), Hanson's critique of Origen's views of inspiration as having been proven false by the modern method looks strangely out of place, and even, perhaps, a little naïve, as if he does not properly understand the modern paradigm to which he negatively compares its ancient counterpart. Such likely misunderstanding aside, however, Hanson's rhetoric does sound flush with confidence in the progress of exegetical science, seems concomitantly jaundiced towards the sensibilities of earlier times, and brackets out the concerns of properly theological hermeneutics. In these he seems remarkably modern, not just as opposed to premodern sensibilities but as opposed by modernity's self-proclaimed successor.

---

23. John J. Collins, "Biblical Theology and the History of Israelite Religion," in *Encounters with Biblical Theology* (Minneapolis: Fortress, 2005), 24–33 and esp. 26–27.

Postmodern Meta-Allergy

Postmodernity is a vast subject. Perhaps it is best not even to define the term except loosely as referring to an intellectual culture that resists further definition out of profound suspicion that the effort to define obfuscates as much as (or even more than) it clarifies. A.K.M. Adam, in a larger treatment of what a postmodern climate begins to mean for biblical criticism, is informative about the ethos generally:

> Even if postmodernity is not any one thing, it is some things more than others. It is almost always fair to think of postmodernism as a movement of resistance. The name itself suggests that postmodernity defines itself over against "modernity." Postmodern thinkers have typically discerned a pattern of radical problems with the ways many of us have gotten accustomed to thinking and arguing; they want to resist the bad habits we have fallen into under the influence of modernity.[24]

So, postmodernity is a "movement of resistance." Later, he provides a more thorough explanation following Cornell West:

> Postmodernism is antifoundational in that it resolutely refuses to posit any one premise as the privileged and unassailable starting point for establishing claims to truth. It is antitotalizing because postmodern discourse suspects that any theory that claims to account for everything is suppressing counterexamples, or is applying warped criteria so that it can include recalcitrant cases. Postmodernism is also demystifying: it attends to claims that certain assumptions are "natural" and tries to show that these are in fact ideological projections. All these characteristics deal with one of the most common characteristics of postmodern thinking: postmodern critics characteristically problematize legitimation, the means by which claims about truth or justice or reality are validated or rejected.[25]

But, what does this mean for biblical criticism? First, because postmodernism is resisting something that preceded it—the postmodern person understands her vocation with regard to her *Zeitgeist* more in terms of what she is not than what she is—it is important to spell out what it is reacting against. What "bad habits" does it perceive, or think it perceives? Crucially for our discussion here, the relationship between the past and the present is centrally at issue:

> The Moderns argued that the simple condition of having lived and worked long ago was itself a problem for the Ancients and

---

24. A.K.M. Adam, *What Is Postmodern Biblical Criticism* (Minneapolis: Fortress, 1995), 1.
25. Ibid., 5.

that living and working in the modern world puts us significantly ahead of our forebears.

One conclusion that the moderns drew from this was that
there is an ever-growing gap separating the past from the present. This was not always the way people thought about their
relation to the past.[26]

Consistent with this, *modern* biblical criticism prefers recent to ancient
sources, interpretations and paradigms of interpretation, as Adam observes,
"Articles in the *Journal of Biblical Literature* or *Interpretation* are likely to cite
sources only from the last twenty years or so. Like the first moderns, modern
biblical scholars set themselves over against their past, and defend the newness
of their own conclusions."[27] Related to this is a sense of being rooted in, and
indebted or loyal to the European Enlightenment and its concerns. To the just
previously quoted sentiment Adam adds, "Modern thought looks to the rationalism of the European Enlightenment as its epitome. . . . When biblical interpreters insist on rational, scientific explanations of biblical events, or when they
defy traditional interpretations in the name of free scholarly inquiry, they show
a debt to modernity."[28] We should remind ourselves at this point that biblical
scholars are not the sole or even the primary practitioners of this sort of thinking. If we consider inspiration to be, in some sense, a biblical event (at least under a certain construal of the Bible), R.P.C. Hanson seems clearly an exemplar.
We should also be reminded, when reading Adam's summary of postmodernity's
critique of modernity, that this critique can take more and less strident forms.
A postmodern person can identify her modern colleague as overly loyal to modernity's agenda without asserting that that agenda was wrong. The question
becomes whether that agenda, however important it once was, remains existentially live or whether we need to move on. Thus *post-* is not necessarily *anti-*.

As a reactive movement against this modern ethos, the postmodern reader
engages in a calculated rebellion on several points. First, and perhaps most importantly, Adam states succinctly but mysteriously, "There is no '*the* text.'"[29]
Postmodern readers are going to feel *contra* Jowett that pursuing one authoritative meaning or interpretation is a sham.[30] The Bible is not a container of static
meaning; it is an occasion for dynamic conversation. The postmodern mind does
not share Jowett's fear that a text that can mean many things therefore can

---

26. Ibid., 2–3.

27. Ibid., 3.

28. Ibid.

29. Ibid., 19.

30. Although, again, it is important to note that postmodernity as Adam describes it
does not necessarily abhor what Jowett is trying to do in the face of the crisis apparently
on his horizon (if Jowett's rhetoric is taken seriously): sectarian strife. Rather, the postmodern person as Adam describes him will likely state that Jowett's hermeneutical science is a mystification designed to cast a spell over and thereby disable a real evil of his
world. To the postmodern, politics can be (at least almost) everything.

mean anything at all; likewise it is not offended by Hanson's observation that Origen reads his own speculative genius into the scriptures—for why should he not? That he does so is simply a function of the sort of event communication is, even (and perhaps especially) when it is textually mediated. Second, and entirely consistent with this more dynamic understanding of texts, Adam observes that "For postmodern readers, 'the author' is a fragmented, contested range of possible identities; the modern unified, unambiguous author who authorizes only particular, correct interpretations, no longer exists."[31] This is not to say that there is *only* the reader solipsistically projecting herself onto an imaginary stage whereon communication is illusory. Such is a misreading of the implications of postmodernity's anti-foundationalism. Although Adam does not state this directly himself, I might interpret him by noting that, with regard at least to texts if not communication generally, reader and writer alike occupy analogous locations in the event, which is a live negotiation or ongoing discovery of meaning. Therefore, the significance of the communicative event (in this case the *text*) is negotiable and, again, intrinsically dynamic.

However, finally and perhaps most immediately important for providing essential background to this book, the postmodern reader will not necessarily accept the modern reader's preference for recent developments over traditional ones and likely will more positively appraise that landmark that modernity abhorred as a great, ugly ditch. Adam writes:

> Indeed, as postmodern criticism escapes modernity's fascination with time, the many assumptions modern people make about "originality," "progress," and "time-conditioning" are more problematic. For example, the modern biblical interpreter assumes that there is a great gap between past and present, which he must valiantly bridge using the tools of historical analysis. The postmodern interpreter, however, may point out that there is already a substantial bridge, inasmuch as the Bible has been interpreted continuously for the whole time that the modern critic is concerned with. The expositions of these intermediary interpreters offer testimonies to the text's meaning, which are invalid only on the modern assumption that one has to reckon with the chronological gap. If, with a postmodern interpreter, we decline to make the chronological assumption, then our need to reckon with the gap disappears, and we can once again learn about the text from our premodern colleagues.[32]

Now, if this paradigmatically postmodern reader is describing *interpretation*, not only am I free, *contra* Jowett and Hanson, to consider Origen genuinely to be an interpreter, I may even be ethically beholden seriously to grapple both with the history of interpretation and with my own existential *Sitz im Leben*. This is

---

31. Ibid., 20.
32. Ibid., 20–21.

especially and obviously the case with books such as the Bible because of their religious potency. We have just gotten slightly ahead of ourselves by alluding to paradigms of ideological criticism, reader response theory, and deconstruction, all of which are characteristic of the postmodern *modus operandi*. However, to return to what texts actually are, Dale Martin gives a somewhat illuminating discussion in his *Pedagogy of the Bible*. He writes:

> Texts are not just containers that hold meaning. The meaning of a text is a result of the interpretive process itself, which is not possible apart from the activities of human interpreters. And texts are not agents who speak. No text has ever spoken. What people mean when they talk that way about texts is that they, the human interpreters, have imagined their own reading practices as if they were listening to a voice coming from the text or from the author imagined to stand behind the text. But these metaphors give people the false impression that texts can control their own interpretation. If we believe someone else is "misreading" a text, we can take the person back to that text, ask the text again what it is "saying," and demonstrate to that person by the text's own agency that his or her interpretation is incorrect and ours is better. Contrary to this common misconception, however, if we are in fact successful in changing another person's mind about the text's meaning, it will have been our agency that affected our friend's reading of the text, not any fictitious agency of the text itself. Texts cannot dispense their meaning, and they cannot control their interpretation. Those activities are done by human beings.[33]

Martin adds, "Thus one of my favorite slogans: Texts don't mean; people mean with texts."[34]

Two characteristically postmodern paradigms, or schools of paradigms, just peered at us from over the hedge in the above paragraphs. First, postmodern critics will be concerned for the ethical implications of reading against the backdrop of *our* scene where that stage, again, involves an interconnected past, present and future for the text and not separately reified and sundered periods of reception. If a text potentially connotes or affects violence in readers, it might not be enough simply for the critic to say "this is what this text means" let alone "this is what the text meant."[35] She might also aggressively seek out where the text is potentially violent—in Martin's terms what violence people might work

---

33. Dale Martin, *Pedagogy of the Bible* (Louisville: Westminster John Knox Press, 2008), 30.

34. Ibid., 31.

35. This now canonical (for biblical studies, at least of a kind) distinction was first proposed by Krister Stendahl in his seminal essay "Biblical Theology, Contemporary," in *Interpreter's Dictionary of the Bible*, vol. 1 (Nashville, TN: Abingdon, 1962): 418–32; reprinted in H. Räisänen et al., *Reading the Bible in the Global Village: Helsinki* (Society for Biblical Literature: 2000), 67–106.

with the text—and disarm the bomb before someone gets hurt; what I might term the interpreter-as-James-Bond (in *Goldfinger*) theory of the critic's primary vocation. David Clines states this concern with clarity:

> The question of the effect of our texts has rarely been raised in our scholarly tradition. This is perhaps the worst consequence of the historical-critical method (which was all very necessary in its own day and remains valid, please don't misunderstand me), since in its quest for origins it screened out the present, and, with that, the ethics of interpretation—including the ethics of keeping alive these texts by study and commentary and writing. The practitioners of the historical-critical method, like the inventors of the atomic bomb, were ethically irresponsible. Their commitment was to the 'truth', whatever that might be and wherever it might lead. And that is unquestionably a whole sight better than a commitment to falsity. But it systematically ignored the question of effects on readers, and it is about time we regarded such study as part of our scholarly discipline and task.[36]

Note that Clines is not claiming texts can mean anything at all. Also, he at least seems to think that the Bible actually is a dangerous book, at least in parts. He would prefer modes of criticism designed to disarm, not to appropriate within a living tradition. In this sense he seems decidedly distinct from Martin, and also, probably, from Adam. What stands out, however, is important. He exemplifies the postmodern mood from the angle of the question of how the Bible affects readers—what it *does* as opposed to what it once *meant* to a supposedly bygone author and original historical setting.

Second, if postmodernity were a slope down a plateau and the vision of the critic's vocation represented by Clines went down the left side of that slope, there is a side opposite his that is particularly important for this book because of the way in which it comes explicitly to value the history of interpretation and particularly what that history termed "the Rule of Faith." By a certain popular reckoning, Karl Barth stands at the head of this path,[37] and the most famous guide into it (among biblical scholars) is Brevard Childs. Childs's proposals are complex and involved, and in their totality are beyond the scope of this book. However, aspects of his core thesis, which to my ear also echoes Hans Urs von Balthasar's reverence for the *gestalt*, cannot not be mentioned in any fair précis of the background we are considering. That thesis says that *canon* must be taken seriously by biblical critics if they wish their interpretive efforts to participate

---

36. David A.J. Clines, "Why Is There a Song of Songs and What Does It Do To You If You Read It?," in *Interested Parties: The Ideology of Writers and Readers of the Hebrew Bible*, Journal for the Study of the Old Testament Supplement 205 (Sheffield, UK: Sheffield Academic Press, 1995), 94–121.

37. The work usually associated with Barth on this score is his commentary on *Epistle to the Romans* (Oxford: Oxford University Press, 1968).

in the larger tasks of Christian theology. The Bible overlays a dynamic process that must be considered in its irreducible complexity as well as through philological and literary analysis; in Childs's words:

> Perhaps the basic theological issue at stake can be best formulated in terms of the church's ongoing search for the Christian Bible. The church struggles with the task of continually discerning the truth of God being revealed in scripture and at the same time she stands within a fully human, ecclesiastical tradition which remains the tradent [i.e., that which preserves and transmits] of the Word. The hearing of God's Word is repeatedly confirmed by the Holy Spirit through its resonance with the church's christological rule-of-faith. At the same time the church confesses the inadequacy of its reception while rejoicing over the sheer wonder of the divine accommodation to limited human capacity.[38]

Search is the operative word. Also clearly in view is one human community that is engaged in, if not in part identified with, that search. That community is mutually engaged with transcendent givens that presumably cannot be reduced to words: God, the Word, the Holy Spirit. It experiences confirmation from those givens and responds with confession and wonder. Rather than a static and clearly delineated text, we have a web of relationships receding into a still living past, "a fully human, ecclesiastical tradition."[39] The approach promised still understands itself as served by criticism as modernity practiced it, but where that modernity set itself, as it were, in the mode of a hermeneutical outsider examining processes solely external to and even distant from it, Childs sees the interpreter as at least potentially an insider participating in the same processes that produced the Bible to begin with, and those processes are identified using terms richly laden with theological connotations. Of key interest here is that this approach fairly easily occupies the ethos of the postmodern situation as I have been outlining it, albeit in a mode quite distinct from Clines's trajectory.

Revisiting the Fathers in the Context of Postmodernity

A few pages back we peered briefly into R.P.C. Hanson's evaluation of Origen of Alexandria. It was very much a modern evaluation, albeit one that, as we saw through brief interaction with John Collins, involved an arguable misreading of historical criticism's theological implications. For Hanson, Origen had an inadequate sense of history; therefore, he could not really inhabit the world of the Bible. However, we have just seen that, at least with regard to biblical studies, a sea-change has been occurring over the past several decades and is still on-going. What implications might that have for scholars seeking to appreciate premodern exegesis anew?

---

38. Brevard Childs, *Biblical Theology of the Old and New Testaments: Theological Reflection on the Christian Bible* (Minneapolis: Fortress, 1992), 67.
    39. Ibid.

Reconsidering allegorical or "figural" reading, as David Dawson calls it,[40] turns out to be key, as is that ancient Christian savant, Origen. Dawson's interest in his book on the subject immediately strikes us as postmodern in at least one respect in that he is existentially motivated in a self-confessed way.[41] Christian reading of Old Testament texts along a certain trajectory has participated in anti-semitism. He wants to explore whether there is not an arguably Christian hermeneutical outlook that eschews this trajectory:

> In the pages that follow, I ask whether there is a kind of Chris-
> tian reading of the Old Testament that might express Christi-
> anity's relation to Judaism while respecting the independent
> religious identity of Jews, and, more broadly, the diverse iden-
> tities of all human beings. I look for the possibility of this kind
> of biblical interpretation in the writings of Jewish and Chris-
> tian thinkers, both ancient and modern, who have reflected
> on the form of traditional Christian biblical interpretation
> known as "typological" or "figural" reading.[42]

His interest is not anti-philological, however, or anti-historical. He even aims to outdo modernity for objectivity of a kind. Setting evaluation of his subject matter to the side—and even trying to suspend basic categories such as *text* and *meaning*—he turns to early Christian primary sources that in turn interpret scripture. He then asks what his ancient Christian interlocutor is seeing, and even how he or she sees the interpretive task. Turning to the seminal early Christian *Book of Acts* chapter 8 ("The Ethiopian Eunuch" pericope), he uncovers a significant difference between ancient Christian and modern interpretive priorities:

> We are told that the Ethiopian is reading the prophet Isaiah,
> and Philip asks whether the Ethiopian understands what he
> reads. Philip does not ask him whether he understands the
> meaning of a text. As presented in this story, Isaiah is not a

---

40. John David Dawson, *Christian Figural Reading and the Fashioning of Identity* (Berkeley: University of California Press).

41. It is important to note that modernist reading is not unmotivated existentially, and, also, that it is not monolithic. Hanson, for example, is even somewhat clear about his motives—he wants to know, as an Anglican, whether and how Origen might be received within his tradition. Hanson also shows significant admiration for the biblical scholar Rudolf Bultmann whose larger program (of which Hanson apparently approved) manifests its motivations clearly. (For one example, see Bultmann's "New Testament and Mythology: The Problem of Demythologizing the New Testament Proclamation," in *New Testament and Mythology and Other Basic Writings*, ed. and trans. Schubert M. Ogden [Philadelphia: Fortress, 1984], 1–44.) However, postmodernity, as we have seen it with the help of A.K.M. Adam, celebrates these motivations in a way modernity did not. Along these lines, one of the accusations the postmodern reader may make against her modern colleague is the charge of hypocrisy on this very issue.

42. Dawson, *Christian Figural Reading*, 3–4.

text but a prophet, and neither he nor the text that records his prophecy offers a "meaning." Instead, the prophet speaks about, that is refers to, a person, either himself or someone else. The prophet's utterance is unquestionably accepted as referential by both Philip and the Ethiopian, and the key interpretive question concerns the proper identification of that referent. . . . The question ultimately concerns the intelligibility of a divine performance: God is doing something by means of an obscure person to whom the prophet refers.[43]

The modern and postmodern worlds, in Dawson's estimation, fail to appreciate this ancient interpretive paradigm and, so, tend not even to understand what ancient interpreters were doing. His solution is:

. . . to de-privilege from the outset the peculiarly modernist and postmodernist assumptions we contemporary readers are apt to bring to any account of Christian figural reading. Whether we still think naively that texts "have" their meanings, the way capitalists own their property, or—with more sophistication or readerly effort—that textual meaning is forever distanced and deferred—we still instinctively bring to Christian figural reading the assumption that, whatever else it may be about, it must concern texts and meanings. The question about the intelligibility of a divine performance is something we would rather not consider, for the idea that the prophet Isaiah had, in his own right and not only as a consequence of some later reader's strange interpretation, once referred in some oblique fashion to the person of Jesus who had not yet appeared in history and, in so doing, sought to render intelligible a certain divine performance, is, for most of us, historiographically absurd; it is, in fact, the height of unintelligibility. Yet any effort to understand Christian figural reading as fundamentally a matter of texts and the presence or absence of meaning, rather than a matter of rendering God's historical performances intelligible, is doomed to theological irrelevance, however much contemporary theoretical sense it might make.[44]

In this way, Dawson's reading, this side of the sea-change, is not less critical but, in some respects, more so. When we take seriously his challenge, we discover that premodern readers had not only different understandings of *texts* and *meanings,* but also, as with postmodernity itself, of history and the relationship between past and present:

---

43. Ibid., 5.

44. Ibid., 6. As an aside, Dawson's use of the term "unintelligibility" seems somewhat strained, at least to me, although "implausibility" does seem to name the anxiety many present-day readers experience upon encountering ancient figural readings and his overall point remains compelling.

Auerbach presents Origen as the preeminent allegorist who undermines the figural imagination, in this case by dissolving the historical reality of the text's representations. I take issue with Auerbach's characterization of Origen's engagement with history, arguing instead that Origen has as strong an interest in history as does Auerbach. But for Origen, the history that one should worry about preserving is the history of divine interactions with human beings, especially interactions that can continue to take place in the present. Any history worth preserving deals with occurrences that are not simply over and done with but are instead part of a larger performance that is potentially ongoing.[45]

Once we have thus used the primary sources to engage the postmodern concern for escaping modernity's mental habits, we discover a world from which we can retrace the trajectory of Christian theological method and hermeneutics for scripture. In the process, we do not forget why we retraced our steps to begin with, nor do we stay in or repristinate the ancient world we hope to have rediscovered, but we move forward from that world self-consciously with the aim of achieving something different—in Dawson's case, attempting to realize a Christianity without supersessionism and concomitant antisemitism:

Origenist allegorical reading, as Boyarin, Auerbach, and Frei criticize it, construes the text as a set of tropes, replacing literal with nonliteral meaning. . . . I argue that Christian interpretation of the Old Testament, as Auerbach, Frei, and Origen conceive of it, is figural—that is, rather than predicated on an anti-literalism, Scripture's figurativeness is not nonliteral; its figurative character is an extension rather than obliteration of the literal sense of texts. This seemingly paradoxical conception of figurative meaning that is not nonliteral is the basis for a conception of Christian figural reading that, consistent with a performative rather than semiotic construal of Scripture, might avoid the supersessionist hermeneutic Boyarin rightly deplores.[46]

Many other writers illustrate, in a variety of ways, this shift in which we have just seen Dawson participate. The conclusions of these writers differ; they cannot and should not be assimilated to one another. Nonetheless, they demonstrate a mood. That attitude includes a determination to discover categories helpful for representing early Christians in a more robust, empathic (though not necessarily sympathetic) light. Often those categories are explicitly mined from postmodern philosophers of language such as Stanley Fish and Michel Foucault. Elizabeth Clark illustrates this sort of dependence well, in the process also showing how the dialectic can run the other way—from using the postmodern

---

45. Ibid., 11.
46. Ibid., 14–15.

world to re-engage early Christians, to using Christianity in its early phase to illustrate (and thereby interpret) the possibilities of which postmodernity dreams:

> If (with Barthes and Foucault) we assume that readers are decisive to the production of a text's meaning, how has the multitude of readers across the ages ever agreed on what that meaning might be? Stanley Fish, the prime theoretician of the notion of 'interpretive communities', answers: to imagine that each reader lives in a world unto himself or herself assumes a solipsistic view of reading that ignores the process by which 'communities of readers' are formed and direct the 'proper' interpretation of texts. The notion of 'interpretive communities', Fish explains, was originally intended as an answer to a question that had long seemed crucial to literary studies. What is the source of interpretive authority: the text or the reader? Yet readers need not fear that they will lose themselves in an 'infinite plurality of meanings', for 'sentences emerge only in situations', statements are 'institutionally nested'. A person in a particular situation, Fish argues, always already possesses 'a structure of assumptions' that guide his or her interpretation. Since language is a social phenomenon, practices that create meaning are 'community property'. When critics argue that Fish's thesis fails to explain how change in interpretation arises, Fish counters that such critiques presuppose a monolithic view of interpretive communities. Although an interpretive community may be homogeneous in respect to its general aims, Fish argues, it also can entertain considerable heterogeneity regarding the various practices it accommodates. Indeed, the interpretive community itself can function as 'an engine of change'. Early Christian communities, I posit, provide a ready arena for exploring the limits within which a diversity of interpretation was tolerated.[47]

Dale Martin, who, like Clark, also makes much of Stanley Fish, similarly considers it valuable to return in a serious way to premodern interpretations for inspiring responsible, creative engagement with the Bible in our context.[48] He admits that ancient interpretation dances to a different piper than interpretation in modernity—but, (perhaps?) consistent with the postmodern sea-change, so what? If the shoe fits, wear it. Historical critical method, though abidingly useful, ought not to claim a hermeneutical monopoly.

---

47. Elizabeth Clark, "Creating Foundations, Creating Authorities: Reading Practices and Christian Identities," in *Religious Identity and the Problem of Historical Foundation* (Boston: Brill, 2004), 555–56.

48. See Martin's chapter entitled "Premodern Biblical Interpretation," 47–70.

As this mood deepens, the tones of openness to modes of interpretation (concomitantly differing understandings of *texts, meaning, interpretation* and *history*) other than the modern can become transposed from natural to sharp. David Steinmetz provides one example in his famous foray into the debates in a paper ambitiously titled "The Superiority of Precritical Exegesis":

> The medieval theory of levels of meaning in the biblical text, with all its undoubted defects, flourished because it is true, while the modern theory of a single meaning, with all its demonstrable virtues, is false. Until the historical-critical method becomes critical of its own theoretical foundations and develops a hermeneutical theory adequate to the nature of the text which it is interpreting, it will remain restricted—as it deserves to be—to the guild and the academy, where the question of truth can endlessly be deferred.[49]

Not all voices come across quite as dramatically as does Steinmetz's; however, the charged oppositions he draws do echo in more nuanced ways throughout the larger setting. Thus Brian Daley will ask whether patristic exegesis is still useable and, in asking that question, charges the modern critic with being "methodologically atheist."[50] R.R. Reno, to whom I will return in chapter 4 of this book, also protests what he sees as some biblical scholars' claim to a hermeneutical monopoly for historical criticism.[51] Notable and nuanced among modern criticism's critics, who wishes (somehow or other) creatively to re-engage the premodern world, is Andrew Louth. In *Discerning the Mystery*, Louth is in contest with the epistemological priority the modern age assigns to the natural sciences, specifically the way in which modern culture extends that epistemology into domains for which it is inappropriate, namely the humanities. In the process, the early Church Fathers become a resource for seeing how things might be done instead. In giving advance précis of his own argument, he writes:

> First, consideration is given to the notion of tradition, which has an important role in Patristic theology. Then attention is focused on the Fathers' use of allegory in the interpretation of Scripture, for, as we shall see, this is part of the tradition, both in the obvious sense that it is a traditional way of interpreting Scripture, and in a deeper sense, in that allegory draws on the notion of tradition, plays on it (as it were) in such a way as to draw out the hidden depths of the tradition. But I also concentrate on allegory for another reason: because it is the Fathers'

---

49. David Steinmetz, "The Superiority of Pre-Critical Exegesis," *Theology Today* 37 (April 1980): 38.

50. Brian Daley, "Is Patristic Exegesis Still Usable? Some Reflections on Early Christian Interpretation of the Psalms," in *The Art of Reading Scripture*, ed. Davis and Hays (Grand Rapids, MI: Eerdmans, 2003), 72.

51. See R.R. Reno's author's introduction to his own offering in the Brazos Theological Commentaries on Scripture series, *Genesis* (Grand Rapids, MI: Brazos, 2010), 26.

use of allegory which, more than anything else, renders their theology suspect, and even frankly incredible, to those who have imbibed the presuppositions of the Enlightenment, presuppositions which I have argued to be increasingly incredible and naïve. . . .[52]

It is important to note that in adducing these various voices, I am not describing a shared project or monolithic perspective. All the writers I have briefly surveyed in this subsection are distinct: in aims, in motivations, in the degree to which they would embrace postmodern identities, even and especially perhaps in their sympathies. Some significant unifying factors or shared characteristics, however, include that they see modernity's legacy as tarnished, wish to play with (or at least understand) different paradigms of interpretation than the modern one, and perceive a valuable dialogue partner for that purpose in early Christian hermeneutics for scripture.

Enter the Theological Interpreters and Reconsidering the "Rule of Faith"

So, postmodernity appears to be a changed context, raising new possibilities and imposing new demands. Intentional re-encounter with premodern readers is often heralded as a desideratum, and one emerging school, often termed *theological interpretation*,[53] particularly wants to engage that encounter by making methodological room for what early and medieval Christians termed the *rule* (Greek: *Canon*, Latin: *regula*) *of faith*. Inspired by the work of Brevard Childs and encouraged by contributions to debates on hermeneutics by theologians such as Robert Jenson, John Webster, and others, present-day advocates of theological interpretation tend to regard historical criticism as practiced in modernity as having achieved important things and made abiding contributions. However, where the critics leaned heavily upon approaches that bracketed out questions, say, of canonicity and living reception of doctrinal traditions, the theological interpreters want also to consider approaches that, to use R.W.L. Moberly's term, "incorporate" such factors.[54] For example, the editorial staff of the *Journal of Theological Interpretation* describe their general aims in precisely such terms in their marketing of the *JTI*:

> Critical biblical scholarship as developed and defined since the mid-eighteenth century has played a significant and welcome role in pressing us to take biblical texts seriously on their own terms and diverse contexts. With the postmodern

---

52. Andrew Louth, *Discerning the Mystery* (Oxford: Oxford University Press, 1990), xiii.

53. For more thorough overviews of the various contributors to this school of thought (for lack of a better category), see Daniel Treier's recent treatment in *Introducing Theological Interpretation of Scripture: Recovering a Christian Practice* (Grand Rapids, MI: Baker Academic, 2008) and also Stephen Fowl, *Theological Interpretation of Scripture* (Eugene, OR: Cascade, 2009).

54. R.W.L. Moberly, *Theology of Genesis* (Cambridge: Cambridge University Press, 2009), 12.

turn, additional questions have surfaced—including the theological and ecclesial location of biblical interpretation, the significance of canon and creed for biblical hermeneutics, the
historical reception of biblical texts, and other more pointedly
theological interests. How might we engage interpretively
with the Christian Scriptures so as to hear and attend to God's
voice?[55]

What, for example, of "the theological and ecclesial location of biblical interpretation"? Moberly appeals to this concern often in his works under the ru-
bric of *(a) rule(s) of faith*,[56] language which is also used by Robert Wall.[57] At issue
here are two related concerns. First, the Bible remains of interest not as a library
of ancient texts haphazardly rescued from obscurity—the *Enuma Elish* hardly receives such attention—but because of the legacy of Christianity (*mutatis mutandis*, Judaism). Second, the lion's share of interpretation occurs for the sake of
institutional investment in worshiping communities, many of which operate
with respect to each other as sibling rivals in dialogue. As partisans of those
traditions position themselves *vis a vis* each other and what they perceive to be
religion's shifting frontier with a wider culture, they value the Bible primarily
as a resource for living, theological discernment within that dialogue and not
just as witness to ever only partially reconstructed events long past. Thus, Wall
envisions Christianity's canonical deposit as a pluriform witness wherein apparent disagreements between past tradents (his chief example involves the canonical Paul vs. James and the catholic epistles) are juxtaposed with each other and
conjointly commended to the faithful through the ecumenical Rule of Faith to
which all scriptural threads, together with present-day traditions of interpretation, must then cohere. Those present-day traditions (small c- churches or worshiping communities with small r- "rules of faith") then, on analogy to that ostensibly canonized pattern of debate,[58] utilize the ecumenical Rule of Faith as a

---

55. "Journal of Theological Interpretation," https://www.eisenbrauns.org/Jour-
nals/jnls_JTI.html.

56. For one such place see R.W.L Moberly, *The Bible, Theology, and Faith: A Study of
Abraham and Jesus* (Cambridge: Cambridge University Press, 2004), 42–43.

57. The interpretation of Wall I am about to give synthesizes his contributions to
Joel B. Green and Max Turner, eds., *Between Two Horizons: Spanning New Testament Studies
and Systematic Theology* (Grand Rapids, MI: Eerdmans, 2000), including "Reading the Bible
from within our Traditions: The 'Rule of Faith' in Theological Hermeneutics," (88–108)
and "Canonical Context and Canonical Conversations" (165–83). Wall's proposals are notably indebted to William J. Abraham, *Canon and Criterion in Christian Theology: From the
Fathers to Feminism* (Oxford: Clarendon, 1998).

58. However, for my part I question whether debate or other synonyms of disagreement best describe scriptures' internal diversity. I can imagine strong voices in the Christian tradition, including from the present-day, who would find such categorization existentially incompatible with the patterns of devotion to Christianity's scriptures com-

kind of "grammar" to generate theological proposals that express their own, distinct spiritual gifts for the larger Church.

All this begs the question as to what the Rule of Faith is, or even what sort of thing it is. As already mentioned, Wall treats it as analogous to a grammar. Paul Blowers, in turn inspired by the work of N.T. Wright, argues strongly that for early Christianity the Rule of Faith is a kind of narrative.[59] Robert Jenson argues in much the same vein, going so far as to assert that, for Christian hermeneutical purposes, the biblical *gestalt* in its totality is about this narrative, internal diversity (one dimension of the aforementioned pluriformity?) in genres aside.[60] In Jenson's historical argument, creed and biblical canon grew up together with the support of the Rule of Faith, and they need each other if they are to function hermeneutically for Christian readers. Without the creed, the canon's doctrinal inner logic—its ability to claim the Church for the Bible by narrating the story of the people of God—becomes opaque. Without the canon, the creed's broad strokes narrative fails adequately to flesh out that story in its richness and totality.[61]

Jenson, especially when he is joined by fellow Lutheran theologian Carl Braaten, is engaged polemically against the culture of historical (or higher) criticism; together Braaten and Jenson accuse the critics of stealing the Bible from the Church. These polemics and counter-polemics take diverse forms between various advocates of theological interpretation in the wake of Brevard Childs, on the one hand, and biblical critics of the traditional, modernist sort, on the other. However, this inner-academic rivalry is not always the primary stage on which paradigms of theological interpretation are methodologically laid out. Jenson reserves some of his sharpest rebukes for present-day Christian communities, charging them with inadequate attention to catechesis and the dynamics of worship.[62] The work of the Reformed theologian J. Todd Billings moves this sort of concern to the foreground. In setting forth the motivations behind his writing *The Word of God for the People of God* Billings describes two, paradigmatic

---

mended to them by their traditions. My own conclusion will explore an alternative taking its cues from the ontology of scripture developed through dialogue with various early Church fathers in my opening chapters.

59. Paul Blowers, "The Regula Fidei and the Narrative Character of Early Christian Faith," *Pro Ecclesia* 6 (1997): 199–228,

60. Though Jenson's writings pervasively illustrate and flesh out this claim, I here am thinking particularly of this sentence: "Scripture is a whole because . . . it is one long narrative. All Scripture's detours and extensions and varieties of literary genre are to be read as moves within the telling of a single story." See Jenson's "Hermeneutics and the Life of the Church," in *Reclaiming the Bible for the Church*, ed. Carl Braaten and Robert Jenson (Eugene, OR: Wipf and Stock, 1995), 89–106 and esp. 97.

61. Jenson argues this extensively in his *Canon and Creed* (Louisville: Westminster John Knox Press, 2010).

62. Jenson, "Hermeneutics and the Life of the Church," 91.

species of hermeneutical approach in contrast to each other and a third *via media*.[63] One approach so imposes dogmatic systems on the Bible that the hearer ends up not so much encountering the scriptures as she does some systematic theology utilizing the Bible as a source of proofs or evidence. Opposite that approach, the detailed apparatus of systematic theology might be bracketed out to allow an inductive, "smorgasbord" approach. Ironically, this stance invariably smuggles in other thought systems than those of systematic theology, however, generating shallow, banal, topical teaching that likewise leaves us unaware of the Bible's larger message and largely turns individual passages into proofs for generic moralities. The middle way is to take the Church's Rule of Faith, with its Trinitarian and Christological themes, as a broad-strokes big picture, then engage that picture to produce far-reaching readings of Scripture's epic. Billings's concern is, as such, for the depth and quality of Christian formation.

In all these proposals the Bible and (the) Rule (rules) of Faith (faith) are constructed through relationship to each other in ways that seem to echo the debates classically separating Roman Catholicism from Protestantism, over the respective authorities of scripture and tradition, obliquely considered. One might expect that an ontology of Scripture more mindful of classically Protestant concerns might demur and pursue alternative proposals and, indeed, that is what John Webster is apparently about in *Holy Scripture: A Dogmatic Sketch*.[64] He takes Jenson to task for advancing a vision wherein "the canon of Scripture . . . is . . . a dogmatic decision of the church."[65] However, this does not mean that the nature of Scripture—what Scripture *is*—should be left dogmatically underspecified in Christian consciousness; the ontological parameters of Scripture demand explicit formulation in order to commend it to its hearers and readers as the *viva vox dei*. Thus considered, the Church's act of canonization is one of recognition, confession, and obedience whereby the Church as the listening, reading people of God, abide in the same salvific processes by which the Scriptures themselves are holy. Scriptural text is sanctified creature, its inspiration flowing from the providence of the Spirit to set apart the very words to the self-revealing Word of God. This providential sanctification covers every moment of Holy Scripture's

---

63. This contrast of these three approaches, which Billings categorizes as "translat[ing] Scripture into propositional building blocks," "pick[ing] over Scripture . . . as we choose what seems to fit out questions and needs," and, finally, "receiv[ing] Scripture as part of a Trinitarian-shaped journey of faith seeking understanding," organizes the flow of Billing's arguments in *The Word of God for the People of God: An Entryway to the Theological Interpretation of Scripture* (Grand Rapids, MI: Eerdmans, 2010). See esp. xv in his introduction.

64. John Webster, *Holy Scripture: A Dogmatic Sketch* (Cambridge: Cambridge University Press, 2003).

65. Webster quotes from and critiques Jenson, *Systematic Theology*, vol. 1 (Oxford: Oxford University Press, 1997), 27–28. Webster's critique of Jenson can be found in Holy Scripture, 63–64.

origin, existence, and ecclesial recognition, generating a written form as the Church's Bible and thus continues to order Scripture's existence now. Categories such as *Rule of Faith* fade to the background or even disappear, but Webster's reader is rendered attentive to Scripture via questions that appear to have been drawn from that Rule (those rules?) as she attends to the sacred letter. In the Rule's disappearance, however, the Bible now appears to be both a chief artifact of and abiding means whereby the salvation of the creature for the Creator might advance; in this way, the Bible now seems to function in some sense *as* Rule of Faith for Christian formation.[66]

In these sorts of ways, often when the emerging school of theological interpretation ventures its vision of a post-critical future it wants to consider the Rule of Faith and its possible role today. We are ready to turn in earnest to the aims, method, and subject matter of this book.

Précis, Thesis, and Approach

This book will pursue two interrelated goals one after the other and coordinate those goals at its conclusion. The first takes its cues from the concern highlighted in my last subsection for relating Holy Scripture to Christianity's Rule of Faith by looking at how an important sample of early Church fathers described the origins, nature, and right interpretation of Scripture in their context. My second goal will be to discern modern biblical criticism's allergy to these seminal interpreters and their commitment to read according to the Rule of Faith, then offer an *apologia* arguing that premodern commitment to the Rule has not properly been understood by modernist critique. As a final, coordinating reflection, I want to consider how reading at once both robustly critical and fully "ruled" might look in a postmodern setting.

Chapters one and two will pursue the first goal outlined above, and will take the form of a revisionist history of early Christian ontology of scripture. To provide both a sampling of early Christian perspectives and a sense of development over the first several centuries, several different fathers from different periods will be considered, starting with texts now canonized for Christians in the New Testament, then running through Irenaeus, Origen, Hilary (of Poitiers), and Augustine. Starting from the observation that different communities bring distinct preunderstandings to events, processes, and artifacts of communication, I will explore early Christian preunderstandings where they related to scripture and argue that the Bible was woven into existence through the dialectical engagement of those preunderstandings with Christianity's emerging library of sacred texts, primarily in the context of worship and catechesis. Chapter 1 will consider

---

66. It is interesting to me as an ordained Presbyterian minister of Word and Sacrament that John Webster is also a Reformed theologian and that one classically Reformed creed names the sixty-six-book Protestant canon as "the Rule of Faith." See the Westminster Confession of Faith 1.2.

the Bible in its ancient context through the window of ecclesiology in the first four centuries, examining ways in which the Bible emerged as *identity story of the people of God*; chapter 2 will reconsider this definition of Holy Scripture by looking at early doctrines of salvation, revising chapter 1's definition to speak of the Bible as *the identity story of God himself, with God's people.*

From there, to approach my second goal I will attempt a flying leap into the modern and postmodern worlds where the Bible now firmly exists as a discrete object in the consciousness of Western culture—a world where the perception also has become that the classical outlooks outlined in my first two chapters are substantially incompatible with biblical criticism. My method here will shift from historical exploration of primary source texts to critical review of four present-day scholars as they muse on biblical criticism as it emerged in modernity and might now be changing. I will spend chapter 3 with the biblical scholar John Barton[67] and historical theologian Michael Legaspi[68] as each regards from his own angle the nature and roots of modern biblical criticism and what each sees as the essential incompatibility of that paradigm with classical, theological approaches to the Bible. In the process I will highlight particularly where Barton's reading of postmodern theological interpreters such as R.W.L. Moberly also pits him against the early father Origen, and, by analogy, other ancient readers. Crucially, I will argue that Barton's opposition to Origen—and therefore today's theological interpreters—involves serious misunderstanding of ancient ruled reading. From there chapter 4 will review contributions from two theological interpreters, R.R. Reno[69] and R.W.L. Moberly,[70] as each tries to offer proposals for engaging the Rule of Faith today in critical-yet-classical treatments of the opening chapters of Genesis. Differences between and features internal to each of these proposals will underscore and even possibly name that impasse, feared by late modern and postmodern interpreters, to advancing a theory of interpretation that is at once both critical and "ruled."

By this point I hope to have set the stage for a synthetic conclusion. The first half of this book will have argued that classical outlooks on Holy Scripture identified it as canonical discernment of, and therefore orientation to, the unfolding story of God with God's people—a story paradigmatically "heard" in the dynamics of catechesis and worship. The second half will have claimed that the specifically dialectical, open-ended character of this vision of scriptural interpretation was misunderstood by modern biblical criticism and dismissed with prejudice, and that interesting experiments have been made by postmodern theological interpreters in retrieving and redeploying aspects of the ancient

---

67. I review his *The Nature of Biblical Criticism* (Louisville: Westminster John Knox Press, 2007).

68. Michael Legaspi, *The Death of Scripture and the Rise of Biblical Studies* (New York: Oxford University Press, 2010).

69. R.R. Reno, *Genesis*, Brazos Theological Commentary on the Bible Series (Grand Rapids, MI: Brazos, 2010).

70. R.W.L. Moberly, *Theology of Genesis* (Cambridge University Press, 2009).

view. However, as chapter 4 hopefully will make clear, I wish to push back on an assumption that appears to me to be at play in both Reno's and Moberly's struggles to retrieve a properly theological hermeneutic. I will suggest that that assumption is peculiarly modernist, that it remains largely uncontested in our now postmodern condition, and that it relates to the core, existential commitment motivating what Brian Daley has termed criticism's methodological atheism: that *critical* yet *unswerving* devotion to the Rule of Faith is a contradiction in terms, impossible to enact. Since Childs's "search for the Christian Bible" in the early period arguably entailed species of just such critical devotion, the strategies for retrieval outlined by Reno and Moberly are potently suggestive. Through their tacit struggle against the modernist assumption, they suggest that dialogue with early Christian interpreters is promising at least partially in the ways in which they imagine critical devotion as an exercise in discovering and inhabiting a world canonically outlined by scripture. In this sense, the best sort of reader is paradoxically at once both critically aware of and yet committed unswervingly to the Rule, which in its essence is a narrative-shaped sense of vocation and stable-yet-mysterious identity in God's story. This mindfulness may in principle utilize every tool—including those celebrated as critical in modernity—to perceive the communion of saints and angels under the unswerving persuasion that this communion exists and that its identity is stable, but also with profound, critical openness to what abiding participation in that communion's unfolding reality entails.

As the above précis shows, my approach involves primarily a focus on select figures read deeply rather than on the twin forests of interpretation premodern and late modern. In this respect, I aim for this book to be somewhat different than related studies that are structured by large literature searches. One reason is simply that even the one forest of premodern ruled reading is already vast. Two such woodlands would likely guarantee we would lose our way, and I want to guide my reader along one, very particular road-less-travelled to a crucial and largely unvisited destination. While the above paragraphs number my goals as two, the coordination attempted in the conclusion identifies one aim in the final analysis: to display how a paradigm often designated as noncritical or precritical—Christian reading mindful of the dynamics of mission, conversion, and faith formation—is in actual fact, profoundly critical in its method, consciousness, and ends. To do this requires that the contours of the classic outlook be amply and convincingly explored (chapters 1 and 2), the charge of modernity against that outlook be named and motivated clearly (chapter 3's review of Legaspi and Barton), and tentative, heuristic experiments in revisiting the ancient outlook be considered in their details and not just broad strokes (chapter 4's review of Reno and Moberly). My hope is that the proposals of the conclusion will, then, be convincing enough as a hypothesis that my reader will be persuaded to continue to discover ruled reading as an open-ended and evolving, living paradigm.

Chapter 1
Communion, Canon, and
the Bible of the Church

One way to begin any inquiry is to rediscover ways in which the familiar is, in fact, actually quite strange. As it happens, that rediscovery is, perhaps discomfortingly, low-hanging fruit when the subject is the Bible. The strangeness has to do with the Bible's status for Christianity. The point can be seen easily enough even when described just from the vantage point of the liturgy, as it is celebrated in many of Christianity's denominations, where, after most every Bible reading, the reader confesses that this is "the word of the Lord." Yet, in a seemingly important way (nonetheless deserving of important qualification), the Bible as we know it has not always been the object of this confession. One—evangelical protestant!—scholar even puts it bluntly in these words: " . . . one cannot properly speak of a Bible for the first several centuries of the church's existence."[1] The process that took the Bible from being a disputed collection of scriptures to being a less disputed(!) library ("canonization") took centuries, and, even during that period, was extending a process of redaction and collection that went back further yet. The result is a book marked with a historical contingency and literary messiness that, for some, seems to fit somewhat awkwardly with its having a normative character. Hermeneutics is the usual solution.

This chapter will not be about the canonization process, although observations relating to that process will turn out to be centrally relevant. Rather than being about how canonization transpired, the concern here is more for what canonization is and was. The questions are: What is biblical authority? Whence

---

1. Craig D. Allert, *A High View of Scripture: The Authority of the Bible and the formation of the New Testament Canon* (Grand Rapids, MI: Baker Academic, 2007), 51. In context, Allert is alerting his reader to the intellectual problems raised by positing a closed canon as the sole basis for doctrine. His point deserves consideration although on its face his statement somewhat caricatures the state of the biblical canon for earliest Christianity which, as a sect of second temple Judaism in its earliest phase, inherited a recognizable form of what Christianity now terms its Old Testament, with vital implications for the nature and progress of doctrine in the centuries I will discuss in these first two chapters.

biblical authority? What is the Bible? Christianity as we know it today got its Bible and doctrine concerning the Bible through Christianity of the past. The strategy here, at least initially, will be to use that observation and the questions above to probe the developing hermeneutics of Christianity in its first four centuries, considering that *what* a thing is believed to be intuitively has implications for how it is interpreted and engaged. Since, however, the Bible lacked as thoroughly developed a form in its ancient context, I will begin by taking a footnote from the canon debate: the frequent observation that canonical scriptures were distinguished from noncanonical writings by "apostolicity."[2] It may seem an odd place to start, but, by the time we get to the second century, the act of recognizing texts as apostolic will turn out to have had remarkable and surprising significance. Although other heuristics, centrally how texts were used in public worship, ranked more highly in the canonization process, they did so not in competition with apostolicity, but in such a way as to spell out what apostolicity meant when scripture was in question: in essence, Holy Scripture functioned, for early Christians, as a mode of abiding communion with the prophetic and apostolic emissaries of God whose witness to Jesus Christ was considered foundational for Christian identity. Implications for what it meant for scripture to be related to Christian initiation or enculturation developed from there. My entry point into perceiving this process is the first century. After starting there, I will proceed to explore ways in which the first century's outlook on apostolic communion evolved in the second century with Irenaeus of Lyon and his approbation of the "Rule of Faith" and, later, in the third century with Origen of Alexandria and his concern for a dialectical relationship between the Rule and scripture.

The "Apostolos" Concept and Communion with God

To begin our explorations into how the category of apostolic communion played into the development of the doctrine of scripture in the early Church, we will begin with the gospels, focusing for convenience and brevity on the Matthean and Johannine traditions. A coherent complex of features leaps out to the eye

---

2. Harry Y. Gamble, *The New Testament Canon: Its Making and Meaning* (Philadelphia: Fortress, 1985), 68. Gamble's discussion in that book provides an accessible and interesting window into the canonization process in the early centuries. A more concise treatment, with consideration specifically of the canon's implications for the history of biblical interpretation, can be found in his "The Formation of the New Testament Canon and Its Significance for the History of Biblical Interpretation," in *The Ancient Period*, vol. 1 of *A History of Biblical Interpretation*, ed. Alan J. Hauser and Duane F. Watson (Grand Rapids, MI: Eerdmans, 2003), 409–29. Another standard treatment is Bruce M. Metzger, *The Canon of the New Testament: Its Origin, Development, and Significance* (New York: Oxford University Press, 1987). Finally, the interested reader will find a succinct survey of current debates in Stephen Chapman, "The Canon Debate: What It Is and Why It Matters," *Journal of Theological Interpretation* 4.2 (2010): 273–94.

from Matthew's account in chapter 10 of that gospel. Jesus gives the Twelve an authority which at least resembles Jesus's own "over unclean spirits, to cast them out, and to cure every disease and every sickness" (v. 1). Their message, "the kingdom of heaven has come near" (7), is identical to that of their master (4:17). Their missionary charter extends to them the power to bless with peace those who receive them worthily (10:13), and, where personally rejected, they are to proclaim the coming judgment of God by dusting off their feet as they leave (14–15). In the light of the rest of Matthew's narrative, the suffering the disciples are to experience resembles the sufferings of Jesus (17–18) because the disciple is to be like the teacher (25). Finally, having bequeathed to the Twelve this mission, the Teacher finally states the reason for the disciples' resemblance to himself:

> Whoever welcomes you welcomes me, and whoever welcomes me welcomes the one who sent me. Whoever welcomes a prophet in the name of a prophet will receive a prophet's reward; and whoever welcomes a righteous person in the name of a righteous person will receive the reward of the righteous; and whoever gives even a cup of cold water to one of these little ones in the name of a disciple—truly I tell you, none of these will lose their reward.[3]

The disciples do not merely resemble Jesus; they are co-participants in his ministry with communion extended through them to those who respond positively to the message of Jesus which they bring. A claim is being made by the evangelist for his own community; his narrative's readers are being drawn into a self-awareness as a people defined by receptivity and active response to the apostolic message.[4] A similar set of motifs can be observed in the very different context of the tradition's mention in John's gospel beginning with the narrative before the Supper discourse in chapters 13–17. On the surface, the Master's setting aside of his garments to wash his disciples' feet seems largely to be a recollection of the radical humility of Jesus. Closer attention to the whole narrative and the discourse that follows, however, reveals more. After washing the disciples' feet, the Master states, in a manner reminiscent of the call to be like the teacher in Matthew, "So if I, your Lord and Teacher, have washed your feet, you also ought to wash one another's feet" (13:14). The rationale given is that "servants are not greater than their master, nor are messengers greater than the one who sent them" (16). Thus, the disciples are to love one another as Jesus has loved them in fulfilling the mission bequeathed him by his Father. Participation

---

3. Mt. 10:40–42.

4. In the words of commentators Davies and Allison: "The proclamation of 10.7 is not only the proclamation of Jesus's twelve but also the proclamation of Matthew's church. This follows from the obvious transparency of chapter 10: while it is addressed to the historical twelve, it is simultaneously addressed to later missionaries." See W.D. Davies and Dale C. Allison, *A Critical and Exegetical Commentary on the Gospel According to Saint Matthew* (Edinburgh: T&T Clark, 1988), 170.

in this love is described in organic terms as well as in the categories of fulfilling mission and obeying commandment, as Jesus speaks of himself as a vine and his disciples as branches abiding in him (15:1–8). As branches abide in their vine so the disciples are to abide in Jesus's love by following his commandment to love one another as he has heeded his Father's commandment and abides in the Father's love (15:9–10). The correspondence extends to Jesus's humiliation in death. Regarding the foot-washing, Raymond Brown observes that "in demeaning himself to wash his disciples' feet Jesus is acting out beforehand his humiliation in death, even as Mary acted out beforehand the anointing of his body for burial (xii 1–8)."[5] The analogy he notes might be strengthened by recognizing in Jesus's symbolic act a call to a cruciform destiny like his own, for Mary, in washing Jesus's feet with precious ointment, readied *Jesus* for burial rather than herself, and here Jesus both cleanses his disciples and enjoins them to imitate and abide in the love of their Lord and Teacher. This sobering resonance with the larger gospel is given explicit form in Jesus's call to mutual love after his own pattern, described in terms of self-sacrificial death: "No one has greater love than this, to lay down one's life for one's friends" (15:13). We are reminded of the motif of suffering from Matthew's gospel where Jesus prophesies, in the earlier discussed sending discourse, his disciples' coming persecution (Mt. 10:16–25).

The tradition of receiving those sent by Jesus, thus, in two distinct witnesses from the first century, develops a picture of apostolicity wherein the one sent is a representative—even, as it were, a mode of presence—of Jesus himself. Furthermore, the form in which the tradition is presented, especially in Matthew, seems designed to draw its community of readers into a similarly apostolic identity.[6] As our interest here is in apostolic communion as it was viewed by patristic witnesses, these observations would be moot if they were visible only to present-day readers. As Ulrich Luz observes, however, the ecclesiological import of the principle woven into Matthew's narrative is also observed closely in the early history of interpretation.[7] He notes particularly Ignatius of Antioch, one of the Apostolic Fathers, where Ignatius writes in his *Epistle to the Ephesians* chapter 6:

> The more reserved a bishop is seen to be, the more he ought to be respected. When someone is sent by the master of a house to manage his household for him, it is our duty to give him the same kind of reception as we should give to the

---

5. Raymond E. Brown, *The Gospel According to John, XII–XXI*, The Anchor Bible (New Haven: Yale University Press, 1970), 562.

6. Ulrich Luz even sees a general ecclesiological principle, see his *Matthew 8–20*, trans. by James E. Crouch (Minneapolis: Fortress, 2007), 63.

7. In his own words "Our saying was very widespread even in early Christianity. Ignatius applied it to the bishop (Eph. 6.1); the Didache to the apostles, as the itinerant preachers are generally called there (11.4, cf. 12.1); 1 Clement to the apostles, who then appointed bishops and deacons in the cities and villages (42.1, 4)." Luz, *Matthew 8–20*, 120.

sender; and therefore it is clear that we must regard a bishop as the Lord Himself.[8]

Here, the one sent by Jesus is the bishop, Onesimus. Ignatius charges the Ephesians to revere Onesimus, receiving him as they would the Lord Jesus Christ. In so doing, they are hearing not merely Onesimus, but Jesus Christ himself present through Onesimus's fulfillment of the charge given him in Jesus's name. The immediate concern is the then-developing episcopacy, which, at this point, was, together with the colleges of presbyters and deacons, in an intermediate stage between being subordinate to and embodying continuity with the more obviously charismatic offices of the period that produced the earlier *Acts*, epistles of Paul, and the *Didache*.[9] Ignatius addresses this concern by evoking the same tradition that lies at the heart of Mt. 10 and Jn. 13–17. The implication, given what we have seen, is that communion with Jesus is an organic reality rooted in the past as it unfolds in the present. Onesimus is one who has received and responded positively to the apostolic witness to Jesus which goes back to the very beginning. Sever that tie—say by receiving and hearkening to someone who has rejected or corrupted the apostolic teaching—and communion with Jesus stands to be threatened. In this way the saving mission of Jesus, the developing apostolic tradition, and even concrete human persons are held together and associated so strongly with each other that to reject any one of them is to reject the others.

At this stage it might appear that the above is by and large unrelated to the topic of scripture. The sending discourse in Matthew, the supper discourse in John, and Ignatius of Antioch's charge to the Ephesians are all three concerned with receiving and submitting to concrete human persons, with the teachings and witness that they convey, to whom fellowship and obedient hearing can be extended or denied in person rather than through a written text. We are observing a realm wherein *oral* tradition is obviously very important. This point should not be underestimated. However, already as the apostolic period came

---

8. Ignatius of Antioch, *Epistle to the Ephesians* 6, emphasis mine.

9. For a fascinating treatment of this development in the first two centuries see James Tunstead Burtchaell, *From Synagogue to Church: Public Services and Offices in the Earliest Christian Communities* (Cambridge: Cambridge University Press, 1992). Burtchaell's thesis is that the core offices of what will come to be called the ecclesiastical hierarchy (bishop, priest, deacon) were not later developments, but were part of the inheritance of primitive Christianity from the synagogue, and that, over time, these offices came to be more central to Christianity's survival and maturation than the charismatic roles (apostle, prophet) more obviously dominant in the early decades represented by the NT and the Didache. As we will see, this observation becomes important for the subject of this chapter with perhaps one or two points of nuance: the ecclesiastical hierarchy's emerging importance did not so much take place to displace the charismatic as to safeguard access to it, as the hierarchy took up the responsibility to initiate each new generation of the faithful into the Holy Spirit's fellowship and gift, with implications for being able to interpret scripture.

to a close and the time of the apostolic fathers, such as Ignatius, progressed, the nature, authority, and proper interpretation of scripture was beginning to come into view. Already, the early text known today as 2 Peter numbers some of the Pauline corpus among "the scriptures,"[10] apparently paradigmatically Old Testament texts.[11] This emergent sense connecting apostolic texts and scriptural authority may have been marginal at the time. Frances Young notes how Ignatius's trump card against his own doctrinal opponents is to refer to Christ's "cross and death and the faith that comes through him" as his "sacrosanct records,"[12] and goes so far as to posit that a "descralisation" of written scripture is occurring in Christianity during this transitional time.[13] However, regardless of whether that is true, the formula for apostolic authority ("the one who receives you receives me") will be explicitly applied to the reception and interpretation of scripture in the controversies of succeeding decades, and in 2 Peter, marginal witness or no, we see that already occurring in an inchoate way.

Irenaeus of Lyon: Reading in Communion and the Emergence of the Rule of Truth / Faith

Already as the time of the apostolic fathers was drawing to a close, two crises lay along the horizon for a young Christianity, along with two (perhaps related) opportunities. Along the lines of crisis, even before this point there were, in the language of Paul from the first century, divisions (*schismata*) and factions (*haireseis*).[14] Paul's first century context in Corinth apparently was focused around questions of eucharistic celebration and disordered table fellowship while, in the background, confusion reigned on a host of issues ranging from the permissibility of eating meat (possibly) sacrificed to idols to the liturgical place and behavior of women to the regulation of *charismata* and to the scandal of incest. While confusion over these practical matters raged, the apostle's own

---

10. 2 Pt. 3:15–16.

11. 2 Pt. 2.

12. Frances Young, *Biblical Exegesis and the Formation of Christian Culture* (Cambridge: Cambridge University Press, 1997), 16. She quotes and reflects upon Ignatius of Antioch's *Epistle to the Philadelphians* 8.

13. Young, *Biblical Exegesis*, 59, 62, 69. While her argument helpfully orients to some of the dynamics of the period and is luminous of the larger development, which Young terms "the Formation of Christian Culture" in her title, additional nuance seems called for in order to explain from the early Christians' own vantage point why that putative "desacralisation" will, in short order, give way to what Young terms a phase of "resacralisation" (69). For my part, I prefer, in a somewhat different key from Young, to take early Christian devotion to scripture in this period as something that remains unquestioned; the issue in these decades is not sanctity but reference and, derivatively, what is needed to discern that reference.

14. 1 Cor. 11:18, 19.

authority was also challenged by super-apostle upstarts,[15] a rivalry that underscores the profoundly social nature of the debates. At issue were not simply community practices but wherein lay the power to discern and authorize them. As time wore on, of course, other issues came to the fore, doubtless as natural development of these sorts of conflicts already attested in the New Testament. By the second half of the second century a particularly high profile attended, on the one hand, the discernment and interpretation of Christianity's genuine sources for doctrine and, on the other, the living, social nexus wherein those sources could be reliably received. To return us to the way in which these crises developed alongside related opportunities, the success of the Gentile mission, so central to Paul's vocation, took the nascent religion into yet deeper engagement, both positive and critical, with the cultural and intellectual traditions of the wider Graeco-Roman world such as that world's rhetorical and philosophical schools.[16] This engagement took place alongside, and so involved, the evolution of the earliest ecclesiastical hierarchies from being apparently parallel but subordinate structures to apostles and prophets, to being sophisticated and super-ordinate fellowships for ensuring stability and continuity. The period deserves close observation for these reasons.

Among the exigencies facing the Church during that time was a complex of movements grouped together under the name of *gnosticism* by present-day scholars.[17] These groups varied widely, rendering a concise definition overarching all of them difficult, and complicating the matter further was that various other movements, also recognized as sub- or quasi-Christian by the Church, while not clearly gnostic, nonetheless seem to have participated in a shared ethos. Particularly important for his participation in that ethos, to the eyes of

---

15. 2 Cor. 11:5.

16. Interaction with the rhetorical school, in particular, has interested scholars who study early Christian theological and exegetical method, as examination of recent literature makes plain. Frances Young's *Biblical Exegesis*, which I interact with throughout this book's first two chapters, deals with this development (see esp. her second section, titled "The Bible as Classic"), as does Robert Grant, in his work on Irenaeus (see *Irenaeus of Lyons* [London: Routledge, 1997], esp. his chapters 5 [41–45] and 6 [46–53]). (This section of the book will deal especially with Irenaeus with help from Grant.) Lewis Ayres, also, in his *Nicaea and its Legacy: An Approach to Fourth-Century Trinitarian Theology* (Oxford: Oxford University Press, 2004), argues for the importance of contextualizing early Christian theological commitments and debates against the backdrop of critical interaction of early Christian theologians with the Graeco-Roman schools. Finally, succinct treatment of implications for interaction between Christianity and the rhetorical school, both in the ancient and early modern worlds, is found in Kathy Eden's *Hermeneutics and the Rhetorical Tradition: Chapters in the Ancient Legacy and Its Humanist Reception* (New Haven: Yale University Press, 1997).

17. One relatively recent work on the topic of the gnostics is that of Alastair H.B. Logan, *The Gnostics: Identifying an Early Christian Cult* (London: T&T Clark, 2006). The topic of gnosticism is beyond the scope of this book; the mention is made here primarily to set the historical stage for understanding Irenaeus.

many scholars, was a wealthy merchant turned would-be-Christian teacher named Marcion. Of less clear but nonetheless intriguing possible significance was an emerging sect of millenarian prophets called Montanists, after their founder. Scholars who study and debate the progress of scripture canonization in the early centuries have long noted these three movements as factors deserving of attention in the period.[18]

Two of these groups—the gnostics and the Marcionites—deserve special attention by this study because they embodied, in their respective practices, takes on the discernment and interpretation of scripture (and, *mutatis mutandis*, what we might term *tradition*) that clashed dramatically with a strong element within the ecclesiastical hierarchy, with its prescribed catechetical pattern, that would emerge dominant as the second century matured into the third. I will return in more detail to a broad overview of the gnostics' outlooks in the next chapter, but, for the purpose of highlighting how gnostic and Marcionite claims—and, more importantly, their catholic or orthodox opponents—contributed to connecting doctrines of apostolic communion with the nature and authority of scripture, a few brief words seem in order here. For the sectarians, what scholars term the young Church's emerging, apparently organic, canon of scripture presented an insoluble problem: the vision of deity central to its inherited core, i.e., the Old Testament. The gnostics' approach to Genesis is illustrative. The creator deity, apparently also the God of Israel,[19] begs the question when he demands exclusive loyalty to himself and asserts that he is the only god.[20] A higher spiritual orbit than he must exist beckoning those capable of illumination. Marcion, though in important ways different, also contrasts what seem to him the visions of God painted in OT texts with the God and Father of Jesus; Israel's God may be just, but he seems not good. In other words, both the gnostics and Marcion posit that the traditional scriptures of the Church must have their origin in diverse spiritual geniuses. For the gnostics, that apparently meant teasing apart the layers of significance in the scriptures with the aim of achieving enlightenment and escape from the prison of mundane, quotidian existence. For Marcion, a core Pauline gospel had to be distinguished from and advanced over a corrupt pattern of reception stemming from Christianity in its previous phase as a sect of second temple Judaism. Extent and ontology of scripture, and hermeneutics appropriate to it, are all clearly implicated.

Probably the most important primary source for reverse engineering particularly the gnostics' views is the second century apologist, Irenaeus, bishop of

---

18. See Metzger's chapter 4, "Influences Bearing on the Development of the Canon," in *Canon of the New Testament*, 74–112.

19. This connection likely seems overwhelmingly obvious to any reader of this book. However, as we will see over the next two chapters whenever we visit the gnostics, their total approach to scripture was somewhat atomizing. Indeed, had their perspective become dominant, it is doubtful whether the literary gestalt we call the Bible would have survived to emerge, more fully developed, from these early centuries.

20. Isa. 43:10

Lyon, whose five books *On the Detection and Refutation of the Knowledge Falsely So-Called* (more popularly, *Against the Heresies*) were written sometime in the span ca. 175–189 C.E.[21] His title immediately informs; the opponents are not really gnostics, but pseudo-gnostics. By distinguishing his opponents as having so-called knowledge, he raises tacitly the possibility of a true gnostic, someone actually positioned rightly to discern and interpret truth. He will even, in the course of his argument, raise explicitly where he believes that true gnosticism can be found: the apostolic Church.[22] Already from his title, then, communion is tacitly in view. The question is how did he develop and apply this concern? The canon—a term the natural referent of which will turn out to be somewhat different for Irenaeus than it is for us—appears, in his day, significantly less developed, regardless of the position one takes in scholarly debates on scripture canonization.[23] The reception and interpretation of scripture was in a state of flux, perhaps even crisis, and distinguishing true from false teacher (to make up a term that captures the ways their world sometimes categorized teaching, "*traditioners*"[24]) was not without its challenges, both facts that the acknowledged trouble of the hour underscores. Frances Young points out that the young Christian faith's total stance towards scripture, both aesthetic and hermeneutical,[25] clashed with the dominant culture in ways that were on a trajectory of a supersessionist claim, not only with respect to ethnic Judaism but, in important ways, with respect to all culture and cultures in the Graeco-Roman world.[26] The ethos of religion along the Mediterranean rim almost certainly made what Irenaeus saw as false claimants to gnostic status look potentially legitimate to others. In view of all this, Irenaeus's task was, to speak with a methodologically intentional empathy to him, one that saw the bishop participating in the tradition as a pro-

---

21. Grant, *Irenaeus of Lyon*, 6.

22. Irenaeus, *Against the Heresies* 4.33.8.

23. Allert's discussion is informative, see his "Introducing New Testament Canon Formation," 37–66, and also "A Closed 2nd Century Canon?," 87–130.

24. I acknowledge gratitude to Edith M. Humphrey, professor of New Testament studies at Pittsburgh Seminary, for this turn of phrase. Her own exploration of the New Testament's idiom, connecting "teaching" and "tradition" from a perspective rooted in both the discipline of biblical criticism and Eastern Orthodox spirituality, illustrates her outlook on the subject, see *Scripture and Tradition: What the Bible Really Says* (Grand Rapids, MI: Baker Academic, 2013).

25. On what I here term the aesthetic dimensions of the clash of cultures, I might note particularly the apparent preference Christianity developed fairly early on for codices instead of scrolls. For illuminating discussion on this point, see Young, *Biblical Exegesis*, 12–14; also Harry Y. Gamble, "The Early Christian Book," in *Books and Their Readers in the Early Church: a History of Early Christian Texts* (New Haven: Yale University Press, 1995), 42–81.

26. The entire discussion constituting part 2 of Young, *Biblical Exegesis*, starting at 49, is illuminating in this regard.

foundly involved tradent. He had to embody apostolic communion, in the process recontextualizing it, forming (to use Young's term) a Christian culture or, to borrow a related heuristic from the field of missiology, translating it.[27]

One way to look at how Irenaeus participated in and recontextualized the tradition he inherited is to take a closer look at the inheritance itself. He has a body of scriptures.[28] He is of a generation of early Christian that has greater access to the philosophical and rhetorical schools of polite Graeco-Roman society. Finally, he is a bishop and so is existentially invested in and carries responsibility for the ecclesiastical hierarchy and the ministries it oversaw, importantly catechesis and Christian initiation. To successfully advance the tradition, so to speak, he has to relate these three factors in response to the tradition's rivals. Also, I should note from the outset that, when he identifies the (pseudo-)gnostics *et alii* as rivals, Irenaeus is already involved in a dialectic, or hermeneutical spiral, because that diagnosis was, historically speaking, still in process. Only after the fact are they clearly so and so clearly rejected.

With that part of the picture in view, Robert Grant brings before our vision Irenaeus's use of the traditions of the Graeco-Roman schools, particularly the rhetorical.[29] The early father's use of the term *hypothesis*, a category that was widely used to designate the flow and structure of narrative, particularly stands out.[30] One quote from the early father demonstrates his point well:

> They [i.e., the pseudo-gnostics] try to adapt to their own sayings in a manner worthy of credence, either the Lord's parables, or the prophets' sayings, or the apostles' words, so that their fabrication might not appear to be without witness. They

---

27. Andrew Walls makes an evocative case for the utility of this category in his seminal *The Missionary Movement in Christian History: Studies in the Transmission of Faith* (Maryknoll, NY: Orbis, 1996), especially his third essay, "The Translation Principle in Christian History," 26–42. One important difference between his use of the category and the use I suggest here is that he presupposes a relatively complete NT canon. The principle, however, seems heuristic, changing what needs to be changed for the context of the second century C.E.

28. In addition to Allert's discussion and Metzger's overall discussion, see also Metzger, *Canon of the New Testament*, 153–56.

29. Grant, *Irenaeus of Lyon*, 46–53. Grant's previous chapter, "Greek Education Against Gnosticism," 41–45, is also informative.

30. Grant, 48. Paul Blowers also reflects extensively on the (possible) significance of analogy to narrative structure for theology in the early fathers, see "The Regula Fidei and the Narrative Character of Early Christian Faith," *Pro Ecclesia* 6 (1997): 199–228. While I find Blower's arguments helpful, Nathan MacDonald raises cogent arguments cautioning against overuse of the category of narrative for understanding the regula fidei in early Christianity and Irenaeus particularly, see "Israel and the Old Testament Story in Irenaeus's Presentation of the Rule of Faith," *Journal of Theological Interpretation* 3.2 (2009): 281–98. I will attempt in the section below to suggest where the category of narrative can function analogously and heuristically to interpret Irenaeus without oversimplifying what sort of thing the *regula fide* (English: "Rule of Faith") is for him.

disregard the order and the connection of the Scriptures and, as much as in them lies, they disjoint the members of the Truth. They transfer passages and rearrange them; and, making one thing out of another, they deceive many by the badly composed phantasy of the Lord's words that they adapt.[31]

The pseudo-gnostics are "fabricat[ors]" who have "disregard[ed] the order and the connection of the Scriptures." The last sentence should not be allowed to distract us. There are patterns of what we might term transference and rearrangement that Irenaeus and other early Christians on the catholic trajectory regarded as unproblematic, even necessary. Method throughout the patristic period massively attended to intertextuality on several levels,[32] a point to which I will return in chapter 2 and then, again, in the conclusion. At issue is not that his rivals are allowing texts to resonate with one another in ways that blur literary boundaries. The critical point, rather, is that the scriptures *as individual texts and as a gestalt* have an "order and connection" that the pseudo-gnostics have bracketed out. Elsewhere, Irenaeus demonstrates more of what he means:

> By way of illustration, suppose someone would take the beautiful image of a king, carefully made out of precious stones by a skillful artist, and would destroy the features of the man on it and change around and rearrange the jewels, and make the form of a dog, or of a fox, out of them, and that a rather bad piece of work. . . . In the same way these people patch together old women's fables, and then pluck words and sayings and parables from here and there and wish to adapt these words of God to their fables.[33]

To stick with Irenaeus's metaphor, the scriptures have a big picture. The gnostics ignore that design. The result is an interpretation that inadequately relates to the scriptures' subject matter. He reminds us from a nearly two thousand year distance of what we read from von Balthasar in this book's introduction. Theology involves aesthetic perception of a *gestalt*. The gnostics lack that perception. Irenaeus does not stay in the world of analogy to visible, artistic modalities. He will directly turn to literary forms. The gnostics are like those who derange the poet Homer:

> After having entirely fabricated their own system, they gather together sayings and names from scattered places and transfer them, as we have already said, from their natural meaning to an unnatural one. They act like those who would propose themes which they chance upon and then try to put them to

---

31. Irenaeus, *Against the Heresies* 1.8.1.

32. Young discusses this at length, see "Reference and Cross-Reference," in *Biblical Exegesis*, 119–39.

33. Irenaeus, *Against the Heresies* 1.8.1.

verse from Homeric poems, so that the inexperienced think that Homer composed the poems with that theme, which in reality are of recent composition.[34]

I am reminded of a website that generates plausible papers on postmodernism—at random, for every new visitor to the page![35] The backbone of the website is a computer program that has been taught what grammatical English sentences on topics of typical deconstructionist interest (Foucault, sex, consumerism, whatever) look like. The results, complete with bibliography, are in actual fact intelligent, fashionable gibberish. To Irenaeus's eye, the gnostics' method seems rather analogous.

Irenaeus claims, then, that the scriptures cohere with one another by analogy to an aesthetic scheme and narrative structure. The question is, why does he think he can make this claim? From whence his epistemic warrant? From the perspective of a world where the Bible is a more definitely delineated object and where Christianity is a major world religion, the claim seems so plausible that a reader might not, at first, make much of it. In Irenaeus's setting, however, this is an involved claim, not a common-sense apologetic move—hence, perhaps, why he appeals to objects more well-known to a typical audience (mosaics, Homer).

It is at this point, where Irenaeus's definitions, as it were, for *heresy* and *orthodoxy* become apparent, that our third factor—his career as bishop—comes to the fore. For the (pseudo-)gnostics, exegetical method entailed, primarily, revisionist activity born of the gnostic teacher's individual charismatic claim. Irenaeus will not deny *charismata* but claims the true Spirit's gifts are manifest where organic continuity with the apostles, stretching back into the Church's past, has come to be embodied by the presbyters, functioning as the apostles' legitimate successors. In this way, the bishop throws his lot in with a development from a generation before: the maturation of the ecclesiastical hierarchy as an organ of communion and a culture for maintaining fidelity to the seminal, apostolic deposit. That culture, and, more importantly, the state of communion it represents, are therefore of supreme epistemological significance. With that commitment in view, heresy turns out not so much to be failure to dot every doctrinal *i* and cross every liturgical *t*, but, rather, a total attitude or disorientation of mind and soul towards the Truth Himself, Jesus Christ, and those who bore witness to Him:

> Indeed, when they are exposed by means of the Scriptures, they turn round and make accusations against the Scriptures themselves.... When, however, we refer them again to the tradition that derives from the apostles and is guarded in the

---

34. Irenaeus, *Against the Heresies* 1.9.4.

35. Andrew C. Bulhak and Josh Larios, "Communications from Elsewhere." http://www.elsewhere.org/pomo.

Churches by the succession of the presbyters, they are opposed to tradition and claim that they are wiser not only than
the presbyters but even than the apostles, and have found the
unadulterated truth.[36]

Heresy consisted in not just beliefs that were false from Irenaeus's perspective—although they certainly were that—but in their caustically revisionist
stance towards apostolic communion received in a three-fold form: *succession of
the presbyters, tradition, Scriptures.* His complaint against them fits what we have
already seen from Ignatius, Matthew, and John. Through explicit mention of
written scriptures, however, Irenaeus now recognizes those scriptures as functioning in the same way that personal encounter with the apostles functioned
some decades earlier. Elsewhere in *Against the Heresies*, he makes this association
yet more explicit:

> Recall what we said in the first two books; and if you add to
> them the following, you will have from us a most complete
> refutation of all the heresies, and you will resist them confi-
> dently and most insistently in favor of the only true and living
> faith, which the Church received from the apostles and dis-
> tributes to her children.
>
> For the Lord of all things gave to his apostles the power of the
> Gospel, and through them we, too, know the truth, that is, the
> doctrine of God's Son. To them the Lord also said, *He who hears
> you hears me; and he who despises you, despises me and Him who
> sent me.*[37]

Irenaeus juxtaposes the scriptures, the apostles of Jesus, and the Church
which received and passed on their word, finally alluding to the defining formula (itself scriptural) for the *apostolos*. And, lest we think that he is only talking
about the mode of oral discourse here, the bishop immediately returns to the
topic of written scriptures in his next chapter:

> In point of fact, we received the knowledge of the economy of
> our salvation through no others than those through whom the
> Gospel has come down to us. This Gospel they first preached
> orally, but later by God's will they handed it on [*tradiderunt*] to
> us in the Scriptures, so it would be *the foundation and pillar of
> our faith.*[38]

The scriptures themselves are apostolic. For this reason, to reject those
scriptures (or to twist them) is to reject the apostles—and, consistent with the
antecedent tradition regarding the sent-ones of Jesus, the saint adds: "Whoever
does not give assent to these things despises the Father and is self-condemned,

---

36. Irenaeus, *Against the Heresies* 3.2.1–2.
37. Irenaeus, *Against the Heresies* 3.preface.
38. Irenaeus, *Against the Heresies* 3.1.1.

for he resists and opposes his own salvation—which is precisely what is done by the heretics."[39] Fascinatingly, Irenaeus even refers to the scriptures as "the foundation and pillar of our faith," alluding to 1 Tim. 3:15, where that ascription is referred not to the scriptures but to the church itself, the larger context describing a primitive form of the ecclesiastical hierarchy. By adapting that passage to speak of the scriptures, Irenaeus has tacitly identified the church, with her ecclesiastical hierarchy, and the scriptures with each other. Communion with Jesus has taken written form.

It is at this point that it becomes invaluable to observe closely what the term *canon* connotes for Irenaeus. His is no mere analogy tightly relating *scripture* as a literary form with *communion*. We can see this by returning to Irenaeus's arguments concerning the "order and connection" of the scriptures and the analogy between the gnostics and those who wrote pseudo-Homeric poems. In that context, Irenaeus refers to that "order and connection"—scripture's big picture or narrative thrust—as "the Rule of the Truth."[40] He indicates that this rule is learned through baptism—sacramental initiation to the mystery of Christian faith. The Latin and Greek underlying the English is *regula / kanōn*. Scholars debate what this rule was in its liturgical and catechetical modality: was it a creed? A proto-creed? A creed *cum* narrative structure?[41] The primary sources give little indication. What Irenaeus does, clearly, tell us here is that, whatever the rule's form in instruction and Christian ritual, the initiate is in a place to discern true from false *gnōsis* after she or he has received it. She has an intellectual structure, a sensibility, a world-view or cultivated aesthetic that enables her to complain if she sees a fox rather than the king depicted or an alien narrative *hypothesis* imposed on scriptural texts. Effectively, the canon for Irenaeus is first and foremost this catechetically inculcated sensibility. Elsewhere, Irenaeus will command a friend in Christ to cling to this canon unswervingly, for

---

39. Irenaeus, *Against the Heresies* 3.1.2.

40. Irenaeus, *Against the Heresies* 3.1.2. In another of his writings, *The Demonstration of the Apostolic Preaching*, Irenaeus uses the more common phrase, "Rule of Faith." The terms are apparently equivalent for him.

41. Paul Blowers believes this was a proto-creed with a narrative logic. See his "Regula fidei." W.J. Abraham, on the other hand, and the school of canonical theism associated with him, inexplicably says the word canon originally meant *list*. See his *Canonical Theism: A Proposal for Theology and the Church* (Grand Rapids, MI: Eerdmans, 2008), 4. I find this unlikely given the fluid character of the rule's exposition, even in only one father such as Irenaeus, who gives the rule different descriptions in *Against the Heresies* and the *Demonstration*. See also Leonard Finn, "Reflections on the Rule of Faith," in *The Bible as Christian Scripture*, ed. Christopher Seitz and Kent Harold Richards (Atlanta: Society for Biblical Literature, 2013), 221–42. The position taken here is perhaps closest to that of Tomas Bokedal ("The Rule of Faith: Tracing its Origins," *Journal of Theological Interpretation* 7 [2007]: 233–55), who locates the regula in Irenaeus's exercise of catechesis more than in apologetics, a point I feel is rather clear given the relation Irenaeus describes between the Rule and baptism.

it is the hermeneutical key whereby bedrock reality may be perceived.[42] We are looking here at Irenaeus's epistemic warrant spelled out.

We are, however, from our perspective, probably still faced with an awkward, rather circular picture with a sense of perspective that may feel like it was produced by M.C. Escher. At times, Irenaeus speaks of this canon as if it were an ecclesiastical tradition handed down in catechesis, as when it is imparted through baptism. When he tacitly identifies church and scripture, however, and when he identifies it as the scriptures' inner aesthetic, their "order and connection,"[43] he comes at least close to identifying the Rule with the scriptures themselves. We are perhaps plausibly seeing the beginning of the process whereby the term *canon* undergoes a semantic shift, on the other side of which *canon* designates the authoritative list of acknowledged scriptures. Simply put, we are left sensitized to the natural order of the scriptures *as* a state of living communion and reception of tradition and *vice versa.* The social (church) and literary (scripture) contexts are, as it were, one with each other. By indwelling the scriptures interpreted according to the rule received in baptism, the faithful, according to Irenaeus, adopt a total perspective that makes them hermeneutical insiders, as it were, or characters living in the scriptures' story. The baptized receive a privileged perspective onto the scriptures' inner logic, a kind of big-picture view that encompasses both those saints who wrote the sacred texts and the churches of God in one common life.

Origen of Alexandria on the Coherence of the Scriptures and the Rule

From the apostles' witness to Jesus Christ through the reception of their teachings in the Church over the first two centuries, communion with Jesus thus took as its written form a set of scriptures with an accompanying Rule of Truth received in baptism. Interpretation of these writings often went awry, however, leading some early Christians to articulate not just the Rule, but a *theology* of the interpretive task. This is, in substantial part, what Irenaeus was already concerned with in *Against the Heresies.* A bare few decades later this same task would be revisited with vigor by the Alexandrian, later Caesarean, teacher, Origen, to whose influence we now turn.

Origen was what might today be called, in some circles, a catechist. He was responsible for instructing others in the elements of Christian faith, a task to which he was eminently suited as a churchman of outstanding devotion and almost overwhelming intellectual command. One of his own students admiringly recalled how Origen worked "socratically" to guide students into the Christian

---

42. Irenaeus, *Demonstration of the Apostolic Preaching* 3.
43. Irenaeus, *Against the Heresies* 1.8.1.

mysteries;[44] as with Irenaeus, Origen had interacted with the grammatical and rhetorical schools of Graeco-Roman culture.[45] He also wrote prolifically, bequeathing to the Church a voluminous corpus of which comparatively little remains to us today. Among those writings is *On First Principles*, a work preserved in its entirety in a somewhat free Latin translation by the fourth-century monk Rufinus, although portions of the originally Greek text survive elsewhere. We will use Rufinus's translation here when we must, using the original Greek where it has been preserved.[46]

On First Principles extensively summarizes Origen's understanding of what the scriptures are and how they are to be interpreted and systematically coordinates this with a range of other topics. His program for coordinating the various subjects, which he sets in writing in the preface to book 1, is instructive and illustrates well what he means by the work's title. First, he observes that, although "All who . . . know Christ to be the truth . . . derive the knowledge which calls men to lead a good and blessed life from . . . the words and teaching of Christ . . . ":[47]

> Many of those, however, who profess to believe in Christ, hold conflicting opinions not only on small and trivial questions but also on some that are great and important. . . . In view of

---

44. Origen saw God as a great teacher who ordered the universe and his own interactions with it to guide souls through a process of ethical and spiritual transformation; Origen ordered his own pedagogy to participate in those ends, see Joseph Trigg, *Origen* (London: Routledge, 1998), 37–38: "Gregory's account of Origen's teaching practice demonstrates how he exercised God's providence along with human care for his pupil. Its fundamental concern was integrating the student's personality, or, more precisely, reintegrating it, into the image and likeness of God. . . . Evidently the genuine teacher's goal is not to have the student reproduce his ideas but to become like himself. In the Socratic tradition, such a teacher's role is not to inculcate ideas but to serve as a midwife, enabling the student to develop his own. Origen must have selfconsciously [sic] placed himself in this tradition, since his student described him as attaching himself 'very Socratically' to his students, his words being like the bit to a wild horse."

45. Young, "The Advent of Scholarship," in *Biblical Exegesis*, 76–96.

46. The comments made on Origen throughout the book are partly dependent on the fourth-century Origenist Rufinus, and, also, on those of Origen's writings preserved in their original Greek through the editorial efforts of other early fathers. Rufinus, in particular, is well known for his freedom in rendering the Alexandrian teacher's writings, which presents to Origen scholars no insignificant methodological difficulty. However great that difficulty may be, though, that has not dissuaded other scholars from making serious use of Rufinus's translation, and I will follow that consensus's lead here. (For one discussion of the problems in assessing Rufinus's translation of Origen's various works, interested readers might consult Mark Vessey, "Jerome and Rufinus," in *The Cambridge History of Early Christian Literature*, ed. Frances Young, Lewis Ayres and Andrew Louth [Cambridge: Cambridge University Press, 2004], 318–27.)

47. Origen, *On First Principles* 1.preface.1.

this it seems necessary first to lay down a definite line and unmistakable rule in regard to each of these, and to postpone the
inquiry into other matters until afterwards.[48]

Where is this "unmistakable rule" to be found? He adds that "we maintain
that that only is to be believed as the truth which in no way conflicts with the
tradition of the church and the apostles."[49] Origen's opening comments cohere
with those of Irenaeus. The "words and teaching of Christ" are the source of
spiritual direction, but those words are encountered reliably only in communion, interpreted within the tradition "preserved . . . in the churches"—a tradition that constitutes an "unmistakable rule."

This, however, raises an additional question. Does the Rule prescribe every
single item to be acknowledged, or does it supply an outline or framework for
discovery and growth? Origen raises and answers that question:

> But the following fact should be understood. The holy apos-
> tles, when preaching the faith of Christ, took certain doc-
> trines, those namely which they believed to be necessary
> ones, and delivered them in the plainest terms to all believers,
> even to such as appeared to be somewhat dull in the investi-
> gation of divine knowledge. The grounds of their statements
> they left to be investigated by such as should merit the higher
> gifts of the Spirit and in particular by such as should after-
> wards receive through the Holy Spirit himself the graces of
> language, wisdom and knowledge. There were other doc-
> trines, however, about which the apostles simply said that
> things were so, keeping silence as to the how or the why; their
> intention undoubtedly being to supply the more diligent of
> those who came after them, such as should prove to be lovers
> of wisdom, with an exercise on which to display the fruit of
> their ability.[50]

Origen's philosophical, Socratic engagements are coming forward as tools
for appreciating the apostolic tradition. He sees his own pedagogy built upon an
apostolic approach stretching into the Church's past, to all Christian origins
whatsoever, as a pattern of catechesis directed differently to three distinct
groups arranged in a hierarchy. The apostles are teachers; their "unmistakable
rule" guides believers, now understood as students enrolling themselves in the
school of Christ. It does this by providing certain clear doctrines with accompanying explanations while leaving other matters to be searched out by the power
of the same Spirit of Christ at work in the apostolic instructors. Origen goes on
to list the clearly delineated teachings and then concludes his preface by explaining his theme:

---

48. Origen, *On First Principles* 1.preface.1.
49. Origen, *On First Principles* 1.preface.1.
50. Origen, *On First Principles* 1.preface.3.

> Everyone therefore who is desirous of constructing out of the
> foregoing a connected body of doctrine must use points like
> these as elementary and foundation principles, in accordance
> with the commandment which says, 'Enlighten yourselves
> with the light of knowledge.' Thus by clear and cogent argu-
> ments he will discover the truth about each particular point
> and so will produce, as we have said, a single body of doctrine,
> with the aid of such illustrations and declarations as he shall
> find in the holy scriptures and of such conclusions as he shall
> ascertain to follow logically from them when rightly under-
> stood.[51]

The apostolic Rule of Faith turns out to be for the spiritual life what axioms
are for geometry: with them, deducing warranted conclusions from evidence is
possible. The Rule empowers investigation. Origen lists eight such principles,
two of which are of particular importance for this discussion because they concern Holy Scripture and its interpretation. First, "the scriptures were composed
through the Spirit of God"[52] and "they have not only that meaning which is obvious, but another which is hidden from the majority of readers."[53] Second,
"the contents of scripture are the outward forms of certain mysteries and the
images of divine things. On this point the entire Church is unanimous, that
while the whole law is spiritual, the inspired meaning is not recognized by all,
but only by those who are gifted with the grace of the Holy Spirit in the word of
wisdom and knowledge."[54] Much could be said regarding these principles, some
of which we will revisit in chapter 2, particularly how "the inspired meaning" is
hidden. One key observation to make now, however, is that a doctrine of Holy
Scripture is one element of the Rule of Faith. The scriptures are received in the
Church as Holy Scripture according to a particular way of construing, or perceiving, them and their meanings, and the commendation of this way of reading, along with commendation of the scriptures themselves, is set forth as a universally received, apostolically grounded dogma of the churches.

The peculiar relationship of the scriptures to the Rule can be examined further by considering how Origen as an apologist defends the Church's claim of
inspiration for the scriptures, which is the topic of the opening chapter of book
4 in *On First Principles*. The Alexandrian begins by contrasting the teachings of
the pagan philosophers with those of the scriptures. He writes:

> For although there have been very many lawgivers among
> both Greeks and barbarians, as well as innumerable teachers
> or philosophers who professed that they taught the truth, we
> remember no lawgiver who has succeeded in instilling into
> the minds of foreign nations a desire and enthusiasm either to

---

51. Origen, *On First Principles* 1.preface.10.
52. Origen, *On First Principles* 1.preface.8.
53. Origen, *On First Principles* 1.preface.8.
54. Origen, *On First Principles* 1.preface.8.

adopt his laws voluntarily or to defend them whole-heart-edly.... Yet all over the world, in the whole of Greece and in every foreign nation, there are innumerable people who have abandoned their ancestral laws and their recognized gods and have submitted themselves to the observance of the law of Moses and to the discipleship of Christ, and this in spite of the fact that an intense hatred has been aroused against them by those who worship images, to such an extent that they are of-ten subjected to tortures at the hands of these men and some-times even led to death.[55]

The success of the philosophers, the leading pagans, is contrasted with the success of the Church. The truth of the scriptures is seen in light of the existen-tial viability of the churches and their life in, and mutual opposition with, the world. This by itself is not a reference to the Rule and so does not yet tell us anything about the relationship between the Rule and the scriptures, but Origen continues:

Now if we consider how in a very few years ... the word has been able, in spite of the fewness of its teachers, to be 'preached everywhere in the world' [Mt. 24:14], so that Greeks and barbarians, wise and foolish [Rom. 1:14] have adopted the religion of Jesus, we shall not hesitate to say that this achieve-ment is more than human, *remembering that Jesus taught with all authority and convincing power that his word should prevail*. . . . [W]hen words spoken with such authority have come to pass it shows that God has really become man and delivered to men the doctrines of salvation.[56]

The proof of the scriptures, then, is not simply evidenced by the success of the apostolic mission but in how that success was prophesied in scripture. The scriptures, then, are demonstrated to be inspired as their content is realized in the very churches that read and revere them. This demonstration does not ap-ply to the gospels merely but extends to Old Testament texts:

And what need is there to say also that it was predicted that those who are called 'rulers' 'shall fail from Judah and the leaders from his thighs, when he shall come for whom it'—that is, clearly, the kingdom—'is reserved', and when 'the expecta-tion of the gentiles shall dwell here' [Gen. 69:10, LXX]. For it is abundantly clear from history and from what we see at the present day that after the times of Jesus there were no longer any who were called kings of the Jews, and that all those Jew-ish customs on which they prided themselves, I mean those connected with the temple and the altar and the performance

---

55. Origen, *On First Principles* 4.1.1.
56. Origen, *On First Principles* 4.1.2. Emphasis mine.

of worship and the garments of the high priest, have been destroyed.[57]

This Old Testament example, together with the many others Origen raises at this point in his argument, underscores the fact that the scriptures are being received by him as they are construed according to the Rule of Faith in the churches, for the passages quoted are not at all interpreted in Origen's way by other communities. This becomes apparent even in *On First Principles* itself when, immediately after the argument cited above, Origen departs from his scriptural proofs in order to address a counter-argument, apparently rabbinical.[58] Thus, when Origen argues for the inspiration of the scriptures, he argues for it with respect to those scriptures particularly construed according to the apostolic Rule.

Does Origen, then, in circular fashion predetermine what the meaning of Holy Scripture must be and then find only whatever he has already decided must be there? The fact that he troubles himself to provide counter-arguments in which he cites scripture under his interpretation and then points to fulfillment in history and in the life of the churches demonstrates how mindful he is of the importance of external evidence and existential viability. The relationship between the Rule and the scriptures, therefore, is not circular. One might expect, then, that, just as the scriptures are interpreted in the light of the Rule, the Rule must be spelled out in scriptural terms.

Indeed, this proves to be the case. After discussing the importance—especially for escaping heresy—of rightly interpreting scripture (i.e., the importance of interpreting the scripture according to the Rule, as we have seen), Origen discusses more narrowly prescriptive rules for theological interpretation. However, now, rather than simply turning to the Rule, Origen turns directly to sacred texts to learn hermeneutics appropriate to the scriptures *a posteriori* of an encounter with them:

> The right way, therefore, as it appears to us, of approaching the scriptures and gathering their meaning, is the following, *which is extracted from the writings themselves.* We find some such rule as this laid down by Solomon in the Proverbs concerning the divine doctrines written therein: 'Do thou portray them threefold in counsel and knowledge, that thou mayest answer words of truth to those who question thee' [Prov. 22:20, 21, LXX].[59]

Origen reminds us of his preface, where he indicated the apostles' instruction implicated three categories of people, as he will quickly clarify:

---

57. Origen, *On First Principles* 4.1.3.
58. Origen, *On First Principles* 4.1.3.
59. Origen, *On First Principles* 4.2.4.

We therefore read in this light the passage in The Shepherd[60] ... where Hermas is bidden to 'write two books', and after this to announce to the presbyters of the Church' what he has learned from the Spirit. This is the wording: 'Thou shalt write two books, and shalt give one to Clement and one to Grapte. And Grapte shall admonish the widows and the orphans. But Clement shall send to the cities without, and thou shalt announce to the presbyters of the Church.' [*The Shepherd of Hermas* 2.4.3.]

Now Grapte ... is the bare letter [of the scriptures], which admonishes those child souls that are not yet able to enroll God as their Father and are on this account called orphans, and which also admonishes those who while no longer associating with the unlawful bridegroom and are in widowhood. . . . But Clement, who has already gone beyond the letter, is said to send the sayings 'to the cities without', as if to say, to the souls that are outside all bodily and lower thoughts; while the disciple of the Spirit is bidden to announce the message in person, no longer through letters but through living words, to the presbyters or elders of the whole church of God, to men who have grown grey through wisdom.[61]

In chapter 2 I will revisit Origen's allegorizing technique; for the moment, however, and for the purposes of discussing the relationship of the scriptures to the Rule, I want to note how Origen is turning to texts that he regards as scriptures not just to justify, but to flesh out his method. He approaches the text with a principle taken from the Rule—that the scriptures are designed to support dynamic, engaged catechesis—and then turns to the texts themselves to see how that principle provides a fruitful angle for interpreting and applying them. In the process, what that principle is comes to be spelled out in concrete terms.

Origen illustrates this dialectical approach for us again when he learns from Paul in Romans how to interpret seemingly ahistorical references to known historical nations and rulers:

The accounts tell us that God chose out a certain nation on the earth, and they call this nation by many names. For the nation as a whole is called Israel, and it is also spoken of as Jacob. . . . This being so, the apostle [Paul], raising our spiritual apprehension to a high level, says somewhere: 'Behold Israel after the flesh', inferring that there is an Israel after the spirit. He says also in another place: 'For it is not the children of the

---

60. Origen here refers to *The Shepherd of Hermas*, an early Christian writing widely, although not universally, regarded by the churches of his day as divinely inspired.

61. Origen, *On First Principles* 4.2.4.

flesh that are children of God', nor are 'all they Israel, who are of Israel.' [Rom. 9:6][62]

In the material immediately preceding this point in Origen's discussions, he has related how numerous passages cannot be taken literally when the plain sense is ahistorical, unedifying, or nonsensical. The concern of the immediate passage is how to refine the method indicated by the Rule so as to help readers discern spiritual referents of texts in the light of this fact. Rather than trying to manufacture an approach entirely out of his own intellectual powers and background knowledge, however, he turns to the scriptures themselves to try to find some explicit clue as to what sorts of spiritual referents can genuinely be expected. The Apostle Paul's discussions of the relationship between national-ethnic Israel with her ancestral laws and the trans-ethnic Church with her Gospel provides Origen with just such a clue. Origen goes on to see how and whether Paul's relating the literal-historical Israel to allegorical-spiritual Israel can serve as a hermeneutical principle more broadly:

> If therefore the prophecies relating to Judaea, to Jerusalem, and to Israel, Judah and Jacob suggest to us, because we do not interpret them in a fleshly sense, mysteries such as these, it will follow also that the prophecies which relate to Egypt and the Egyptians, to Babylon and the Babylonians, to Tyre and the Tyrians, to Sidon and the Sidonians, or to any of the other nations, are not spoken solely of the bodily Egyptians, Babylonians, Tyrians and Sidonians. If the Israelites are spiritual, it follows that the Egyptians and Babylonians are also spiritual. *For the statements made in Ezekiel about Pharaoh king of Egypt entirely fail to apply to any particular man who was or will be ruler of Egypt, as will be clear to those who study the passage carefully.*[63]

From there, he attempts to trace those prophecies to spiritual referents analogically similar to spiritual Israel. Evidence is found in various prophecies indicating the rationality of extending Paul's spiritualizing and allegorizing hermeneutics to deal with any *ethnos,* and not just Israel. It is important to note, here, that not only did Origen not construct a method out of his own resources, but even after he consulted the scriptures to find a method, he carefully tested to see whether the method seemed apropos in the particular contexts he was investigating. Paul's spiritualizing references to Israel could apply by analogy to Egypt and Babylon only after examining closely the context of the prophecies in question and observing clues internal to those prophesies that seemed to preclude a literal, historical interpretation.

In these ways the Rule serves as a guide into the meaning of Holy Scripture and not as a determinant of that meaning. Origen's approach implicitly makes the Rule dependent for its own interpretation on the very scriptures which it

---

62. Origen, *On First Principles* 4.3.6.
63. Origen, *On First Principles* 4.3.9, italics mine.

serves as an introduction; what it means to follow and apply the Rule, particularly with respect to scriptural interpretation, is spelled out in terms learned from the scriptures in an open-ended investigation of the sacred letter. The relationship of the scriptures to the Rule is, thus, not a static circle but a dynamic spiral, the inward slope of which is designed to converge ever deeper in the Spirit's councils unto salvation, for the Rule was as scriptural as the scriptures were *ruled*, or as the next century would put it, canonical.

The Fellowship of the Holy Spirit and Illumination of the Inspired

The ground was now paved for defining the Bible of the Christian Church as the Holy Scriptures discerned and interpreted according to the *scriptural* Rule of Faith. Athanasius and other early bishops, such as Augustine of Hippo, would publish official lists of books to be regarded as authoritative or *canonical* for their districts. Illuminatingly, Augustine prefaces his list, known from his seminal *De doctrina Christiana*, with heuristic rules to empower preachers to discern lists of their own by way of comparing the practices of the various episcopal sees.[64] In this way, the canonical lists remain transparent to the underlying ontology relating the scriptures and the canon of the apostolic Church. It is perhaps even helpful not to think of *canon as list of books* (the dominant sense of the word today) as having replaced *canon as summary teaching*, but rather *canon as list* as a metonym for the entire Rule, where the Rule remains what it had been since the days of Irenaeus: the Church's determination to preserve, pass on, and live out the implications of the apostolic deposit. Held together in this way, ruled scripture and scriptural Rule were together one mode, even the prime mode, of communion with the patriarchs, prophets, apostles and all the righteous—the whole communion of saints—and, through them, with the Word and Spirit of God who had sanctified those saints unto God's revelation. I might even say that this one object, canonical scripture, functioned as the authorized version, so to speak, of the identity story of the people of God, although I shall have to nuance that description in the next chapter. By functioning as a mode of communion with the saints, the scriptures initiated each new generation of Christians into the mystery of the Church. They told the Church and the Christian who she was, where she came from, and into what future she was on pilgrimage.

Nowhere was this more true than in the corporate worship of the Lord's Day liturgy. As pointed out by Gamble and as is apparent in Augustine's instructions in *De doctrina Christiana*, one highly ranked heuristic applied by early Christians in discerning Holy Scripture from noncanonical writing was how regularly they were used by the churches,[65] and use at that time primarily meant public

---

64. Augustine of Hippo, *De Doctrina* 2.12.
65. Gamble, *New Testament Canon*, 70–71.

reading during worship[66]—a use demonstrable from some of those very writings. Public reading in corporate worship is anticipated by liturgical instruction to "greet one another with a holy kiss,"[67] and the mysterious *Apocalypse* pronounces blessing on "he who reads aloud the words of the prophecy, and . . . those who hear."[68] One major setting for such reading, if not *the* major setting, was the eucharistic gathering celebrated on "the Lord's Day" mentioned in the *Apocalypse* itself. Justin Martyr, a seminal second century apologist, writes somewhat at length on this early liturgical reading in his *First Apology*. He tells his non-Christian audience that:

> And on the day called Sunday all who live in cities or in the country gather together in one place, and the memoirs of the Apostles or the writings of the prophets are read, as long as time permits. Then when the reader has finished, the Ruler in a discourse instructs and exhorts to the imitation of these good things. Then we all stand up together and offer prayers; and, as we said before, when we have finished the prayer, bread is brought and wine and water, and the Ruler likewise offers up prayers and thanksgivings to the best of his ability, and the people assent, saying the Amen. . . .[69]

Thus, texts at that time categorized as apostolic and prophetic, most likely corresponding to some subset of writings now comprising our New Testament and likewise for the Old, were strongly associated with the flow and logic of the Eucharistic liturgy. Indeed, such reading was considered partly constitutive of the liturgy, with the Eucharist itself taking place after the readings and the homily that, presumably, judging from the practices of later centuries, was an interpretation of those readings. This shaping of the liturgy followed naturally from the inner logic of ruled reading of scripture, as argued here, for the Eucharist, Justin tells us in allusion to Jn. 1, is "the flesh and blood of that Jesus who became incarnate,"[70] or, as various other early Christian writings describe it, deifying encounter with Jesus himself.[71] The point of these gatherings was transforming, renewing, converting fellowship with the risen and ascended Lord Jesus—and he, as already discussed at length, could be received by way of receiving those sent by him. The scriptures interpreted and discerned within the Church according to her Rule were principle means whereby those sent by Jesus Christ, the Word of God, were continually received in fellowship and so quite reasonably preceded reception of Christ's Eucharistic presence.

---

66. Gamble, *Books and Their Readers*, 205.

67. Rom. 16:16; 2 Cor. 13:12.

68. Apoc. 1:3.

69. Justin Martyr, *First Apology* 67.

70. Justin Martyr, *First Apology* 66, cf. Jn. 1:14.

71. One particular early Christian writer who makes this point is Hilary of Poitiers, who says that eating the Church's Eucharist deifies the communicant. See Hilary of Poitiers, *De Trinitate* 8.12–13.

Indeed, remembrance of Jesus and hope for experience of his in-breaking presence at the Eucharist, arguably, formed the *Sitz im Leben* of at least those texts that eventually comprised the New Testament, as Denis Farkasfalvy, a historical theologian who has worked on the development of the New Testament canon, demonstrates. Speaking specifically regarding the written Gospels, he writes:

> The first Eucharistic assemblies came about as Jesus' original disciples were prompted to meet after experiencing the first evidences of the resurrection and there they were led to begin a process of recalling and retelling the memories of Jesus' ministry. The narrative tradition that stands behind the Synoptics was formed and shaped in this "eucharistic cradle" of early Christian liturgy. From its beginning, the Synoptic tradition stood in live exchange with an audience gathered for hearing about Jesus because they wanted to meet Jesus by means of the liturgical assemblies where they experienced the past encounters as being re-enacted and relived. Consequently, the narratives were formed for audiences that identified themselves with those described in the narratives as meeting Jesus, being brought to him, or approaching him for healing, teaching, or some other benefit. In such presentation of episodic material, Jesus is necessarily featured not as a figure of an objective past, defined and isolated in the context of a *mere* historical past, but as the one who, at the beginning of an episode, both arrives and is being approached, encounters a human need or religious problem—a human situation of "crisis"—and brings an experience of salvation, i.e., a manifestation of divine mercy resulting in a solution unexplainable from mere human resources.[72]

Farkasfalvy's argument, if I may put it in words suggested by Mary Carruthers's study in *The Book of Memory*, to which I will return in chapter 2, is that the New Testament texts and those oral traditions that stood behind them functioned as a kind of communal memory,[73] intentionally stirred up as a means of waiting upon and receiving Christ anew. The implications of such a reading are enormous, for it demonstrates that communal meditation on Holy Scripture, orally recited and interpreted, functioned to name and renew the identity and sense of vocation shared by the gathered worshipers—namely, an identity and vocation organically continuous with that of the saints of old. On this matter Farkasfalvy observes:

---

72. Denis Farkasfalvy, "The Eucharistic Provenance of New Testament Texts," in *Rediscovering the Eucharist: Ecumenical Conversations*, ed. Roch A. Kereszty (Mahwah, NJ: Paulist, 2003), 34–35.

73. Mary Carruthers, *The Book of Memory* (Cambridge: Cambridge University Press, 1990).

The eucharistic practice of the church constitutes the medium in which ongoing continuity can be legitimately perceived and claimed between the historical past and the present on its way into the future. The Eucharist is the context in which history does not undergo a *rigor mortis* by becoming both stiff and irrelevant, hopelessly and irredeemably glued to long-past events and states of mind. Instead, in this medium of the church's continued sacramental practice, Jesus' universal mission (Matt 28:16–20) successfully extends the chain of the gospel episodes so as to reach all times and all places and make his journey transcend the limits of history without rendering it ahistorical. This would, of course, mean that, in this way, the last words of Matthew's gospel, "I will be with you always until the completion of the aeon" (*synteleia tou aionos*) becomes a highest expression of eucharistic theology.[74]

He alludes to the closing discourse of Matthew's gospel, in which Jesus reinvests his apostles with his own authority for the sake of mission among the nations, an authority that is cosmic in scope ("all authority in heaven and on earth").[75] Thus, in recognizing and even producing scriptures so as to be amenable to an "ecclesial and sacramental exegesis," as Farkasfalvy puts it,[76] Christians sought no mere record of the past but a connection to it, or rather, through their forebears in it, to the eternal Lord who was ever the same throughout its scope.[77] In publicly reading these texts and reciting these traditions in public worship, the early Church sought a reminder of, encounter with, and re-investment in the authority of Jesus, reconstituting the churches in their apostolic identity. Those who were, by participating in that Church, sharers in the apostolic mission were thus uniquely positioned to appreciate and enter into the full mystery of holy scripture. They were reading their own story when they read the apostolic and prophetic deposit.

---

74. Farkasfalvy, "Eucharistic Provenance of New Testament Texts," 45.

75. Mt. 28:18.

76. Farkasfalvy, "Eucharistic Provenance of New Testament Texts," 45.

77. Heb. 13:8. Note also, in this connection, the repeated motif of the unity of the Law and the Prophets and the God of both the Old and New Testaments in Irenaeus at, e.g., *Against the Heresies* 4.2.1–2.

Chapter 2
Ontology of Scripture and Indwelling Salvation's Epic (Or, Whose Identity Story?)

My previous chapter described an evolving *ethos* wherein scripture was constructed, together with the rule of faith that supplied its true *hypothesis*, as the identity story of all the faithful—a mode of communal memory whereby emerging generations of Christians were initiated to a eucharistic identity receding into the apostolic past. I intended that description to be heuristic and now propose a second go around the dialectical spiral to refine it.

Critical re-consideration of the nature and definition of apostolic figures, the Word's plenipotentiary emissaries, can underscore why. In the first century, Paul describes his ministry in terms that nuance and expand the *apostolos* principle discussed in chapter 1. He writes in 2 Corinthians:

> For we do not proclaim ourselves; we proclaim Jesus Christ as Lord and ourselves as your slaves for Jesus' sake. For it is the God who said, 'Let light shine out of darkness', who has shone in our hearts to give the light of the knowledge of the glory of God in the face of Jesus Christ. But we have this treasure in clay jars, so that it may be made clear that this extraordinary power belongs to God *and does not come from us.*[1]

Were we to start naïvely from the early Church's high regard for apostolic authority, we might conclude that the Church's message is one of obedience to the apostles or to the Church itself, perhaps understood as vicars of an absentee lord. Paul's words sharply militate against that possibility. The apostle's authority is not the primary content of his own preaching ("we do not proclaim ourselves"), and becomes part of the proclamation only once qualified as a form of slavery ("and ourselves as your slaves") on behalf of Christ ("for Jesus' sake").

---

1. 2 Cor. 4:5–7, emphasis mine. As an important aside, it is interesting to note that Origen of Alexandria cites explicitly from this passage in *On First Principles* 4.1.7 in describing the divinity of the scriptures.

The reason given for why this is the case is that God is revealing himself ("For it is the God who said, 'Let light shine out of darkness', who has shone in our hearts to give the light of the knowledge of the glory of God . . . "). The apostles' ministry, then, is not so much a delegation from an absent God in Christ as it is a participation in the ministry of the Christ who is ever present in the Spirit, or, as Matthew's gospel puts it, "Remember, I [Jesus] am with you always, to the end of the age."[2]

Implications abound if scripture was, in early Christianity, a mode of communion with the apostles, as I have argued here. Were the scriptures to constitute the Church as a place of blessing external to the life of God, we might expect to find eternal life in devotion to the scriptures themselves or to other modes of ritual participation in the Church's / Israel's community life—as, indeed, some misguided (from the perspective of the early Church) Israelites did believe and received a rebuke from Jesus: "You search the scriptures because you think that in them you have eternal life; and it is they that testify on my behalf. Yet you refuse to come to me to have life."[3] Given especially how early Christians read the person of Christ Jesus, verses such as this one amount to a denial that the scriptures refer primarily to the community's past or present sense of identity, vocation, and order. Jesus is the Word made flesh and he who has received the Name above every name.[4] We should expect divine transcendence to attend the text, the story it tells to be that of God, and not just that of a human society, however sacred. At the least, this is something we should anticipate as we aim to penetrate into early Christian understandings of what it meant to read Holy Scripture faithfully. As with the preceding chapter, we will begin by considering some of the earliest traditions available to our perusal—those preserved in the New Testament.

The New Testament on the Spirit,
the Scriptures, and Prophecy

The New Testament is riddled with reflection on the Holy Spirit's role in elevating the reference of human speech and writing. For the sake of brevity of introduction, two passages come particularly to mind. The first is Paul's discussion (in 1 Cor. 14) of pneumatically empowered prophecy and the implications of the Spirit's presence and empowerment for corporate worship. Although his discussion does not explicitly deal with written scriptures, by exploring the nature of the human relationship with the Spirit and the implications of that relationship for humans' relationships with each other in the Church Paul's discussions there illuminate early Christian understandings of prophecy in every mode including the written one, which tended to be received communally and in worship no

---

2. Mt. 28:20.
3. Jn. 5:39–40.
4. Jn. 1:1–14, Phil. 2:5–11.

less than charismatic prophecy. The second is the discussion of written prophecy in 2 Pt. 1, where the divine character of scripture is explicitly tied to its interpretation and both discussions are set in the larger context of human salvation particularly construed as Christ-followers coming to share in the divine nature itself. This second passage is explicitly cited in the fourth-century christological debates by Hilary of Poitiers as significant for distinguishing authentic from inauthentic explorations of the scriptures' witness,[5] underscoring 2 Peter as a vital bridge between the first and succeeding centuries.

Second Cor. 14 rather famously lays down practical instruction for the utterance of ecstatic tongues and intelligible prophecy, both understood as gifts of the Spirit in the larger context of 12–14. The *Sitz im Leben* of Paul's instruction to the Corinthian church, as disclosed by the persistent polemic of the epistle, is communal disunity rooted in one-upmanship.[6] Playing into this disunity, especially in the context of corporate worship, was, apparently, a view of spirit-inspiration in modes like that of some pagan cults that also prized ecstatic displays.[7] Liturgical chaos ensued, so Paul addressed it:

> If anyone speaks in a tongue, let there be only two or at most three, and each in turn; and let one interpret. But if there is no one to interpret, let them be silent in church and speak to themselves and to God. Let two or three prophets speak, and let the others weigh what is said. If a revelation is made to someone else sitting nearby, let the first person be silent. For you can all prophesy one by one, so that all may learn and all be encouraged. And the spirits of prophets are subject to the prophets, for God is a God not of disorder but of peace.[8]

Significant for our focus here is the relationship of the Spirit and the speakers. One might be tempted to think that the Spirit's and the speaker's responsibilities for the utterance are inversely related: that as the Spirit's involvement becomes more direct, the speaker's self-control and rational/volitional involvement decreases. Paul asserts the opposite. Because "God is a God not of disorder but of peace," persons inspired by his Spirit retain their self-control, even in their ecstasy, and are responsible to partner with him to build up the gathered worshipers. Fee believes this unveils an opposition between pagan and Christian

---

5. Hilary of Poitiers, *De Trinitate* 1.18.

6. For extended discussion of the problems of the Corinthian community, one good commentary is that of Gordon Fee, *The First Epistle to the Corinthians* (Grand Rapids, Michigan: Eerdmans, 1987).

7. This is the position of Fee (ibid., 692). B. Witherington notes that pagan cults could, however, differ in their oracular practices; the Pythia of Delphi, for example, tended towards a more ordered and intelligible mode than the initiates to the mysteries of Dionysus, see *Conflict and Community in Corinth* (Grand Rapids, MI: Eerdmans, 1995), 276–79.

8. 1 Cor. 14:27–33a.

understandings of (s/S)pirit-inspiration that was partly to blame for the Corinthians' anti-social behavior:

> Not only did they [the Corinthians] have a singular passion for this gift [glossolalia], but apparently they had allowed it to dominate their gatherings *in a way that reflected pagan ecstasy far more than the gospel of Christ.* This [Paul's] guideline clearly removes tongues from all forms of pagan ecstasy, as far as Paul's understanding is concerned. The admonition in v. 32 is probably intended as much for this gift as for prophecy. Whatever else, Christian inspiration, including both tongues and prophecy, is not "out of control." The Spirit does not "possess" or "overpower" the speaker; he is subject to the prophet or tongues-speaker, in the sense that what the Spirit has to say will be said in an orderly and intelligible way. It is indeed the Spirit who speaks, but he speaks through the controlled instrumentality of the believer's own mind and tongue.[9]

So, there is a partnership, a synergy, and even a sort of mystic union in view. At least the occasion, if not the content, of prophecy is to be mapped not on a continuum opposing divine to human, but against a backdrop that unites them, foreshadowing the christological reflection of forthcoming centuries. This theme of partnership leads us seamlessly to 2 Pt. 1, where discussion of such partnership is closely juxtaposed with a rebuke to inauthentic readings of Holy Scripture. The author opens with a discussion of what it means for humans to "become participants in the divine nature,"[10] followed by what at least resembles a terse reference to the Transfiguration of Jesus seen by Peter and finally opens up into a castigation of false prophets and teachers with the words: "First of all you must understand this, that no prophecy of scripture is a matter of one's own interpretation, because no prophecy ever came by human will, but men and women moved by the Holy Spirit spoke from God."[11] The relationship of the divine emissary to God renders the reference of his or her writings into something transcendent of the community devoted to those writings' exegesis—namely, to the life and activity of the Spirit of God.[12] The Spirit is the author, so to speak, of prophecy, such that its true interpretation lies in the Spirit's

---

9. Fee, *First Epistle to the Corinthians*, 692. Emphasis mine.

10. 2 Pt. 1:4. This verse was commonly understood in the early period that is the focus of this chapter to refer to human deification in Christ; see, for example, Hilary of Poitiers, *On the Trinity* 1.18; also A.L. Kolp, "Partakers of the Divine Nature: The Use of II Peter 1:4 by Athanasius," in *Studia Patristica* 17 (Oxford: Pergamon Press, 1982), 1018–23.

11. 2 Pt. 1:20–21.

12. It is important to note that this passage is ambiguous in the Greek, the pronoun for self being in context open to referring either to the inspired person or to the reader. The reading adopted here is that not only is scripture's meaning not determined by the subjectivity of the individual reader, but scripture's meaning is determined by no mortal agent, but by the Spirit of God who gave it. This interpretation coheres with the devel-

purposes, but those purposes are the salvation of the Christ-follower conceived of as sublime union and communion with God. Lightning has struck the same spot twice, albeit from different angles: in 1 Corinthians divine inspiration empowered and did not diminish human participation; here human participation coheres with the self-disclosure of God without corrupting, diluting, or diminishing the revelation. Apply this model heuristically to the question of ontology of scripture, and we might say that the scriptures serve not only as the identity story of the Church but as the story of God in his pursuit of union and communion with humankind—and, therefore, derivatively the story of the Church, the communion of the Holy Spirit. I now have a hypothesis for refining the heuristic definition developed in chapter 1. Will reflection on biblical interpretation confirm or discount that hypothesis?

Irenaeus on the Rationality of Prophetic Reference and the Dramatic Coherence of the Economies of God

If the hypothesis is right, the next place to look would be soteriological doctrine from the second century, preferably from a father who is also concerned to reflect on right interpretation of holy writ. Given what we have already seen, Irenaeus demands another visit. Besides *Against the Heresies*, he also wrote the *Demonstration of the Apostolic Preaching*, apparently a sort of correspondence with a friend in Christ designed to reinforce his devotion to the aforementioned Rule of Faith / Truth. The opening, catechetical summary of this rule in the *Demonstration* turns out immediately promising:

> Well also does Paul His apostle say: *One God, the Father, who is over all and through all and in us all.*[13] For *over all* is the Father: and *through all* is the Son, for through Him all things were made by the Father; and *in us all* is the Spirit, who cries *Abba Father*,[14] and fashions man into the likeness of God. Now the Spirit shows forth the Word, and therefore the prophets announced the Son of God; and the Word utters the Spirit, and therefore is Himself the announcer of the prophets, and leads and draws man to the Father.[15]

The Spirit shows forth the Word by crying out "Abba Father." Irenaeus echoes Paul's words in Rom. 8 where the speaker of the filial cry is a symphony of voices both creaturely and divine, and the "spirit of adoption" is described empowering the prayers of those who are being saved—prayers which, ultimately,

---

oping patristic tradition, as we will show throughout this chapter. For extended discussion, see Richard J. Bauckham, *Jude, 2 Peter*, Word Biblical Commentary Series 50 (Waco, Texas: Word, 1983), 228–35.

13. Eph. 4:6.

14. Rom. 8:15.

15. Irenaeus, *Demonstration of the Apostolic Preaching* 5.

express the longings of the entire creation for redemption and life.[16] It is this context that Irenaeus has in mind when he says that "the prophets announced the *Son* of God." The description of the Spirit's ministry as "fashion[ing] man to the likeness of God" is also telling in that it positions the ministries of the prophets in a single, overarching plot stretching backwards to creation and forwards to redemption, for the reference to the "likeness of God" evokes a motif that resonates across the scriptures from the Genesis creation accounts (wherein human beings are said to be created in the image and likeness of God, Gen. 1:26–27) to the description of Christ Jesus as "the image of the invisible God" (Col. 1:15). Thus, Irenaeus describes the Spirit as the divine patron of the prophets and positions the prophets as participants in the Spirit's ministry in the mystery of salvation, a ministry that continues to advance into the present hour. The content of the prophets' message is the same as that of the Spirit-empowered creation's cry in Rom. 8 and thus is an oracle that, ultimately, is about the Word and Son of God, Jesus Christ. In this sense the direct recipient of the Spirit's ministry is the Word Himself, in the soteriological partnership of the Father, Word, and Spirit:

> For this reason the baptism of our regeneration proceeds through these three points: God the Father bestowing on us regeneration through His Son by the Holy Spirit. For as many as carry [in them] the Spirit of God are led to the Word, that is to the Son; and the Son brings them to the Father; and the Father causes them to possess incorruption.[17]

Just prior to the quote given, the Holy Spirit is described as the divine patron not only of explicit prophecy, but also of the patriarchs and the righteous. His patronage leads them specifically to the Word. The Word, therefore, is the ultimate subject of the prophets' oracles and the goal of the patriarchs' and righteous persons' spiritual pilgrimage regardless of whether the subjects of the texts involved be Abraham's or Israel's Levant itineraries, the exile of Jerusalem, etc. Irenaeus understands the careers of the prophets, patriarchs, and righteous of old—and the Church of his day—to participate in a larger providence, the guiding and empowering architect of which is the Spirit and the goal of which is communion between God and humanity realized through (and as?) the Word made flesh, the Lord Jesus Christ. The hypothesis stated earlier—that the reference of scripture was to God and humanity in communion—is already receiving verification. Irenaeus calls this communion generating providence the dispensation or *ekonomia* of the Father.[18]

---

16. Rom. 8:15. The underlying Greek has the word *huithesias*, a compound involving *huios* (English: "son") and thereby evokes thoughts of patrimony and inheritance. Irenaeus apparently has picked up that theme from the text of Romans and set it in a larger theological context involving Jn. 1.

17. Irenaeus, *Demonstration of the Apostolic Preaching* 6–7.

18. Irenaeus, *Demonstration of the Apostolic Preaching* 6.

The dispensation of God again becomes a focus in *Against the Heresies*. To see how requires some exposition. We already saw in chapter 1 how the bishop describes his approach to scripture in terms of the apostolic Rule. Irenaeus's articulation of this rule is substantially directed to unmasking the pseudo-gnostics by presenting a contrast to their pattern. This pattern, represented diversely by teachers ranging from Valentinus to Marcion, posited, among other things, all sorts of divisions:[19] between 'Jesus' and 'Christ', between the God of Israel and the Father of 'Christ', and between the Creator, standing over the ruinous creation, and the Redeemer, associated exclusively with a non-created order. Groups such as the Valentinians, Irenaeus tells us, developed complex mythologies populated by various divinities, some of which were associated with the transcendent, spiritual orbit, others with the gross material creation, and yet others with an intermediate state between those two extremes. As divinities hailed from different orbits, so also was the meaning of the scriptures polarized by origin in different ultimate sources.[20]

The whole of *Against the Heresies* is, in many respects, an extended discussion of the opposite view set in a polemical context against this worldview of the Valentinians, Marcionites, and those of their ilk. Apparently shifting the accent of his apology more in the direction of Marcion yet still in the larger context of this total polemic, Irenaeus describes God as "one and the same" throughout:

> All things therefore are of one and the same substance, that is, from one and the same God; as also the Lord says to the disciples "Therefore every scribe, which is instructed unto the kingdom of heaven, is like unto a man that is an householder, which bringeth forth out of his treasure things new and old."[21] He did not teach that he who brought forth the old was one, and he that brought forth the new, another; but that they were one and the same. For the Lord is the good man of the house, who rules the entire house of His Father; and who delivers a law suited both for slaves and those who are as yet undisciplined; and gives fitting precepts to those that are free, and have been justified by faith, as well as throws His own inheritance open to those that are sons.[22]

God is one, so God's saving providence is integrated. The Law's character as law is relationally apropos for slaves and the undisciplined, while the Gospel is directed towards those now adopted as heirs in God's house—a reference to the

---

19. We will cover, in extremely brief summary, below, some of the main features of Irenaeus's opponents. His own treatment of them can be found at length in book 1 of *Against the Heresies*, but is far too detailed to be successfully represented here by direct quotation.

20. See Irenaeus, *Against the Heresies* 1.7.3.

21. Mt. 13:52.

22. Irenaeus, *Against the Heresies* 4.9.1.

temporal priority of the Law and its succession by the Gospel of Jesus Christ with, perhaps, another passing allusion to the adoption theology of Rom. 8. Irenaeus continues, describing the providence of God as salvation achieved through two covenants:

> Now, without contradiction, He means by those things which are brought forth from the treasure new and old, the two covenants; the old, that giving of the law which took place formerly; and He points out as the new, that manner of life required by the Gospel.... But one and the same householder produced both covenants, the Word of God, our Lord Jesus Christ, who spake with both Abraham and Moses, and who has restored us anew to liberty, and has multiplied that grace which is from Himself.[23]

As there is one God and one Lord so there is one salvation brought to fruition through two great covenant interactions with humanity. Furthermore, these covenants relate to each other not in complementary ways, as if there were one goal arrived at by two roads, but through a divinely guided progression, one covenant preparing for and leading into its successor:

> He declares: "For in this place is One greater than the temple."[24] ... Greater, therefore, is that legislation which has been given in order to liberty than that given in order to bondage; and therefore it has also been diffused, not throughout one nation [only], but over the whole world. For one and the same Lord, who is greater than the temple, greater than Solomon, and greater than Jonah, confers gifts upon men, that is, His own presence, and the resurrection from the dead; but He does not change God, nor proclaim another Father, but that very same one, who always has more to measure out to those of His household. And as their love towards God increases, He bestows more and greater [gifts]; as also the Lord said to His disciples: "Ye shall see greater things than these."[25]

The Gospel is more to the Law's less. By alluding to Jesus's words to his disciples that they would see him perform yet greater miracles than they had yet seen him work, furthermore, this single divine goal for the covenants is seen, by a kind of analogy, to be the self-expression of the One Lord's invariant character and identity: as Christ Jesus in his earthly career demonstrated ever more of his power and divine identity, so has he been doing throughout his saving engagement with humankind.

The most important observation we might draw from these paragraphs, however, is that this united, salvific engagement of God with humankind that

---

23. Irenaeus, *Against the Heresies* 4.9.1.

24. Mt. 12:6.

25. Irenaeus, *Against the Heresies* 4.9.2. The scripture reference with which this quote ends is to Jn. 1:50.

Irenaeus discusses in *Against the Heresies* is none other than the *ekonomia* referred to in the *Demonstration*.[26] This is made clear in how Irenaeus continues in
this immediate section with words that identify the Spirit received by the
Church under the new covenant with the Spirit of adoption from Rom. 8:

> And Paul declares: "Not that I have already attained, or that I
> am justified, or already have been made perfect. For we know
> in part, and we prophesy in part; but when that which is per-
> fect has come, the things which are in part shall be done
> away."[27] As, therefore, when that which is perfect is come, we
> shall not see another Father, but Him whom we now desire to
> see . . . *neither do we receive another Holy Spirit, besides Him who is
> with us, and who cries, "Abba, Father;"*[28] and we shall make in-
> crease in the very same things [as now], and shall make pro-
> gress, so that no longer through a glass, or by means of enig-
> mas, but face to face, we shall enjoy the gifts of God. . . .[29]

This passage clearly relates to the same subject matter as the opening chapters of the *Demonstration* because it identifies the Holy Spirit received by the
Church with the Spirit of adoption from Rom. 8. In the *Demonstration*, however,
that Spirit was the patron of prophecy and divine executor, together with the
Word, of the *ekonomia* of the Father. All this means that the *ekonomia* discussed
in the *Demonstration*—the context of prophecy and of the careers of the patriarchs and all the righteous—are one and the same as the Old and New Testaments, where those Testaments are two covenants related to each other in a
single, unfolding saga of salvation. The inscripturation of prophecy described in
Against the Heresies, therefore, occurs in the economic context of the Spirit's
bringing human persons, now, apparently, with their histories and literary tal-
ents, to the Word, uniting them to God.

Furthermore—and, though it is a subtle point, it is one well worth stating
clearly—the material contents of Old Testament scripture are not, for Irenaeus,
merely literary representation of events occurring along God's unfolding plan.
They are a record of the saving God's dispensation set down in words at the behest and patronage of the Spirit of adoption to accomplish his ministry to the
Word of God. That Word, the Son of God, will take flesh as the virgin-born Lord
Jesus Christ as the climax of prophecy and incarnate Savior. While the events
recorded, then, project human history forward to his great epiphany, the scriptures, as the events' literary record, likewise participate in the dispensation by

---

26. Irenaeus, *Demonstration of the Apostolic Preaching* 6.

27. This scriptural reference presents, in impressively condensed fashion, words
taken from Phil. 3:12, 1 Cor. 4:4, and 1 Cor. 13:9–10.

28. Rom. 8:15.

29. Irenaeus, *Against the Heresies* 4.9.2. Emphasis mine.

the Spirit's design. They prepare the way, so to speak, for the Word's incarna-tion, as the Spirit's servants—the prophets, patriarchs and righteous—announce the Son of God as the climax and ultimate subject of all prophecy.[30]

If we read, then, with Irenaeus, we might expect the sub-narratives (e.g., the Exodus) and various prophetic oracles to look forward to Christ as much as (or even more so than) backwards to Egypt or to the immediate *Sitz im Leben* of the text's historical horizon. Indeed, this is precisely how many sub-narratives and prophesies function according to Irenaeus. A few examples to show the ex-egetical implications seem in order. We might start with the dénouement of the Genesis Flood narrative (from Gen. 9, esp. vv. 18–27), where the early careers of Noah's sons Shem, Ham, and Japheth are narrated. Irenaeus notes how Genesis depicts Ham making a mockery of his father, Noah, and Shem and Japheth tak-ing action to restore Noah's honor. For this, Ham's son Canaan is cursed to be the progenitor of slaves, while Shem is given a special relationship to the Lord God and Japheth is given both that he should be enlarged and that he should dwell in the house of Shem.[31] In the larger penteteuch, the *Canaanites* are ethnic rivals of Israel, and Israel is the heir of Shem.[32] The curse of Ham/Canaan is thus seen to play out in the drama of Israel's conquering enmity with her pagan neighbors and the blessing of Shem in the Lord God's covenant with Israel through her ancestors. What of Japheth? Irenaeus writes with particular inter-est in his blessing, for:

> In the end of the ages he blossomed forth, at the appearing of the Lord, through the calling of the Gentiles, when God en-larged unto them the calling; and *their sound went out into all the earth, and their words to the end of the world.*[33] The enlarging, then, is the calling from among the Gentiles, that is to say, the Church. *And he dwells in the house of Shem;*[34] that is, in the in-heritance of the fathers, receiving in Christ Jesus the right of the firstborn.[35]

Japheth is the progenitor of those who are not physically descended from the patriarchs but who, nonetheless, come to share the patriarchs' call and vo-cation, 'enlarged' to include them as they come into relationship with the patri-archs' God as the Church. This, in turn, has implications for seeing a yet deeper layer of blessing accruing to Shem, for the call of God goes out to the Gentiles through Christ Jesus, the descendant of Shem and the righteous patriarchs *par excellence*, and Jesus is, in the big picture, the victorious Lord who came "to com-plete and gather up all things . . . in order to abolish death and show forth life

---

30. Irenaeus, *Demonstration of the Apostolic Preaching* 5.
31. Irenaeus, *Demonstration of the Apostolic Preaching* 20–21.
32. Irenaeus, *Demonstration of the Apostolic Preaching* 20.
33. Ps. 19:4, possibly by way of Paul's allusion to that verse in Rom. 10:18.
34. Gen. 9:27.
35. Irenaeus, *Demonstration of the Apostolic Preaching* 21.

and produce a community of union between God and man."[36] Since the inheritance of the patriarchs is that which is inherited by Jesus, Shem and Japheth's righteous action is understood in retrospect to have participated in God's purposes unto salvation, and Noah's prophetic blessing of them (and, in the inverse sense, his curse on Ham/Canaan) is seen to have surprising consequences reaching far into the dénouement of the ages. The meaning of Noah's curses and blessings unfold in open-ended ways as the divine dispensation progresses. Exegesis likewise requires a future-oriented openness.

A different interpretive move grounded in the same set of assumptions regarding the Spirit's role in forming the scriptures is made of the end of the Pentateuch, the Book of Deuteronomy. First, Irenaeus provides an abstract for the entire book with the words:

> Here Moses gathered the people together, and summed up all afresh, proclaiming the mighty works of God even unto that day, fashioning and preparing those that had grown up in the wilderness to fear God and keep His commandments, imposing on them as it were a new legislation, adding to that which was made before.[37]

With this summary of Deuteronomy still ringing in his hearers' ears, Irenaeus describes Jesus as the climax of prophecy and of Israel's relationship to God:

> And, when Moses had finished his course, it was said to him by God: *Get thee up into the mountain, and die*: for thou shalt not bring in my people into the land.[38] So he *died according to the word of the Lord*;[39] and Jesus the son of Nun succeeded him.[40] He divided the Jordan and made the people to pass over into the land....
>
> Hither were the prophets sent by God through the Holy Spirit; and they instructed the people and turned them to the God of their fathers, the Almighty; and they became heralds of the revelation of our Lord Jesus Christ the Son of God, declaring that from the posterity of David His flesh should blossom forth; that after the flesh He might be the son of David, who was the son of Abraham by a long succession; but according to

---

36. Irenaeus, *Demonstration of the Apostolic Preaching* 6.

37. Irenaeus, *Demonstration of the Apostolic Preaching* 28.

38. Deut. 32:49.

39. Deut. 34:5.

40. MacKenzie, whose translation I am using for this quote, probably chooses to render the reference to Joshua son of Nun from the hexateuch as "Jesus the son of Nun" because, not only are the names the same etymologically but that correspondence is theologically significant to Irenaeus, as we are about to see. In this cluster of paragraphs, however, Ireaneus seems mostly interested in a Moses-Jesus typology rather than a Joshua-Jesus one.

the spirit[41] Son of God, preexisting with the Father, begotten before all the creation of the world, and at the end of the times appearing to all the world as man, the Word of God *gathering up in Himself all things that are in heaven and that are on earth.*[42]

As Moses "gathered up the people, and summed up all afresh" at Israel's journey's end so the Lord Jesus Christ, at the climax of the ages, "gather[ed] up" all earthly and heavenly history in himself so that humanity might receive a new covenant with God and proceed to salvation's goal: "So then He united man with God, and established a community of union between God and man."[43] This second kind of reading, which involves intuitively different strategies then the reading Irenaeus gives to the blessing of the diluvian patriarchs, has been classed as *typological* together with a host of similar readings given of numerous Old Testament narratives.[44] By adopting it, Irenaeus displays Jesus to his reader as accomplishing for all of humanity what Moses and Joshua, in a lesser sense and by analogy, accomplished for Israel at the climax of the Exodus and wilderness wanderings. This particular typological reading is left un-flagged by the church father; elsewhere, however, he engages this interpretive strategy explicitly, and, in the process, bares some of the assumptions behind it. One such example, taken from the third book of *Against the Heresies*, likens Jesus to the rod of Moses which became a serpent:

> On this account also Moses, manifesting a type, threw a rod to the ground, that when it had become enfleshed [*incarnata*] it might expose and swallow up all the sinfulness of the Egyptians that was rising up against God's economy,[45] that even the Egyptians might bear witness that it was God's finger that wrought salvation for the people, and not Joseph's son.[46]

If the wooden rod, which took flesh and swallowed up the witchery of the Egyptian sorcerers to accomplish the Exodus of Israel from Egypt, displayed God's power and not the power of a mere mortal, than surely the greater miracle—the swallowing up of all cosmic rebellion against God whatsoever to bring

---

41. MacKenzie's rending this as a common noun, despite Irenaeus's (fairly clear) reference to the "Spirit" who co-administers the "dispensation of the Father" (i.e., the "Holy Spirit" of later, trinitarian theology), seems inexplicable at this point. It seems likely to me that it is a typographical error.

42. Irenaeus, *Demonstration of the Apostolic Preaching* 29–30. The crucial scriptural allusion with which Irenaeus ends chapter 30 apparently makes involved use of Col. 1:15–20.

43. Irenaeus, *Demonstration of the Apostolic Preaching* 31.

44. For an accessible and winsome treatment of typology and related approaches to interpretation in the early fathers see John J. O'Keefe and R.R. Reno, *Sanctified Vision: An Introduction to Early Christian Interpretation of the Bible* (Baltimore: John Hopkins University Press, 2005).

45. Exod. 4:1–5, 7:8–12.

46. Irenaeus, *Against the Heresies* 3.21.8.

to fruition the entire plan of God for salvation—would require Jesus to be the Word incarnate and virgin-born and not the son of the merely mortal Joseph. Moses's rod thus is a sign twice over. In its immediate narrative context it displays the power of God to the Egyptians. In the larger context of the entire economy of salvation, however, it demonstrates that Jesus is the Word become flesh of the virgin Mary by the power of God.

Typologies of this type do not, intuitively speaking, absolutely require divine inspiration. We might expect any clever literary critic to be able to draw connections between narratives without those narratives having been specifically designed with such connections in view. And, with any particular, proposed typology or narrative analogy Irenaeus might agree. After all, he finds the analogies proposed by the Valentinians unacceptable and absurd. Regarding the possibility of scriptural typology in general, however, Irenaeus is quite clear that its basis is not the eye of the beholding subject but the design of the Spirit after which the prophets labored. Thus, he tells us regarding Jesus, or Oshea, the son of Nun:

> And when they were near to the land . . . Moses chose a man from every tribe, and sent them to search out the land and the cities therein and the dwellers in the cities. At that time God revealed to him the Name which alone is able to save them that beleive thereon; and Moses changed the name of Oshea the son of Nun, one of them that were sent, and named him Jesus: and so he sent them forth with the power of the Name, believing that he should receive them back safe and sound through the guidance of the Name: which came to pass.[47]

Jesus (Joshua), who went with the other spies into the land of Canaan and who, ultimately, would lead all Israel to conquer that land, received his name from Moses in order to typify, or indicate by prophecy, the greater Jesus whose "Name . . . alone is able to save those who believe in it." Irenaeus is explicit: Moses, the prophet, received the Name by revelation, perceiving by the Spirit the Name's saving power towards those who trust it, and renamed Oshea, because of his faith in the Name, as an act of intercessory invocation, seeking divine patronage and protection over the spies' mission. This is the logic of valid typology for Irenaeus, as opposed to the merely subjective, literary whimsy of such as Valentinus.

All true types, then, must be prophetic in the sense of indicating some other event or player in the economy; it does not follow, however, that all prophesies must function by way of types. We have already seen this, in a way, by looking at Irenaeus's reading of the deluvian patriarchs Shem, Ham, and Japheth. Irenaeus supplies another example from the Book of Isaiah and the second psalm:

---

47. Irenaeus, *Demonstration of the Apostolic Preaching* 27. The scripture being interpreted by Irenaeus is Num. 13, esp. v. 16.

And again Isaiah the prophet says: *Thus says the Lord God to my anointed the Lord, whose right hand I have held, that the Gentiles should hearken before him.*[48] And how the Christ is called Son of God and King of the Gentiles, that is, of all mankind; and that He not only is called but is Son of God and King of all, David declares thus: *The Lord said unto me: Thou art my Son, this day have I begotten thee. Ask of me and I will give thee the Gentiles for thy inheritance, and for a possession the utmost parts of the earth.*[49] These things were not said of David; for neither over the Gentiles nor over the utmost parts did he rule, but only over the Jews. So then it is plain that the promise to the Anointed to reign over the utmost parts of the earth is to the Son of God, whom David himself acknowledges as his Lord, saying thus: *the Lord said unto my Lord, Sit on my right hand,*[50] and so forth, as we have said above. For he means that the Father speaks with the Son; as we showed a little before as to Isaiah, that he said thus: *God saith to my Anointed the Lord, that the Gentiles should hearken before him.* For the promise is the same by the two prophets, that He should be King: so that the speech of God is addressed to one and the same, I mean, to Christ the Son of God. Forasmuch as David says: *The Lord said unto me*, it is necessary to say that it is not David who speaks, nor any one of the prophets, in his own person: for it is not a man who speaks the prophecies; but the Spirit of God, assimilating and likening Himself to the persons represented, speaks in the prophets, and utters the words sometimes from Christ and sometimes from the Father.[51]

Irenaeus rejects a typological reading of the passages just quoted. The speaker of the second psalm, and hearer of both Isaiah's oracle and psalm one hundred and ten, is simply and immediately Christ.[52] The fact that texts such as

---

48. Apparently (and curiously, from our standpoint, given how he interprets Ps. 2) this is a reference to Isa. 45:1.

49. Ps. 2:7–8.

50. Ps. 110:1, read apparently with the same interpretive tradition attested in Mt. 22:41–46 in mind.

51. Irenaeus, *Demonstration of the Apostolic Preaching* 49.

52. However, it seems worth noting that in making this move Irenaeus has seemingly ignored that the Isaiah passage explicitly refers its fulfillment to the historical Persian conqueror Cyrus; in this sense, his reasoning (which, interestingly, seems identical to that given in Mt. 22:41–46) applies intuitively to Ps. 2:7–8, but only in a strained way to Isa. 45. However, perhaps we can read Irenaeus here as being dependent on a typological reading of Isa. 45:1 but not of the second psalm with which he juxtaposes it. In any event, Ps. 2 is here clearly being read in a nontypological fashion as a "direct" prophesy, and, when Isa. 45 is juxtaposed with it as having the same subject, the second passage is effectively rendered through the first—and, therefore, is apparently not functioning typologically under this interpretation.

these function for Irenaeus as direct prophecies, and not what we might term prophecies by way of types, even though he will make use of typological readings elsewhere, demonstrates clearly that the bishop is not woodenly applying one treasured technique such as typology. His commitment, rather, is to the salvation wrought by the Lord Jesus Christ at the behest of God the Father by the power of the Holy Spirit—the dispensation of God in which the sanctification of the ancient righteous, with the inscripturation of the sacred letter, was divinely designed.

If Ireneaus's committment is to the Lord's salvation, then certain ideas left tacit to this point in our treatment of the early father beg to be made explicit and explored. First, Irenaeus's understanding that the "dispensation of the Father" is the ultimate *Sitz im Leben* of the text, with sweeping implications for exegesis, sets forth a dynamic anthropology. The climax of the Spirit's leading humanity to the Word is the Word's incarnation as the man Jesus, the son of the virgin Mary. The divine Word becomes a particular human with the corollary that there is now a man who is also divine and shares supreme executive responsibility, in partnership with the Spirit, for the dispensation of God. The full and final outcome of this is that those led to him are granted immortality by God the Father. Indeed, the total climax is described elsewhere by the early father in the language of divinisation or human beings being made "gods" by grace:

> Now it was necessary that man should in the first instance be created; and having been created, should receive growth; and having received growth, should be strengthened; and having been strengthened, should abound; and having abounded, should recover [from the disease of sin]; and having recovered, should be glorified; and being glorified, should see his Lord. For God is He who is yet to be seen, and the beholding of God is productive of immortality, but *immortality renders one nigh unto God.*

> Irrational, therefore, in every respect, are they who await not the time of increase, but ascribe to God the infirmity of their nature. Such persons know neither God nor themselves, being insatiable and ungrateful, unwilling to be at the outset what they have also been created—men subject to passions; but go beyond the law of the human race, and before that they become men, they wish to be even now like God their Creator. . . . For we cast blame upon Him, because we have not been made gods from the beginning, but at first merely men, *then at length gods.*[53]

There is a lot in these paragraphs, but the key point is clear. The brokenness of our universe and the frailty, both moral and physical, of the human race are neither God's fault, on the one hand, nor beyond God's power, on the other. His

---

53. Irenaeus, *Against the Heresies* 4.38.3–4. Emphasis mine.

view of history is supremely hopeful; Irenaeus regards all things that have happened as working together, in God's wisdom, gradually to perfect humanity, and make us like God. Godlikeness, however, is the very identity of the Son as well as the destiny (and, hence, telic identity) of human persons, for:

> Again, this Word was manifested when the Word of God was made man, assimilating Himself to man, and man to Himself, so that by means of his resemblance to the Son, man might become precious to the Father. For in times long past, it was said that man was created after the image of God, but it was not [actually] shown; for the Word was as yet invisible, after whose image man was created. Wherefore also he did easily lose the similitude. When, however, the Word of God became flesh, He confirmed both these: for He both showed forth the image truly, since He became Himself what was His image; and He re-established the similitude after a sure manner, by assimilating man to the invisible Father through means of the visible Word.[54]

Jesus Christ is the goal, and the source because he is the goal, of the human race. He is the image of God in whose image humanity was created. It is important to note that it is specifically Jesus, the Word *incarnate*, who is the goal of humanity from the beginning. When Genesis says that humanity was made "in the image of God," there is from that point forward a type prophesying Jesus as the fulfillment and destiny of creation, the one who, as we saw earlier, "gather[ed] up" all things in himself.[55] We see here a significant advance on our definition from chapter 1: the story of the Church, the communion of the Holy Spirit, turns out to be the story of all of humanity as humanity is "gathered up" in its archetype, the Word / Son of God. This is how radically integrated the dispensation is for Irenaeus: redemption is not a plan B to accommodate a plan A failure. Redemption in Christ Jesus is the actualization of creation, the accomplishment of plan A in spite of and even by means of every human apostasy and demonic malice committed against it. The plan is a pedagogical strategy executed by the Word and Spirit of God to lead humanity to union and communion with God.

Pedagogy, however, is a gradual process and (especially?) where resisted proceeds with pain. The divine plan, then, moves forward as an eventful process over which humanity is first created and then matures. At least in part this explains another matter tacit in our discussions up to this point. For Irenaeus, prophecies and types proclaim or *demonstrate* the Word upon their fulfillment, but before that point function mysteriously, like events in a suspenseful novel that only click into place at the climax:

---

54. Irenaeus, *Against the Heresies* 5.16.2.
55. Irenaeus, *Demonstration of the Apostolic Preaching* 30.

If any one, therefore, reads the Scriptures with attention, he will find in them an account of Christ, and a foreshadowing of the new calling. . . . For Christ is the treasure which was hid in the field, that is, in this world (for "the field is the world"); but the treasure hid in the Scriptures is Christ, since He was pointed out by means of types and parables. . . .[56] For every prophecy, before its fulfilment, is to men [full of] enigmas and ambiguities. But when the time has arrived, and the prediction has come to pass, then the prophecies have a clear and certain exposition.[57]

This property is referred to as *dramatic coherence*, classically defined as the property whereby a well-written story holds together as a sequence of events that occur "unexpectedly but on account of each other."[58] Just as a reader or hearer of such a story cannot predict events before they happen but can recognize how they had to be after they happen, so it is, also, with prophecy and type for Irenaeus. The Spirit occasions the incarnation of the Word by preparing the ground, so to speak, hiding Jesus Christ in the world as the Word echoing in the mouths of the prophets and in the pilgrim lives of the righteous ancients and, therefore, in the inspired written account of our world, the scriptures, under the form of types and prophesies. That written account, then, is at once a foreshadowing of him, a means for recognizing (and learning to recognize?) him upon his advent, a commendation of the hidden Word to future generations, and a relic of the divine pedagogy, the being-led-to-the-Word, it records.

Origen of Alexandria on the Pedagogy of the Spirit and the Mystery of Inspired Reference

Irenaeus saw the Spirit as a kind of pedagogue in partnership with the Word. His sovereign role in the providence of God the Father is to consecrate the attentions of those chosen by the Father, orienting them to God through the Word and thereby making them the saints they are and sharers in God's holiness. Was this view unique to Irenaeus or was he tuned into a motif that would resonate more widely in the early tradition, perhaps with shades of translation in later fathers? That is to say, we neither need to, nor should, expect to find Irenaeus's outlook and arguments repeated in subsequent decades and centuries. After all, later thinkers will be acting in different situations. However, if Irenaeus was, as he himself suggests, passing on a tradition to which there was deeper, bedrock commitment—a DNA for Christianity, so to speak—succeeding generations might well be expected to express the same or related commitments in new

---

56. Irenaeus is using two parables from Mt. 13, the parable of the sower (vv. 1–23) and of the treasure hidden in the field (vv. 44–46).

57. Irenaeus, *Against the Heresies* 4.26.1.

58. Robert W. Jenson quoting Aristotle, *Peri Poietikes* 1452a, 3. See *The Triune God*, vol. 1 of *Systematic Theology* (New York: Oxford University Press, 1997), 64.

ways, effectively fleshing out their theological and philosophical implications. We might turn in a variety of directions to answer the question; the path I will take here is to turn, as I did in my first chapter, to the witness of Origen, a figure in whom the specifically *pedagogical* aspect of the dispensation of God and its relationship to Holy Scripture becomes explicit.[59]

We have already seen, in passing, how Irenaeus's opening summary, on the economy of salvation, in the *Demonstration* describes the partnership of the persons of the Trinity in human salvation. When Origen comes to discussing the person of the Holy Spirit, this, likewise, becomes his focus:

> God the Father bestows on all the gift of existence; and a participation in Christ, in virtue of his being the word or reason, makes them rational. From this it follows that they are worthy of praise or blame, because they are capable alike of virtue and of wickedness. Accordingly, there is also available the grace of the Holy Spirit, that those beings who are not holy in essence may be made holy by participating in this grace. When therefore they obtain first of all their existence from God the Father, and secondly their rational nature from the Word, and thirdly their holiness from the Holy Spirit, they become capable of receiving Christ afresh in his character of the righteousness of God, those, that is, who have been previously sanctified through the Holy Spirit; and such as have been deemed worthy of advancing to this degree through the sanctification of the Holy Spirit obtain in addition the gift of wisdom by the power of the working of God's Spirit. . . .
>
> Thus the working of the Father, which endows all with existence, is found to be more glorious and splendid, when each one, through participation in Christ in his character of wisdom and knowledge and sanctification, advances and comes to higher degrees of perfection; and when a man, by being sanctified through participation in the Holy Spirit, is made purer and holier, he becomes more worthy to receive the grace of wisdom and knowledge, in order that all stains of pollution and ignorance may be purged and removed and that he may make so great an advance in holiness and purity that the life which he received from God shall be such as is worthy of

---

59. The pedagogical outlook of Origen on questions of inspiration and hermeneutics appropriate to inspired scripture is a topic that receives significant discussion from Karen Jo Torjesen. See "'Body', 'Soul', and 'Spirit' in Origen's Theory of Exegesis," in *The Bible in the Early Church* (New York: Garland, 1993), 287–301; her larger work is *Hermeneutical Procedure and Theological Method in Origen's Exegesis* (Berlin: Walter de Gruyter, 1986). Origen's pedagogical outlook, also, is thereby a soteriological one, as this section of this book will discuss; a recent writer who gives full length treatment to soteriology in Origen's hermeneutics is Peter William Martens, *Origen and Scripture: The Contours of the Exegetical Life* (Oxford: Oxford University Press, 2012).

God, who gave it to be pure and perfect, and that that which exists shall be as worthy as he who caused it to exist. Thus, too, the man who is such as God who made him wished him to be, shall receive from God the power to exist for ever and to endure for eternity.[60]

I have risked a long quote at this point because it spells out a picture that can be perceived only with the whole in view. I want to show that Irenaeus's trinitarian soteriology and summary of the Rule of Faith is cognate to Origen's description in these paragraphs. Recall that, a generation or so earlier, Irenaeus had summed up the dispensation in the words: " . . . those who bear the Spirit of God are led to the Word, that is to the Son, while the Son presents [them] to the Father, and the Father furnishes incorruptibility."[61] Origen's description follows a similar logic but with some illuminating surprises. In order to receive Christ in his capacity as the righteousness, wisdom, and knowledge of God, the rational soul must be oriented towards him by the person of the Spirit. However, once the Spirit has commenced the soul's sanctification, Christ (as righteousness and wisdom) and the Spirit (as sanctification) instruct and purify the soul in stages until it is rendered worthy of the Father, who grants the "power to exist for ever and to endure for eternity." Irenaeus's description left tacit the gifts of wisdom and knowledge but made explicit the body of prophecy, the deposit of Holy Scripture, thereby produced. Origen reverses this order. He leaves tacit the *inscripturation* of the saints' sanctifying and wisdom-inculcating encounter but makes growth in wisdom and holiness clear. The saints, by embracing the Holy Spirit in his particular ministry, receive through the Spirit's power Christ in his capacity as "wisdom and knowledge and sanctification"[62] that eventually unite them to God in incorruption. We have here a deeply coded, but still unmistakable, picture of the salvation of the Lord as laid out in Irenaeus's Rule of Faith.

It is here that another, more specifically Origenistic, motif becomes more clearly coherent with the total picture of early Christian theological and liturgical use of scripture. I noted Origen's allegorical method in passing in chapter 1, promising to say more about it here. The reader may by now, also, have observed some analogy between that method and Irenaeus's use of typology. We might now ask the questions: Why typology? Why allegory? While authorial intention might explain explicit prophecies, it is difficult to see how this could explain types and allegories, especially where the types supplied are acknowledged as in some sense historical events the primary logic of which is the author's interpreting and calling to mind an actual past.[63]

---

60. Origen, *On First Principles* 1.3.8.

61. Irenaeus, *Demonstration of the Apostolic Preaching* 7.

62. Origen, *On First Principles* 1.3.8.

63. Even Origen, with his passion for allegory, writes regarding the historicity of scriptural records, "The passages which are historically true are far more numerous than those which are composed with purely spiritual meanings." *On First Principles* 4.3.4.

In developing and recontextualizing the Rule, Origen has already suggested an answer. Recall from chapter 1 how Origen's hermeneutic is catechetical and dialectical. Clear doctrines are supplied as a set of first principles whereby those worthy of the gifts of wisdom and knowledge flesh out those doctrines (in chapter 1 it was the hermeneutic itself) into a total perspective. In other words, he expects his students not to be passive. Now, in the paragraphs just above, Origen has tacitly subordinated—even expanded upon—his own catechetical approach and hermeneutic in terms of a larger soteriological vision, the patron of which is the Holy Spirit. Later, in book 4, he makes this tacit expansion explicit:

> In the first place we must point out that the aim of the Spirit who, by the providence of God through the Word who was 'in the beginning with God' (Jn. 1:1), enlightened the servants of the truth, that is, the prophets and apostles, was pre-eminently concerned with the unspeakable mysteries connected with the affairs of men . . . his purpose being that the man who is capable of being taught might by 'searching out' and devoting himself to the 'deep things' (1 Cor. 2:10) revealed in the spiritual meaning of the words become partaker of all the doctrines of the Spirit's counsel.[64]

In other words, Origen does what he does because he believes that that is what the Holy Spirit has always been doing. The "servants of the truth" were no more passive in their reception of sanctity and wisdom than Origen's pupils. Every thought, word, and action in such a dispensation—an adventure in which the Spirit's counsels, his own searching all things created and uncreated, are sought actively and won through hard effort—would take the Spirit's probing, testing quest as its own form also. Even explicit prophecies, and not just what we have called prophecy by way of types, would take coded form. All scripture, then, would be riddled with meaning, some of it, to be sure, visible on the surface, but much of it accessible only to the one reading in the same searching Spirit in which its mysteries were inscribed. This suggestion is precisely the model that Origen makes explicit in describing his method:

> When we speak of the needs of souls, who cannot otherwise reach perfection except through the rich and wise truth about God, we attach of necessity pre-eminent importance to the doctrines concerning God and His only-begotten Son. . . . Now while these and similar subjects were in the mind of the Spirit who enlightened the souls of the holy servants of the truth, there was a second aim, pursued for the sake of those who were unable to endure the burden of investigating matters of such importance. This was to conceal the doctrine relating to the before-mentioned subjects in words forming a narrative that contained a record dealing with the visible creation, the formation of man and the successive descendants of the first

---

64. Origen, *On First Principles* 4.2.7.

human beings until the time when they became many; and also in other stories that recorded the acts of righteous men and the sins that these same men occasionally committed, seeing they were but human, and the deeds of wickedness, licentiousness and greed done by lawless and impious men.[65]

It is important to interpret Origen with care. The logic behind his method might sound merely elitist—a way of saying that the Spirit manipulated the representation of history to speak to some but not to others. This is true but with a clarification: those able to perceive the Spirit's deeper meanings attain to that perception by deepening in their intimacy with the Spirit, Word, and Father, what some Christians today term growth in sanctification. The hermeneutic is not elitist but catechetical. This mirrors the sanctification of the saints through and about whom the sacred letter was written. Here the illumined reader adopts an analogous (if not, indeed, identical) orientation as the inspired author and, together with the author, becomes enlightened in wisdom and knowledge. Origen spells out the mystery of this in greater detail:

> But the most wonderful thing is, that by means of stories . . . certain secret truths are revealed to those who are capable of examining these narratives; and, even more marvellous, through a written system of law the laws of truth are prophetically indicated, all these having been recorded in a series with a power which is truly appropriate to the wisdom of God. For the intention was to make even the outer covering of the spiritual truths . . . in many respects not unprofitable but capable of improving the multitude in so far as they receive it.[66]

I have skipped over, for the moment, Origen's discussion of just how and where one might perceive that meaning has been hidden in order to draw him out where he illustrates the parable-like quality of the records of the saints. Not all human activities are amenable to representing the sublime truths of the Spirit's counsels. However, the Spirit still searches mortal history and hearts and minds, discerning within them ways in which history might be rendered so as to represent those truths transcendent of it. In this way, the Word and Spirit thereby shape history in partnership with the saints who the Spirit, in the course of his search, sanctifies. Scripture, as that search's artifact and record, thus reflects the Spirit's counsels twice over: once through his searching out human history to note where and how it might suit his mysterious purposes, and again by his thereby providentially influencing the entire sequence of events. The result is a text and a history that both reveals and conceals, with revelation sufficient to edify and to capture the attention of the as-of-yet uninitiated and also concealment to provoke them to join the Spirit's searching

---

65. Origen, *On First Principles* 4.2.7–8.
66. Origen, *On First Principles* 4.2.8.

of times and thereby become initiated to communion with the God who is beyond all times:

> But if the usefulness of the law and the sequence and ease of the narrative were at first sight clearly discernible throughout, we should be unaware that there was anything beyond the obvious meaning for us to understand in the scriptures. Consequently, the Word of God has arranged for certain stumbling-blocks, as it were, and hindrances and impossibilities to be inserted in the midst of the law and the history, in order that we may not be completely drawn away by the sheer attractiveness of the language, and so either reject the true doctrines absolutely, on the ground that we learn from the scriptures nothing worthy of God, or else by never moving away from the letter fail to learn anything of the more divine element.[67]

The Spirit of God, then, is like a kind of Socratic teacher who provokes his students to critical thinking both by refusing instantly to supply all the answers while yet positively supplying clues in the structure of the discourse that more goes on than meets ear or eye. The situation of the reader of scripture, thus, is at least analogous, if not identical, to the situation of the saint of old, because they take place in the same soteriological partnership or communion named by the Rule of Faith. Both are made partakers of the same Word and Spirit of God; both are involved in working out their salvation in the one economy of salvation; both receive as the prize at the end of the race immortality in full communion with God the Father. This organic continuity supplies the explanation for Origen's allegories. Scripture tells a mystery to the reader because the saints' encounter with the Word of God in the Spirit was itself a mystery, even to them, and the interpretation hidden away in that enigma was, in both cases, the same—Jesus Christ, the wisdom and righteousness of God.

We are led, then, to another heuristic suggestion, one that coheres well with what we have seen of Irenaeus and the New Testament witness: that the reference of Holy Scripture to Christ is to him in his union with humankind. We have seen hints of this already in Origen's soteriological description, showing that the scriptures arise out of the saints' Spirit-mediated encounter with Christ as the righteousness and wisdom of God. There is, perhaps, another hint in his comparing the levels of meaning in scripture to the whole human person in body, soul, and spirit, keeping in mind that, as a Christian, he confesses Christ as the Word made flesh:

> We find some such rule as this laid down by Solomon in the Proverbs concerning the divine doctrines written therein: 'Do thou pourtray [sic] them threefold in counsel and knowledge, that thou mayest answer words of truth to those who question

---

67. Origen, *On First Principles* 4.2.9.

thee.'[68] One must therefore pourtray [sic] the meaning of the sacred writings in a threefold way upon one's own soul. . . . For just as man consists of body, soul and spirit, so in the same way does the scripture, which has been prepared by God to be given for man's salvation.[69]

The high water mark of Origen's theological exegesis arguably makes explicit the suggestion hidden in hints such as these. In his commentary on the Song of Songs, Origen says the reference of the Song is three-fold.[70] On the surface, its bodily meaning is a holy but erotic love between Solomon and the Shunnumite. Two deeper levels beckon, however. One level refers the song to the Word of God in his union with the whole communion of saints, the Church; the other, to the Word of God in his union with the individual soul in its pilgrimage of transformation into the image of God.[71] Of course, we should not extrapolate from Origen's comments on the Song of Songs only that the reference of all Holy Scripture has this two-fold character in his thought, hints otherwise and elsewhere in his writings, as examined, notwithstanding. His soteriological picture, however, clearly makes this conclusion possible, and, by the middle decades of the fourth century, another early patristic witness will make explicit a connection between the divine nature of the scriptures and the reader's participatory union with that nature.

Hilary of Poitiers and the Hermeneutics of Faith

We advance from the third to the fourth century, where hermeneutics for Holy Scripture becomes a major point of contention in the so-called Arian debates.[72]

---

68. Prov. 22:20–21.

69. Origen, *On First Principles* 4.2.4.

70. However, an interesting case—still compatible with and, indeed, suggestive in some ways of the conclusions being drawn here—has been made by J. Christopher King that the Song of Songs is, in Origen's view, "bodiless," having only pneumatic and psychological senses. See *Origen on the Song of Songs as the Spirit of Scripture: The Bridegroom's Perfect Marriage Song* (Oxford: Oxford University Press, 2005).

71. Origen, *Commentary on the Song of Songs*, Prologue, chapter 1.

72. The point of view and entry into the controversies of that period taken here is that of Hilary of Poitiers in his *De Trinitate* and, to a lesser extent, some of his surviving correspondence. Although he wrote on the Trinity, his writings are most often consulted today for the window they supply onto an early Christian theological method. Two major secondary sources consulted here include Carl Beckwith in three of his works, *Hilary of Poitiers on the Trinity: From De Fide to De Trinitate* (Oxford: Oxford University Press, 2008); "The Condemnation and Exile of Hilary of Poitiers at the Synod of Bézier (356 C.E.)," *Journal of Early Christian Studies* 13.1 (2005): 21–38; and "A Theological Reading of Hilary's 'Autobiographical' Narrative in *De Trinitate* I.1–19," *Scottish Journal of Theology* 59.3 (2006): 249–62; and Joseph Emmenegger, *The Functions of Faith and Reason in the Theology of Saint Hilary of Poitiers* (Washington, DC: Catholic University of America Press, 1947). The short historical background given here is due largely to them and, to a lesser extent, to Daniel

The simplified vision of this century's controversies holds forth how an Egyptian presbyter, Arius, scandalized the newly Christian Constantinian empire by denying the deity of Jesus and thereby forced the Church painfully to wrestle with and systematize its convictions. In this version of the story, the two combatants in the wrestling match were those with a *high* Christology and those with a *low* one; at stake was a metaphysical vision of Deity. As might be expected, the actual scenario, one that played out over decades, at least, was considerably more involved than that, and, in its process, touched upon matters and engaged categories far more encompassing than how precisely to describe the Trinity. The questions of how to read Holy Scripture and how to relate faith (the Rule?) with the philosopher's reason were at least as central, if not actually more so.

We see these questions even just glancing at the debates themselves, for the moment setting to the side any particular combatant. Throughout those years most parties agreed that Jesus was in some sense divine—clearly, he was greater than us, even greater than the angels—but a great many wished to describe that divinity in qualified terms so as to preserve the doctrine of the One God. One major category, adopted by some of the participants and used—again, by some— to describe Jesus's divinity as the same as the Father's, *homoousios to patri* (often translated "of one being with the Father" and called simply "the homoousion"), was confusing to many and seems genuinely to have been ambiguous due the material connotations of one of its constituent morphemes, *-ousia*, "substance" or "being." Roughly speaking, there were three patterns of response in the discourse surrounding this category. Some advocates of the homoousion, among them Marcellus of Ancyra and Photinus of Sirmium, seem to have interpreted the material analogy modalistically; that is they acknowledged no eternal, personal distinction between the Father and Son. Monotheism was preserved together with a seemingly high Christology in a fashion that, even to this day, seems intuitive and, therefore, fully rational. Modalism, however, had already been widely condemned in the churches as contrary to the Rule of Faith for almost a century and so invited immediate and vehement censure.[73] Others, taking this Marcellan/Photinian interpretation for granted as *the* meaning of the

---

Williams, *Ambrose of Milan and the End of the Arian-Nicene Conflicts* (Oxford: Clarendon, 1995), acknowledging, also, his alternative reading to Beckwith's of the history surrounding Hilary's exile, "A Reassessment of the Early Career and Exile of Hilary of Poitiers," *Journal of Ecclesiastical History* 42.2 (1991): 202–17. Beckwith and Emmenegger's investigations primarily concern method in Hilary; my explorations here seek to nuance their conclusions not by showcasing Hilary's method, but by examining one motif within it: namely, showing how Hilary's hermeneutic fills out and coheres with the soteriological perspective of Irenaeus and Origen already discussed.

73. Modalism was addressed in the condemnation of Sabellius, a heresiarch of the third century. A simple check can illustrate why this Christology was rejected as contrary to the Rule: the gospels repeatedly and pervasively depict Jesus praying to, worshiping, and, in general, relating to and about the Father as another person. Even considering principles of analogical language, modalism, in light of this, did not take scripture seriously enough. For just one instance, see Jn.14–17.

homoousion, advanced a subordinationist vision in opposition, qualifying Christ's deity as ontologically less than the Father's. Again, an intuitively rational monotheism was seemingly preserved—however, at the cost of a clarion confession of Christ as God. A third party said that this subordinationist response was heterodox; it failed not merely to dot some conceptual *i* or dash some ritual *t*, but to uphold the Rule, the inner logic of Holy Scripture. This third party was left in the unenviable position of defending a paradox.

It is in this context that it is helpful to consider Hilary of Poitiers (ca. 300–ca. 368 C.E.), bishop, apologist, and exegete. For the purposes of this book, most interesting about Hilary's analysis of his and the Church's situation was how he identified a far more serious problem than any failure merely to comprehend a conceptual point, even one so vital as Jesus's divinity. To Hilary's eye, the enemy ultimately at work in the Photinian and subordinationist outlooks alike was an idolatrous *disposition* of the mind that blinded the soul to the glory of God, hindering it from perceiving the sense and reference of the scriptures. His writings often refer to this mental attitude as "philosophy," apparently as an echo of Col. 2:8, as in this quote, taken from a letter he wrote to the emperor Constantius: "Remember it does not exist in a debate on philosophy but in the teaching of the Gospel. Not so much for my sake do I beg a hearing, as for yourself and God's churches."[74] This reference to "debate on philosophy" gets repeated three times elsewhere in Hilary's magisterial *De Trinitate*, once each at the beginning, middle, and end of that work.[75] The larger context for his naming the threat of "philosophy" opposes "faith" and "being made a sharer in the divine nature" to this "philosophical" perspective. One passage, often quoted for its summary of Hilary's theological method,[76] displays what Hilary intends by that opposition:

> The regenerated spirit needs new faculties in order that everyone's conscience may be enlightened by the gift that comes from heaven. Therefore, as holy Jeremias warns [in Jer. 23:22, LXX][77], he must take up his stand by faith in the nature of God so that, when he shall hear about the nature of God, he may direct his mind to the things that are worthy of God, but he must do so in accordance with no other norm for judging except that of infinity. Since he is conscious of being made a sharer in the divine nature, as blessed Peter declares in his second Epistle [1:4], he must measure the nature of God not by the laws of his own nature but evaluate the divine truths in

---

74. Hilary, *Letter to the Emperor Constantius* 8.

75. See Hilary, *De Trinitate* 1.12–13; 8.52–53; 12.19–20.

76. Beckwith appeals to this passage in his treatments, as, also, does T.F. Torrance, see his "Transition to the West: the Interpretation of Biblical and Theological Statements According to Hilary of Poitiers," in *Divine Meaning: Studies in Patristic Hermeneutics* (Edinburgh: T&T Clark, 1995), 392–427.

77. The translation here used, that of Stephen McKenna, inexplicably refers the allusion to Jer. 23:14. Migne refers this to 23:22.

accordance with the magnificence of God's testimony concerning Himself.[78]

The reader is a sharer in the "nature of God," and must read with "faith" in that nature. This sentiment becomes a motif echoed throughout the early tradition when human salvation is under discussion, for example by Hilary's senior colleague, Athanasius.[79] There are important hermeneutical implications flowing from this in Hilary's estimation; as he puts it in *De Trinitate* 1.18, "The best reader is he who looks for the meaning of the words in the words themselves rather than reads his meaning into them, who carries away more than he brought and who does not insist that the words signify what he presupposed before reading them."[80] If the reader is to experience the quality of healing and glory Hilary anticipates, she must let the words take her beyond her own capacities.

The motif of divinization in Christ remains in view throughout *On the Trinity*; its role in 1.18 is no polemically motivated one-off. Take, for example, Hilary's reflections on the full divinity of Jesus, as, for example, when he considers Jn. 17:

> But, because it is proper only to the Father and the Son to be one by their nature, for the God from God and the Only-begotten from the unborn can alone possess the nature of His origin, so He who is born exists in the substance of His own birth, and the birth of the divinity does not have another and different God than that from which it has come. The Lord . . . taught the nature of this complete unity in the whole discourse that follows, for these words come next: 'That the world may believe that thou hast sent me.' The world therefore, will believe that the Son has been sent by the Father because all who will believe in Him will be one in the Father and the Son. And He at once teaches us how they will be one: 'And the glory that Thou hast given me, I have given to them.' [Jn. 17:21, 22][81]

In other words, the "unity" that Christ has with the Father has to be capable of elevating us to unity with the Father also. Why can this unity not be a unity of will or desire? Because it is experienced corporeally in the mystery of the Word made flesh, and, therefore, in the Eucharist:

---

78. Hilary, *De Trinitate* 1.18.

79. Alan L. Kolp, "Partakers of the Divine Nature: The Use of 2 Peter 1:4 by Athanasius." *Studia Patristica* 17 (1982): 1018–23.

80. Hilary, *De Trinitate* 1.18.

81. Hilary, *De Trinitate* 8.12. Immediately at this point, McKenna adds a footnote that explains Hilary's point like so: "From a purely human standpoint it would be rash to hope for union with God, but it is not rash when the hope is based on the promise of God Himself."

If the Word has indeed become flesh, and we indeed receive the Word as flesh in the Lord's food, how are we not to believe that He dwells in us by His nature, He who, when He was born as man, has assumed the nature of our flesh that is bound inseparably with Himself, and has mingled the nature of His flesh to His eternal nature in the mystery of the flesh that was to be communicated to us? All of us are one in this manner because the Father is in Christ and Christ is in us. . . . If, therefore, Christ has truly taken the flesh of our body, and that man who was born from Mary is truly Christ, and we truly receive the flesh of His body in the mystery (and we are one, therefore, because the Father is in Him and He is in us), how can you assert that there is a unity of will, since the attribute of the nature in the sacrament is the mystery of the perfect unity?[82]

Hilary's vision reaches its apex when it bends towards the *eschaton*:

Last of all, after death has been finally conquered, in order that his [the apostle Paul's] explanation of this mystery might be complete, he then said: 'But when he shall say all things are subject, he is excepted who subjected all things to him; then he himself will be made subject to him who subjected all things to him, that God may be all in all.' Hence, the first step in the mystery is that all things have been made subject to Him [Christ], and then He Himself [Christ] becomes subject to Him who subjects all things to Himself [God the Father] in order that, just as we subject ourselves to the glory of His reigning body, the ruler Himself in the same mystery may again subject Himself in the glory of the body to Him who subjects all things to Himself. We are made subject to the glory of His body in order that we may possess that glory with which he reigns in the body, because we shall be conformable to his body.[83]

Hilary reminds us of Irenaeus's and Origen's treatments of the Rule of Faith in which the trinitarian description ends with the Father furnishing eternal life. We can get so caught up in this vision of deification in Christ that we lose sight of where we began with Hilary in 1.18. There the object in view was the right discernment and reading of Holy Scripture, and the alternative—i.e., the wrong reading of scripture—was fleshed out as lack of faith, as reliance upon the merely human nature. Our journey tracing the motif of deification running through *De Trinitate* displays those early comments as no mere polemic but as thoroughly integrated within Hilary's thought. The divine nature referenced in 1.18 is the eternal nature of Jesus Christ which he shares with the Father. The human nature is the nature he took in the incarnation and which he shares with

---

82. Hilary, *De Trinitate* 8.13. McKenna clarifies again by adding in a footnote: "Through the reception of the Body and Blood of Christ in the Eucharist we share in His nature and, through Him, with that of His Heavenly Father."

83. Hilary, *De Trinitate* 11.36.

us. Right reading of scripture, then, is submission to that divine economy, the submissive (or, perhaps better, humbly reliant) recognition that our human nature has been laid hold of by God, the end of which is deification and immortality. Wrong reading is opposition to the divine economy, a soul's arrogant attempt to hold back the intellectual dimensions of its existence from the God who aims to heal and glorify it.

This, in turn, disambiguates the connections between bad reading, "philosophy" and lack of faith, especially given the larger polemical context of the fourth century and the tradition preceding it into the earlier periods. The positive reference to "faith" echoes the tradition's commendation of the Rule, and does not connote a merely stubborn and uncritical fideism; "philosophy" is not critical, rational inquiry into the scriptures but rationalistic attempts at explaining scriptural details away whenever they describe what seems to be impossible from a human perspective. In other words, bad reading involves a mere human projecting his or her limitations through the text onto God. Hilary has clued us in to how he, and the Tradition as he sees it, understands the Holy Scriptures. The final referent of scripture is God as made known in salvation and, therefore, in union with humankind. We have no mere this-worldly identity story in the scriptures but an ascent to the illimitably Transcendent. Implied about the sense and reference of scripture is that scripture's language ought not to be domesticated so as to force it to make sense to a human reader. Its power to clue us into the nature of God (and, therefore, into the possibilities salvifically available to the Christ-believer) rests, partly, in its scandal and paradox.

Augustine of Hippo, the Hermeneutics of Love, and the Sacramental Theory of Reference

What we have just seen makes sense as a development of the soteriological outlook of Origen in the third century. For him, scriptural author and reader alike were in a process of increasing sanctification, of ever deepening union with the Father, Son, and Spirit. One of his metaphors, if metaphor it was, for this deepening relationship was that of a holy eros, the desire of the Church and the soul for marriage union with Christ. In Hilary's translation of this soteriological hermeneutic, love goes backstage while polemic against rationalism trumpets from the fore. A bare few decades after Hilary, however, love will again receive attention as an interpretive norm, in Augustine of Hippo, receiving an accent both distinct from and more aggressive than eros had in Origen. In the process, Augustine will not lose Hilary's concern for scripture's transcendent reference. Rather, he will develop the idea, likely through ministerial use of a neo-Platonic lens, pointing the way to how radically the divinely transcendent reference of scripture, and the invitation to a scripturally mediated spiritual ascent, could be taken by Christians of the first four centuries.

In the preface to *De doctrina Christiana* he describes three objectors to his program of instructing priests in how to interpret Holy Scripture. The first two opponents he dismisses quickly, apparently regarding their protests as insubstantial. He addresses the third, however, at length. This opponent says Augustine's project to teach scriptural interpretation is misguided because authentic understanding is a gift of the Spirit; surely, it cannot be taught. Augustine's first response is to point to his interlocutor's existential condition, as a human person who has already received substantial blessing through the hands of human teachers. Second, he adduces scriptural examples of the same. Finally reaching the climax of his argument, he explains why God should choose to use human intermediaries:

> Moreover, there would be no way for love, which ties people together in the bonds of unity, to make souls overflow and as it were intermingle with each other, if human beings learned nothing from other humans. . . . Is it not true that God spoke with Moses, and yet Moses accepted advice about guiding and governing such a great people from his father-in-law, a man actually of another race, with an abundance of foresight and an absence of pride? He was well aware that true advice, from whatever mind it came, should be ascribed not to man but to the unchangeable God who is the truth.[84]

Two themes leap out of the paragraph. First, and coherent with the earlier sections of this chapter, human advice and teaching is said to be at the behest of God, who is its patron. So radical and utter is the patronage that the advice is attributed to the grace of God rather than to the mortal by whom it was given, even though that human volitionally and intellectually participated in the act. Second, and more immediately important for discussion here, is that God elects to work through human mediators in this way *for the sake of forming a human communion* of love. Should this divine intention arch over all of scripture and the economy through which it arose, then love will prove to be both the meaning of scripture and the spirit in which scripture should be approached. This will, in fact, prove to be the case.

Before turning to that case, however, I must pause to note how Augustine, like Hilary and Origen before him, takes time to develop a theory of scriptural significance. To delve into that theory, I might start by recalling the observation from chapter 1 that, for early Christians, the scriptures functioned as what might be called a eucharistic memory. The medievalist Mary Carruthers draws a distinction in her study of memory as it was understood in the ancient and medieval worlds, contrasting their "memorial" culture with our "documentary"

---

84. Augustine, *De Doctrina*, preface.6–7.

one.[85] In premodern cultures, memory and memorization were not the denigrated things they are for us, " . . . devoid of intellect: 'just memorization,' not 'real thought' or 'true learning.'"[86] She goes on to show throughout the whole book how, although premodern philosophers and other literati recognized memory's foibles and limitations, they prized memory as the seat of creativity and, particularly, the moral imagination. Morals and ethics were implicated in the cultivation and use of memory because personal identity, in this sense, was relational: persons are not atoms but participants in community with other persons. Memory is primarily the share of the individual in the communal well, and, as such belongs not primarily to herself but to all. The mode wherein this communal property exists, however, is not noetic but symbolic: texts (broadly construed as either written or orally transmitted) with their corresponding traditions of reception. Related to this, Carruthers shows that "authors" in the medieval world were not primarily persons but "authorized" texts; even a writer did not truly own the text he or she wrote. The process of authorization, by which a text became a classic and a writer was immortalized, was one of communal reception and rumination. One outcome, besides the authorization itself, was that those texts were authorized that functioned to, in Carruthers's words, "'complete' uninformed individual experience."[87]

The social nature of memory and process of authorization for texts outlined by Carruthers matches neatly what we have already noticed with respect to the reception of the scriptures in our first chapter. Additional details adduced by her bring the picture into yet sharper relief. An astute reader of the above paragraphs might object that her model reduces meaning to consensus—the model fails to account for how the ancients appreciated at least certain texts, such as those which became the Christian Bible, for their *transcendent* reference. It also has not yet described why any particular text would be authorized and not others. Carruthers's analysis answers these questions over the course of her treatment. Memory's symbols are not self-referential, but are "adequate" to matters external, even transcendent, to them:

> If we . . . unpack the metaphor incorporated in the scholastic dictum, "veritas est adaequatio verbi et rei," we find that it embodies what is basically a rhetorical view of the "representational" relationship between word and thing (and we must always remember that the Latin word *res* is not confined to

---

85. Mary Carruthers, *The Book of Memory: A Study of Memory in Medieval Culture* (Cambridge: Cambridge University Press, 1990). My discussion of her here will aim for synthesis rather than analysis, drawing not from particular quotes but with the application of the total picture she draws to an intuitive, rather than formal, theory of textual reference. Quotes will be kept to a minimum; the reader is directed especially, however, to her introduction, chapter 1, and chapters 5–7.

86. Ibid., 1.

87. Ibid., 24.

objects of our senses but includes notions, opinions, and feelings)—that is, a view based on the principle of decorum.
Adaequatio is a word of relationship, "adjustment," "fitting" a
word to what one wants to say. The prefix is crucial to its
meaning, not a "dead" metaphor. *Aequatio* and its adjective,
aequalis, convey the notion of iteration, "equal," identity of a
formal, quantifiable sort. But in this dictum, truth contained
in words is always *ad-aequatio*, getting towards identity but
never achieving it. . . . *Aequatio* conceptually admits only of
true or false; *adaequatio*, being a matter of relationship and not
identity, admits of many grades and degrees of approximation.[88]

There are for medieval and other premodern persons, to partly get ahead
of ourselves, thing (*res*) and sign. Truth is a relationship of adequacy between a
sign and that which that sign represents. Two points are worth noting. First, we
can immediately sense the correspondence between Carruthers's description
and what we have seen from the early Church both regarding the transcendence
of scripture and the necessity of ruled reading. The Rule was handed on in baptism and enacted, as it were, at the Supper and in prayer, especially what we,
today, call liturgical prayer. Under the classical model of texts and readers considered by Carruthers and relevant to our discussions here, not only *can* texts
have hermeneutical insiders and outsiders (e.g., for the Holy Scriptures, Christians were insiders; pagans outsiders), they necessarily have them, for until and
unless one has been introduced to the reality which defines its referring texts,
those texts will be relatively opaque. Second, the significance of a text lies in its
relationship to the reality to which it refers, through its power to orient a reader
and draw her through its words deeper and deeper into the mystery of its referent, effectively making that introduction or initiation possible. This coheres
with the catechetical nature of the Rule and of scripture, with the transformation that catechesis envisages, which we have seen in Irenaeus, Origen, and
Hilary. Frances Young observes something very like this coherence in Gregory
of Nyssa, a near contemporary of Augustine's. Regarding the sacramental character of biblical narratives for Nyssa, she writes:

In one sense this standpoint emphasises the finitude of human
language; in another it hints at the kind of 'infinity' found in
post-modern linguistic and literary discussion. For it ultimately validates an 'expanding' or open-ended sense of ever
more meaning to be discerned, the polyvalence recognized in
poetry, rather than a defining or delimiting reduction of
meaning to propositional definitions produced by deduction—
the process so often assumed to be at work in the formation
of doctrine. Language remains referential: ancient theory . . .
assumed a relationship between Word and World, Logos and

---

88. Ibid., 24–25.

Reality, and this was in some sense a representational relationship. But the reality to which theological language refers
transcends all possible linguistic expression, and so is explosive of both literalism and conceptual deciphering, thus bearing comparison with the generative character of metaphorical
expression as understood in recent discussion.[89]

The language of scripture is sacramental in character and so serves ever to
re-initiate the Church, its authorizing community, to the mystery of Christ
whose body and bride she is. Augustine, we will see, operates with and fleshes
out this model or something very like it. He starts out by distinguishing signs as
a *subset* of things (Latin: sg. *res*, recall Carruthers[90]). He then promises to discuss
these in order, first things, then signs.[91] His definitions are worth quoting in
full:

> All teaching is teaching of either things or signs, but things are
> learnt through signs. What I now call things in the strict sense
> are things such as logs, stones, sheep, and so on, which are not
> employed to signify something; but I do not include the log
> which we read that Moses threw into the bitter waters to
> make them lose their bitter taste, or the stone which Jacob
> placed under his head, or the sheep which Abraham sacrificed
> in place of his son. These are things, but they are at the same
> time signs of other things. There are other signs whose whole

---

89. Frances Young, *Biblical Exegesis and the Formation of Christian Culture* (Cambridge:
Cambridge University Press, 1997), 143–44. A footnote at this point in Young's text refers
to the "contributions of Gadamer, Ricoeur and others." Ibid., 144. As a not unimportant
aside, given the larger ethos we have been exploring in this chapter and the one preceding it, we might note that Young's interest in patristic theories of reference also has in
view a critique of some modern scholarship that, to her eye, has exaggerated the difference between Alexandrian and Antiochene approaches to scripture. Ostensibly, the Al-
exandrians were committed to allegory, while Antiochenes were proto-critics in the
modern sense of the term. Young is concerned to deconstruct this notion. Besides her
Biblical Exegesis, see "Alexandrian and Antiochene Exegesis," in *The Ancient Period*, vol. 1
of *A History of Biblical Interpretation*, ed. Alen J. Hauser and Duane F. Watson (Grand Rapids,
MI: Eerdmans, 2003), 334–54.

90. Carruthers, *Book of Memory*, 24–25.

91. Interestingly, and perhaps importantly, Augustine's treatment of things
throughout his first book will rapidly develop into an evangelical retelling of the economy of salvation, the climax of which is the incarnation of the Word as Jesus. One can
perhaps just discern an intended affect by asking how the treatise would be different
were the topic of signs put before things, and / or by asking the same question should
the treatment of things proceed through a putatively objective starting point outside the
Christian Rule of Faith. Augustine, by putting things first, and construing that subject
entirely within the story of Jesus, the Word made flesh, gives hermeneutical control to
the subject matter, God, rather than to the inquiring subject, be he one of the unin-
structed, a catechumen, a lay baptized Christian, or a member of the hierarchy of the
Church.

function consists in signifying. Words, for example: nobody uses words except in order to signify something. From this it may be understood what I mean by signs: those things which are employed to signify something. So every sign is also a thing, since what is not a thing does not exist. But it is not true that every thing is also a sign.[92]

This so far coheres straightforwardly with the description given by Carruthers. Texts, with their constituent words, are signs for things. We can even perhaps pick up faint promise here of types and allegorical signs, for the examples he has so far adduced are all scriptural signs often referred, in the early Church, to Christ and the events of his life and death. If this pattern of signification should hold, we see the tip of the iceberg, so to speak, of the scriptures' transcendent reference or at least the potential for it. Immediately important for the discussion at hand is what Augustine is setting up to do with these definitions. For now, we note that his distinction is at once both binary ("all teaching . . . is either of things *or* signs"[93]) and designates, at least in the current state of salvation's economy, a proper subset. This binary distinction will give way to yet another, that between *use* and *enjoyment*:

> There are some things which are to be enjoyed, some which are to be used, and some whose function is both to enjoy and use. Those which are to be enjoyed make us happy; those which are to be used assist us and give us a boost, so to speak, as we press on toward our happiness, so that we may reach and hold fast to the things which make us happy. And we, placed as we are among things of both kinds, both enjoy and use them; but if we chose to enjoy things that are to be used, our advance is impeded and sometimes even diverted, and we are held back, or even put off, from attaining things which are to be enjoyed, because we are hamstrung by our love of lower things.[94]

At this point Augustine's reader might have noticed something and raised a question concerning it. *Signs* sound very much like they are useful to get at the *things* to which they refer. With the signs of Holy Scripture, at least, this proves to be the case, as an early chapter of Augustine's second book demonstrates:

> Consequently even divine scripture, *by which assistance is provided for the many serious disorders of the human will*, after starting off in a single language, in which it could have been conveniently spread throughout the world, was circulated far and wide in the various languages of translators and became known to the Gentiles for their salvation. *The aim of its readers is simply to find out the thoughts and wishes of those by whom it was*

---

92. Augustine, *De Doctrina* 1.2.
93. Augustine, *De Doctrina* 1.2. Emphasis mine.
94. Augustine, *De Doctrina* 1.3.

written down and, through them, the will of God, which we believe
these men followed as they spoke.[95]

Scripture is described in categories that designate it as something to be
used to attain, first, to the thing which is the "thoughts and wishes of those by
whom it was written" and, through those, to the "will of God." We have here a
richly relational and dynamic vision of the created order with God. The signs of
scripture evoke the authors of scripture in their relationship to God, such that
those authors, in turn, are signs that evoke the Godhead. We have seen the second pair (authors → Godhead) before, under a cognate form, in our first chapter
where we discussed the *apostolos* principle and communion as a critical norm
for interpreting the scriptures. We have even seen the first pair (scriptures →
authors) in cognate form: the scriptures, when read through the Rule, are communion with the apostles. Augustine places himself squarely in the Tradition as
its representative even as he recontextualizes the Rule and the scriptures in
terms of a sacramental worldview and hermeneutic. The scriptures with their
Rule signify the saints, and the saints in their life signify God, such that the
scriptures interpreted rightly—*used* rightly, to echo Augustine—first refer us to
the communion of saints and through them to communion with the holy Trinity: "The things which are to be enjoyed, then, are the Father and the Son and
the Holy Spirit, and the Trinity that consists of them, which is a kind of single,
supreme thing, shared by all who enjoy it."[96] In this way, communion as a critical norm leads us through the transcendence of the text into union and communion with God. The voyage is one of purifying transformation:

> Since, therefore, we must enjoy to the full that truth which
> lives unchangeably, and since, within it, God the Trinity, the
> author and creator of everything, takes thought for the things
> that he has created, our minds must be purified so that they
> are able to perceive that light and then hold fast to it. Let us
> consider this process of cleansing as a trek, or a voyage, to our
> homeland; though progress towards the one who is ever pre-
> sent is not made through space, but through integrity of pur-
> pose and character.[97]

Unimpeded fellowship with God is our homeland, and we are far from
home. The trail of signs, beginning with Holy Scripture, is the way there. The
trail runs through the Church's and the Christian's life, and is identical to the
purification of the eye of the mind, until it can see God clearly.[98] We have elsewhere, both in Augustine and more explicitly in Irenaeus and Origen, observed
that what Augustine here terms *signs* do not have a one-to-one relationship with

---

95. Augustine, *De Doctrina* 2.5, emphasis mine.

96. Augustine, *De Doctrina* 1.5.

97. Augustine, *De Doctrina* 1.10.

98. It seems likely to this author that, even here, Augustine has scripture in view,
where Mt. 5:8 reads "Blessed are the pure in heart, for they shall see God."

the things to which they refer but are polysemous, possessing layers of meaning. The journey of purification, we should expect, will never leave either the scriptures or the scriptural authors they evoke behind, even in the act of using them, but will instead, in a fashion coherent with Carruthers's and Young's observations with regard to the explosive and sacramental character of (scriptural) texts, behold God in the ever deepening vision of profundity in the sacred page.

It is at this point where the theme of love re-enters Augustine's picture. Among the names he uses to describe "stages" along the journey of purification, "love" holds pride of place. Fear of God and holiness mark the entry to the path of return along the map of signs to home in God's presence, but then comes:

> ... the third stage, that of knowledge, with which I now propose to deal. This is the area in which every student of the divine scriptures exerts himself, and what he will find in them is quite simply that he must love God for himself, and his neighbor for God's sake, and that he must love God with his whole heart, his whole soul, and his whole mind, and his neighbor as himself. It is vital that the reader first learns from the scriptures that he is entangled in a love of this present age, of temporal things, that is, and is far from loving God and his neighbor to the extent that scripture prescribes.... For this knowledge makes a person with good reason to hope not boastful but remorseful.... And so he begins to be at the fourth stage—that of fortitude—which brings a hunger and thirst after righteousness. In this state he extricates himself from all the fatal charms of transient things; turning away from these, he turns to the love of eternal things, namely the unchangeable unity which is also the Trinity. When he beholds this light (as far as he is able) ... and realizes that because of the weakness of his vision he cannot bear its brilliance, he is at the fifth stage—that is, in the resolve of compassion—and purifies his mind, which is somehow turbulent and in conflict with itself because of the impurities accumulated by its desire of what is inferior. Here he strenuously occupies himself with the love of his neighbor.[99]

Once again love is central. Famously, Augustine views love of God and neighbor as the meaning of the scriptures and, therefore, uses the double-love commandment like a kind of shorthand for the Rule of Faith. Just after this quote, he will name the final stage of the purifying pilgrimage, what earlier he termed the soul's homeland. Here, however, Augustine surprises us, for he does not do what we might expect: call the journey's end *God*, perhaps per the biblical 1 Jn. 4:7–8 and its, also famous, dictum "God is love." Instead he names it *wisdom*:

---

99. Augustine, *De Doctrina* 2.7.

> Full of hope now, and at full strength, since he has come to love even his enemy, he rises to the sixth stage, in which he now purifies the eye by which God may actually be seen. . . . At this stage he purifies the eye of his heart so that not even his neighbor is given a higher priority than the truth, or even an equal one; nor does he give priority to himself. . . . Such a son ascends to wisdom, which is the seventh and last stage, enjoyed by those who are calm and peaceful. . . . [T]hese are the stages by which we progress from the one to the other.[100]

Has love been eclipsed? Is there another concern actually more hermeneutically core? The answer will actually turn out to be no, but in a surprising way that fleshes out the very meaning of love in a dialectical spiral back to the scriptures themselves, read according to and for what Irenaeus, centuries before, called their true *hypothesis*. Wisdom for Augustine as for Origen evokes a particular, biblical Person in his capacity of bringing people into fellowship with God the Father—the person of Jesus Christ:

> [This journey of purification "through integrity of purpose and character"[101]] we would be unable to do, if wisdom itself had not deigned to adapt itself to our great weakness and offered us a pattern for living; and it has actually done so in human form because we too are human. But because we act wisely when we come to wisdom, wisdom has been thought by arrogant people to have somehow acted foolishly when it came to us; and because we recover strength when we come to wisdom, wisdom has been reckoned as being somehow weak when it came to us. But 'the foolishness of God is wiser than men, and the weakness of God is stronger than men' [1 Cor. 1:25]. So although it is actually our homeland, it has also made itself the road to our homeland. And although wisdom is everywhere present to the inner eye that is health and pure, it deigned to appear even to the carnal eyes of those whose inner eye was weak and impure. For because 'in the wisdom of God the world was incapable of recognizing God through wisdom, it pleased God to save those who believe through the foolishness of preaching' [1 Cor. 1:21]. It is not, then, by coming in a spatial sense but by appearing to mortals in mortal flesh that wisdom is said to have come to us. So it came to where it already was, because 'it was in this world and the world was made through it' [Jn. 1:10]. . . . And what was the manner of his coming, if not this: 'The word was made flesh and lived among us' [Jn. 1:14]?[102]

---

100. Augustine, *De Doctrina* 2.7.
101. Augustine, *De Doctrina* 1.10.
102. Augustine, *De Doctrina* 1.11.

Jesus Christ is the God who is our homeland, the wisdom in our hearts that grants us fellowship with God, and the path to wisdom. He is the significance of every sign, the tie that binds sign to thing throughout all of God's creation, and so, ultimately, is union and communion with God. Every existentially true sign points to him and derives its meaning, its definition, from him. Jesus, God and yet a human, is this ultimate referent of scripture because he scandalously deigned to descend.

Augustine does not detail Christ's motive in the quote I have just given, but, elsewhere, he does. His *De Catechizandis Rudibus*, or *Instructing Beginners in Faith*, emphasizes that love for God and neighbor is the subject matter and end of all instruction in the scriptures, and in the process defines love with careful precision:

> Thus, before all else, Christ came so that people might learn how much God loves them, and might learn this so that they would catch fire with love for him who first loved them, and so that they would also love their neighbor as he commanded and showed by his example—he who made himself their neighbor by loving them when they were not close to him but were wandering far from him. And all of the divine scripture that was written before the Lord's coming was written to announce that coming; and everything that has since been committed to writing and invested with divine authority tells of Christ and calls to love. If this is so, then it is plain that on the two commandments of love for God and neighbor hinge not only the whole law and the prophets—the only holy scripture that existed when the Lord spoke these words—but also all the other books of divine writings which were later set apart for our salvation and handed down to us.[103]

Quite explicitly, the meaning of all scripture is love—but it is also the advent of Christ Jesus. Less explicitly yet still clearly, the very definition of love is the "humble God," Christ Jesus. This becomes clearer as Augustine writes on:

> Therefore, since nothing is more opposed to love than envy, and since the origin of envy is pride, the same Lord Jesus Christ, God-man, is at the same time the evidence of divine love toward us and the example of human humility among us. In this way the swelling of our arrogance, great as it is, could be reduced by an even stronger antidote. For the proud human being is in a deeply wretched condition, but the humble God brings an even deeper compassion.[104]

Augustine does not define love *a priori* to foist it on the scriptures from without. Rather, the dialectical spiral we observed in Origen continues to hold here, where the soul that encounters the humble God comes to know him as the

---

103. Augustine, *Instructing Beginners in Faith* Section 8.
104. Augustine, *Instructing Beginners in Faith* Section 8.

very definition of Divine Love, and then proceeds to ask this God, in his scriptural self-witness, to disclose more and more what it means for the soul to love God in return and to love neighbor for God's sake. In this way, the meaning of love is never determined apart from a total engagement, through and with the text, of the realities—the things, to use Augustine's category—referred to by the signs of scripture. Indeed, the meaning of love no less than the meaning of wisdom or the types of the Old Testament ultimately is the one finally enjoyable Thing beyond all things: "the Father and the Son and the Holy Spirit, and the Trinity that consists of them."[105]

Conclusion

The heuristic ontology with which I ended the previous chapter and began this one has now taken another level of refinement. From saying that scripture came, over the course of the early period, to be understood to be the Church's eucharistic memory and font of identity, her or our story, approached with an insider's hermeneutic, we have come to discover that scripture also came to be constructed as the story of God with us, the Word in his God-ordained, Spirit-orchestrated union and communion with those he deigns to save. Seeds of this understanding had, arguably, already been sown in the pneumatology of Paul in the first century and had begun to sprout for the author and audience of 2 Peter. By Irenaeus's time, controversy with the gnostics and Marcionites, possibly together with other rivals to the mainstream hierarchy and catechetical pattern, provoked that early father to prune the early growth into a well-developed and integrated application of soteriology to questions of scriptural ontology and interpretation—and, for him, already, the meaning of all scripture was now Christ. A few decades later, the Socratic catechist Origen displayed a related theory of allegory laden and layered scriptural text, with hints that the ultimate reference of all scripture was to holy *eros* uniting human beings and God in a dynamic salvation story. The fourth century would see Hilary of Poitiers polemically redirect this by-now significantly grown hermeneutic to make explicit the christological transcendence and soteriological aim of scripture's reference, and Augustine of Hippo, a generation later, would prune this concern using the categories of neo-Platonic ascent to commend a dialectical spiral that reminds sharply of Origen from a century before.

My preceding paragraph notwithstanding, it is important, in considering this précis of the argument made over the past two chapters, to recognize that none of the fathers here interviewed understood himself to be inventing a hermeneutic. Even cursory glance—much less close reading—shows Irenaeus, Origen, Hilary, and Augustine self-consciously participating in a tradition the architect of which was, to each father's respective vision, not human beings but the same Spirit who, in Irenaeus's words, led the ancient righteous to the Word

---

105. Augustine, *De Doctrina* 1.5.

of God. To express that sentiment in biblical idiom, our patristic interlocutors saw themselves as but men sowing and watering in order to partner with God's giving growth. In this way, the Church's memory, our story, turns out to be curiously explosive in significance, sacramental, as that memory discloses not just a limited, intersubjective, communal religious experience, but the infinite God who, in love, stoops down, in Christ and in the Spirit, to heal and glorify. The implication is that the scriptures are, as sacrament of the Spirit brooding over his saints, a mystic initiator to God's salvation. As sacred sign, they disclose a world in which the reader can cease to be lost and, journeying ever upward, find the embrace of the Trinity that is truly home.

Perhaps the last word in this pair of chapters, then, should be given to Origen of Alexandria. In refining our heuristic from the end of chapter 1 to its present form, we have not found that the early Church denied Holy Scripture as the source of her own identity. Rather, we discover that identity itself is something of a surprise. In the words of him whom all these early fathers reverently termed the Apostle, for her to live was Christ, to die, gain.[106] Although Origen wrote these words regarding just one of the Bible's many books, we might repeat them regarding the whole: "It seems to me that this little book is . . . a marriage-song . . . [written] in the form of a drama and sang under the figure of the Bride, about to wed and burning with heavenly love towards her Bridegroom, who is the Word of God. And deeply indeed did she love Him, whether we take her as the soul made in His image, or as the Church."[107]

---

106. Phil. 1:21.
107. Origen, *Commentary on the Song of Songs*, Prologue, chapter 1.

Chapter 3
The Legacy of Modernity and
the Methodological (Pre?)Occupations
of a Critical Age

"And, then, *everything* changed." Well might this chapter begin with words like those, according to some who see a titanic shift from the hermeneutics of the ancient and medieval Christian Church, the subject of chapters 1 and 2 of this book, to those of the modern age. More important yet for this book are related voices who call questionable the legacy imparted through that shift in what some are calling our postmodern context—that is, with how our world continues to pull upon the legacy of modernity even as the conditions that occasioned it have changed. Whereas the first half of this volume was directed to exploring how early Christianity discerned, received, and interpreted its scriptures, this second half will explore motivations and possibilities for our day's reengagement with that tradition.

This book's introduction outlined a developing hermeneutical controversy, certain modern voices proclaiming the irrelevance of ancient hermeneutics and, now, postmodern voices calling that proclamation into question. The setting of that controversy deserves to be set in greater detail; modern biblical criticism's distancing from its ancient counterpart must be described. The scholars chosen to dialogue with us in this task will be the biblical critic John Barton (*The Nature of Biblical Criticism*) and historian of biblical interpretation Michael Legaspi (*The Death of Scripture and the Rise of Biblical Studies*). The differences between their two pictures of biblical studies are significant as are many of their conclusions and motivating sympathies—and yet, somewhat to anticipate the outcome of their juxtaposition, they reach conjunction at one illuminating point: the relationship each posits between ancient-confessional patterns of reading and modern-critical patterns is one of incompatibility and possibly even opposition. Legaspi and Barton will construct this opposition differently, but both identify it as an unyielding factor in the relationship between biblical studies / criticism, on the one hand, and what I have been calling ruled reading, on the other. It is principally this point of agreement between Legaspi and Barton that interests me and which I want to critique. Legaspi exaggerates the gulf between the paradigms and the culture of modern, critical scholarship as represented by Barton has misunderstood the essentially dialectical, dynamic, open-ended nature of the reading task as such was constructed by ancient Christian readers and is being revisited by postmodern theological interpreters. Thus, my argument, while acknowledging that biblical criticism and classic, ruled reading have been contingently opposed in modernity, will challenge the conclusion that this opposition is necessary or even desirable from the angle of the ideal ruled reader.

Before proceeding to critical review of Legaspi and Barton, a few words of introduction seem in order to explain why they are being used here. Each has been chosen to supply one distinct window on the modern, critical paradigm. Both are biblical scholars, and Legaspi also a historian of biblical interpretation. However, their approaches and sympathies are notably distinct in ways that make them interesting dialogue partners for my larger argument. Barton's work is a nuanced, yet at points polemically sharp, *apologia* for criticism as practiced in modernity; Legaspi, by contrast, stands at the end of the day nostalgically sympathetic to confessional reading strategies and concomitantly ambivalent on the value of modern biblical criticism. Also, where Barton reflects on best practices as he sees them, Legaspi writes as a historian seeking (much as I have done here) the roots of an *ethos* or reading culture. These differences between the two scholars both in methods and sympathies, I hope, will show forth where they agree in bold relief, thereby motivating my argument and chapter 4's review of two experiments in revisiting reading with the Rule of Faith after modernity.

Legaspi and the Rise of Biblical Studies

Michael Legaspi's treatment of the "rise of biblical studies"[1] is "a revisionist account of the early history of biblical scholarship."[2] Partly for that reason, Legaspi's examination of biblical studies is uniquely interesting for our purposes. Like the first half of this book, he has sought out the evolution of an *ethos* for reading in a certain period (the modern one in Legaspi's case)—a total framework wherein texts are discerned and interpreted. Since he is searching out an *ethos*, his analyses are somewhat comparable to those of our earlier chapters.

Legaspi's thesis is perhaps usefully stated in a way as straightforward as it is stark: the Bible that is the object of modern biblical studies is *not* the same as the scriptures of the Christian Church, although it bears some sort of historical relationship to them. The discipline of university biblical studies was *de facto* a

---

1. From the title of his book, see Michael Legaspi, *Death of Scripture and the Rise of Biblical Studies* (New York: Oxford University Press, 2010). As an aside germane to the theme of this book's second half, it is of at least passing interest that Legaspi's method and goal, exercised with respect to the history of biblical studies, is manifestly cognate to the biblical critic's own approach to the Bible.

2. Ibid., 6.

creative literary enterprise in its own right, generating a new, post-confessional literary *gestalt* serving new purposes. Essentially, the Church with her sense of identity, vocation, and understanding of history's trajectory and *telos*—in the ancient and medieval categories explored here, her Rule of Faith—was cut out of the proverbial loop or, perhaps better, hermeneutical spiral. In Legaspi's own words from his preface:

> This book tells the story of the academic Bible.... It begins at a moment when the scriptural Bible ... had receded to the margins of modern Western cultural and public life. The Reformation engendered a crisis of authority in which authority itself ... was contested. As a result of this crisis, the ecclesial underpinnings of the scriptural Bible became too weak, too fragmented to sustain its place.... It was moved to the boundaries, where, throughout the sixteenth and seventeenth centuries, it fueled confessional and anticonfessional theological programs, some critical and others traditional.... The academic Bible was created by scholars who saw that the scriptural Bible, embedded as it was in confessional particularities, was inimical to the socio-political project from which Enlightenment universities drew their purpose and support. Given the choice between the scriptural Bible and something else, university men, the fathers of modern criticism, chose something else.[3]

Legaspi knows this is a controversial claim, even a counter-intuitive one. After all, as Barton points out, biblical scholars of the academy have historically been religious,[4] and, as Legaspi himself admits, early modern biblical scholars "did not manifest the kind of aggressive heterodoxy associated with the radical or early Enlightenment."[5] Rather, they "preserved many traditional moral and religious forms (*for example, the authority of the Bible*)."[6] This remains true today. Ministry students are schooled in biblical studies to help them become effective preachers and teachers. The Bible they study in the classroom is at least ostensibly the Bible they intend to preach from on Sunday morning. However, Legaspi says they actually are not the same Bible; the object approached through critical study is, in a certain sense, no longer the book which is read in worship and devotionally. A more homiletically and pastorally disempowering situation ardly could be imagined.[7] So counter-intuitive is this claim, it might be rejected

---

3. Ibid., viii.

4. Barton, *Nature of Biblical Criticism*, 173.

5. *Death of Scripture*, ix.

6. Ibid., emphasis mine.

7. A similar case was made explicitly, long before Legaspi's revisionist history of the biblical studies academy, by David Steinmetz in his seminal "The Superiority of Pre-Critical Exegesis," *Theology Today* 37.1 (April 1980): 27–38. A difference between them is that Steinmetz says simply and bluntly that "critical exegesis" does not "work" pastorally;

out of hand.[8] If the two Bibles are so radically distinct—indeed, if there are *two* Bibles, an academic and a scriptural one—how could such a state of affairs have arisen with hardly anyone noticing until now, even in schools for training pastors and theologians? By way of acknowledgment, Legaspi briefly apologizes for this, in the process fleshing out in greater detail precisely what he is arguing:

> *The image of the two Bibles may seem too totalizing, too dichotomous to some.* One might object, for example, that there are churchly and academic communities . . . that believe the two are complementary. . . . I do not deny that theologians, biblical scholars, and churchmen of various sorts have worked out constructive relations between the two Bibles and the interpretive modes they represent. Intellectually earnest interpreters often see the two Bibles as representing real and profound antitheses between history and revelation, faith and reason, and the like. And they believe they must be held in a kind of creative tension. However, in actual practice, the relation has not, in my opinion, yielded decisive solutions to perennial theological, moral, and philosophical questions in the history of interpretation. *It tends rather to employ modern criticism as a prophylactic against fundamentalism and to treat traditional belief in biblical authority as a distant source of social and cultural capital* for the academic enterprise. In other words, the intellectual stakes turn out to be low, *and the social ones quite high.*[9]

What were those social stakes? It was those that prompted the organization of the state-sponsored German university in post-Reformation Europe.[10] Thus, Legaspi follows his counter-intuitive two-Bibles hypothesis with a much clearer observation regarding the social dynamics and values of western European societies in modernity, especially the society of academic culture, as new consensuses developed after the Reformation and through the Enlightenment. As he puts it a few lines further down from our quote, above, "Intellectual antinomies were not discovered by modern scholars; they were redeployed by them."[11] Modern biblical criticism involves such redeployment, designed, according to Legasi's analysis, to allow the Bible to continue to function "as a distant source

---

Legaspi supplies one argument why that might be the case, although he denies having the intention to do so.

8. However, the more nuanced but somewhat cognate claim—that the texts anthologically collected as the Bible have been repeatedly recontextualized, that the contexts for interpretation are changed—is quite intuitive. This related claim is made in various ways by one of Legaspi's valued secondary sources, Jon Levenson (see his discussions in any of the essays in *The Hebrew Bible, the Old Testament, and Historical Criticism* [Louisville: Westminster John Knox Press, 1993]) and also by R.W.L. Moberly, to whom we will turn in chapter 4.

9. *Death of Scripture*, viii–ix, emphasis mine.

10. Ibid., viii.

11. Ibid.

of social and cultural capital" (i.e., to create some sort of space for a quasi-tra-
ditional biblical authority) while simultaneously neutralizing the toxin of "fundamentalism," the putative bane of an enlightened society as the new consensus
saw things.[12] This categorization of modern biblical criticism's ethos, perhaps
more than the two-Bibles hypothesis (or at least in more nuanced fashion), describes the heart of Legaspi's analysis. In Legaspi's own words, "the goal was and
is irenicism,"[13] over and against the wars of religion:

> What a close look at the origins of modern criticism shows is
> that the discipline is best understood as a cultural-political
> project shaped by the realities of the university. As an aca-
> demic discipline, it shared in the fundamental paradox at the
> heart of Religionswissenschaft. In order to maintain the criti-
> cal distance necessary for objective understanding, scholars
> of religion created ways of studying their subjects that insu-
> lated them from the thing that gives religion power: its claim
> on the loyalties of the individual. In this way, biblical scholar-
> ship bore a necessary relation to religious communities, pro-
> moting understanding of their bibles. Yet critical scholars also
> reserved the right to modify or reject the beliefs and interpre-
> tive disciplines that gave religious communities their distinc-
> tive confessional shapes. Biblical scholarship, as a discipline,
> had no programmatic interest in theological heterodoxy (or
> orthodoxy). Its overriding concern was the creation of a new
> postconfessional mode of biblical discourse, one that re-
> mained open to religion while opposed to interpretation con-
> sciously shaped by particular religious identities.[14]

That, then, is Legaspi's thesis. It remains for Legaspi to show how that state
of affairs came about. As he sees things, the two Bibles developed serially, the
academic one as the scriptural one became "moribund."[15] This development is
what he calls "the Death of Scripture" in his title. All the rest is built upon the

---

12. Ibid., ix. As an aside, Legaspi's use of the term "fundamentalism" feels somewhat
odd. Properly speaking, the fundamentalist-modernist debates are a late modern development that occurred far down the historical pike from the post-Reformation, German
Enlightenment scene described at the heart of his thesis. Using the category vis-à-vis the
controversial inheritance of the Enlightenment's legacy in the late modern period seems
par for the course (and, for one writer who usefully does just that, again, see Levenson,
"Historical Criticism and the Fate of the Enlightenment Project," in *Hebrew Bible*) but
anachronistic for getting at the motives of early modern readers. However, one can read
Legaspi's use of the term as his way of locating late modern biblical scholarship in a tradition going back to the early modern period; i.e., today's scholars oppose fundamentalism for reasons rooted in previous centuries' rejection of its apparent ancestor, early
modern sectarian strife.

13. Legaspi, *Death of Scripture*, 7.

14. Ibid.

15. Ibid., 3.

presupposition that this death occurred in the centuries immediately preceding the German Enlightenment or at least upon the claim that those responsible for innovating the field of biblical studies in the early modern period were convinced it had. Biblical studies with its academic Bible arose after this death, in Legaspi's almost poetic terms as new growth out of the decomposed compost of late medieval scripture.[16] Given this book's substantial dedication, in its first two chapters, to describe early Christian discernment and reception of Holy Scripture—what Legaspi might term the rise of scripture, at least in its Christian form—first place will be given here to summarizing Legaspi's obituary for the scriptural Bible, followed by more brief discussion of his treatment of the rise of biblical studies and its academic Bible. Finally, before proceeding to discussion of John Barton's *Nature of Biblical Criticism*, I will venture one criticism of Legaspi's discussion, particularly his claim that the scriptural Bible died.

When describing the scriptural Bible's ostensive demise, Legaspi continues to develop a pattern of opening his chapter with affectively charged, stark language followed later by descriptive qualification. He opens his obituary for scripture in the language of accidental manslaughter committed unnoticed and in ignorance by well-intentioned partisans:

> Scripture died a quiet death in Western Christendom some time in the sixteenth century. The death of scripture was attended by two ironies. First, those who brought the scriptural Bible to its death counted themselves among its defenders. Second, the power to revivify a moribund scriptural inheritance arose not from the churches but from the state. The first development was the Reformation, and the second was the rise, two hundred years later, of modern biblical scholarship.[17]

It may be tempting at this point to read Legaspi as a historian of Protestant Christianity and his story as the story perhaps not so much of the academic Bible but of the Bible within Protestantism or at least a certain trajectory along Protestantism's left flank. Not only Legaspi but others, also, show substantial interest in this topic in parallel treatments of the history and nature of biblical studies, for example those of Barton and Levenson. On those grounds, Legaspi's remarks about the Reformation, considering that term's regular connotation of its specifically Protestant genus, deserve to be noted. However, here he appears to use the term with a somewhat broader and simultaneously more temporally periodic sense. The Reformation slaughterers of scripture, as the chapter develops, will turn out to include such devout communicants of Rome as Erasmus. In this sense, the term is perhaps something of a red herring. Still, the plot Legaspi develops begins with internecine conflict between Protestant and Roman Catholic:

---

16. Ibid., 5.
17. Ibid., 3.

> For over a millennium, Western Christians read and revered
> the Christian Bible as Scripture, as an authoritative anthology
> of unified, authoritative writings belonging to the Church.
> The scriptural Bible was neither reducible to a written "text"
> nor intelligible outside a divine economy of meaning. . . . How-
> ever, in the wake of the traumatic religious divisions of the
> sixteenth century, the fractured Church ceased to be a unified
> body capable of maintaining a coherent claim on the Bible as
> its Bible. Because both Roman Catholics and Protestants
> claimed the Bible, in different ways, as their own, the Bible
> could no longer function unproblematically as Scripture.[18]

Therefore, scripture died. Its death was guaranteed by the devastating extent of the early modern European religious conflicts, encompassing as they did
not only the emerging Protestant-Catholic divide but, also, the then equally
novel Protestant-Protestant rivalries (e.g., Lutheran vs. Reformed)[19]—and
more. Before the dust entirely settled, the wars of religion instrumentalized the
by then already ancient rivalry between Christianity and the Synagogue,[20] and
even ultimately occasioned ideological raids against the Judeo-Christian tradition by radical opponents.[21] Furthermore, it is no wonder the death, if death it
was, was quiet. None of the combatants, not even Spinoza, regarded themselves
as anti-Bible. All of them—again, even Spinoza—championed the Bible as a
properly religious vehicle for sublime truth and even salvation.[22] In this respect,

---

18. Ibid., 3–4, emphasis Legaspi's.

19. Hence, Legaspi writes, "[The Bible's] only meanings were confessional meanings:
Catholic, Lutheran, Reformed." (5).

20. For one discussion of this, see Legaspi's discussion on 19–21.

21. Famously, a figure oft discussed in relation to the development of modern biblical hermeneutics: Baruch (Benedict) Spinoza. See Legaspi's treatment on 24–25, where
he discusses the excommunicated Sephardic Jew's *Tractatus Theologico-Politicus.* Spinoza
lived and wrote, however, in the seventeenth century rather than the sixteenth. In this
sense, Legaspi's narrative of scripture's death includes what he might term its immediate
post-mortem situation.

22. Although, this is true only granting first that Spinoza's vision of religion and
revelation was markedly different from his Christian and Jewish opponents, all of whom
were horrified by his *Tractatus.* (See the illuminating treatment by Brad S. Gregory in his
introduction to the translation of the *Tractatus Theologico-Politicus* by Samuel Shirley [Lei-
den: Brill, 1989], 1–44.) However, to observe that Spinoza's self-understanding was pro-
and not anti-Bible or even anti-theistic (unless, of course, he was being deceptive—a distinct, but to my eye unlikely, possibility), we need go no further than his own words
closing his fifteenth chapter: "I wish to emphasise in express terms—though I have said
it before—the importance and necessity of the role that I assign to Scripture, or revelation. For since we cannot perceive by the natural light that simple obedience is a way to
salvation, and since only revelation teaches us that this comes about by God's singular
grace which we cannot attain by reason, it follows that Scripture has brought very great
comfort to mankind." Ibid., 236.

not only we, but the early moderns about whom Legaspi writes might find counter-intuitive the two-Bibles hypothesis and word of scripture's death premature.

When a person dies they leave behind a body. Legaspi's use of the word text,
in scare-quotes, in the just excerpted paragraph turns out to be his favored category for describing the sort of thing the death of scripture left behind. Even his
chapter title reads "From Scripture to Text."[23] He nowhere defines this term,
yet close reading indicates something of what he means by it. The first thing to
note is that, as he uses it, "text," while not actually opposed to "scripture," is
nonetheless not scripture: "In claiming that biblical scholarship operated on the
Bible as text and not as scripture, I wish to . . . mark out distinct but adjacent
hermeneutical territories."[24] Thus, much as he may have apologized for and
qualified his two-Bibles hypothesis, Legaspi has not departed from it. How are
we to describe the border between these territories? Perhaps much as the paradigmatic modality of music is in its performance and not in inert, objective,
written form, so the "scriptural Bible [of Western Christians] was neither reduc-
ible to a written 'text' nor intelligible outside a divine economy of meaning."[25]
In this sense, Legaspi's scriptural bible was not so much an object of perception
as it was a lens, the means through which everything else was seen, having "fur-
nished [the Church's] moral universe, framed its philosophic inquiries" and
"provided the materials for thought, expression, and action."[26] By contrast, as
text the Bible became an object:

> What had functioned centrally in the life of the Church be-
> came, in the early modern period, a kind of textual proving
> ground for the legitimacy of extrascriptural theoretical un-
> derstandings: at first theological and polemical and then, over
> time, literary, philosophical, and cultural. As a text, an object
> of critical analysis, the Bible came into clearer focus; however,
> as Scripture, the Bible became increasingly opaque.[27]

As object—reified and set forth as something the right interpretation and
authority of which could be disputed—the Bible could now be recontextualized

---

23. Legaspi, *Death of Scripture*, 3–26, emphasis mine.

24. Ibid., 10.

25. Ibid., 3. The musical analogy by which I try to interpret Legaspi's comments is
not his, but rather belongs to Frances Young, *Virtuoso Theology: The Bible and Its Interpretation* (Cleveland, Ohio: Pilgrim Press, 1993).

26. *Death of Scripture*, 3. Legaspi's use of the lens metaphor here seems tacit; one denizen of the early modern world he is studying used it explicitly, cf. John Calvin, *Institutes
of the Christian Religion* 1.6.1: "Just as old or bleary-eyed men and those with weak vision,
if you thrust before them a most beautiful volume, even if they recognize it to be some
sort of writing, yet can scarcely construe two words, but with the aid of spectacles will
begin to read distinctly; so Scripture, gathering up the otherwise confused knowledge of
God in our minds, having dispersed our dullness, clearly shows us the true God."

27. Legaspi, *Death of Scripture*, 4, emphasis mine.

vis-a-vis its partisan communities' extrascriptural understandings. Speaking of this specifically with respect to the peculiar alliance of the Protestant Louis Cappel and Roman Catholic Jean Morin, who aided each other as business partners although at confessional cross-ends, Legaspi writes:

> Both [Cappel and Morin] regarded the historically condi-
> tioned character of the biblical text as a first-order problem.
> To Protestants and their Catholic opponents, the Bible was not
> a self-evident scriptural inheritance guiding the faithful but
> rather an indeterminate object whose meaning and authority
> had to be established from outside the Bible itself, either by
> appeal to authority or the exercise of critical judgment. But
> the Bible qua Bible was a disputed book in a confessional no-
> man's-land.[28]

What Legaspi terms "the death of scripture" in affectively charged form, then, might more neutrally be termed the Bible's textualization. It is not that the Bible was in no sense a book during the Middle Ages and earlier; rather, it is a matter of what questions, expectations, procedures for discerning meaning, and paradigmatic context for study (and realization?) were brought to it, or (to use Legaspi's term) in what economy of meaning it cohered and functioned. As we have already seen, for the early and medieval Church the scriptures were read according to the Rule of Faith, the corollary of which was that the Rule of Faith was "read" scripturally. This is because Holy Scripture was definitionally whatever functioned as the written modality of that for which the Church's Rule of Faith—her culture of worship and gospel proclamation—was the living form. For these sorts of reasons, Rule and scripture each played an inalienable role in discerning the other; indeed, they were not separate objects at all, but different forms of the same object which might then also be called variously apostolic communion, devotion to the teaching, or, as I suggested in my first chapter, the Church's identity story. The dialectical spiral this suggests set forth the scriptures as (after a manner of speaking) a "self-authorizing" (the term is Legaspi's) library of sacred literature, for the Rule was not understood to be an extrascriptural principle brought to bear upon the scripture as if from outside. The circularity, if circularity is the best thing to call it, of this situation did not worry the ancient Christian but felt so natural as not even to demand explicit formulation except in rare crises such as those provoked by Marcion or Valentinus. As Legaspi tells it, here interacting with Ephraim Radner, in the early modern period all that profoundly changed:

> Theologian Ephraim Radner, in an insightful and important
> book on the theological consequences of Christian division,
> describes the situation faced by Catholic and Protestant bibli-
> cal interpreters: "That two portions of a divided Church could
> never, in the face of their critics or antagonists, persuasively

---

28. Ibid., 21.

extricate themselves from the circularity of their criteriology was a realization quickly made by both controversialists and religious scoffers."[29] For each group, the presence of the other Christian confession, which also claimed fidelity to the Bible, made it necessary for each group to defend its distinctive mode of biblical interpretation. As Radner points out, though, there was no noncircular way to ground biblical interpretation in distinctive criteria.[30]

It is perhaps important to note—although Legaspi does not, at least explicitly—that the stress was not caused by the circularity *per se*. As noted above, circularity of a kind has always played a role in Christian reading of Holy Scripture because the context in and through which scripture is discerned and read—namely the Church herself, with her Rule of Faith—is itself understood to be profoundly scriptural.[31] The stress in the early modern situation came from the ways in which each community's hermeneutical spiral was set up as a rival of all others. The result was that the conversation shifted from a debate over what the Bible said to one more along the lines of what the Bible was, involving such questions as how it related to tradition, to the Church, to reason and common sense—the full web of relations that could be thought of as defining it. When Legaspi speaks, then, of the "death of scripture," tacit in his analysis is the question "whose scripture?" The answer is "the scripture of the united Church." What immediately replaced it were myriad claimants to the title, just as there were now many splinters each claiming to be, in some sense, the Church or at least the purest declarers of the Faith. Where the original had once stood now gaped a vacuum, for the cultures of Europe still expected the one Bible with the one Church to occupy the crucial social location. Strained as much of Legaspi's thesis is, his observations on this point are clear and helpful. The context in which the Bible was received and read had now changed irrevocably, and that

---

29. Legaspi cites from *The End of the Church: A Pneumatology of Christian Division in the West* (Grand Rapids, MI: Eerdmans, 1998), 15.

30. Legaspi, *Death of Scripture*, 17, emphasis Legaspi's.

31. Robert Jenson observes that this sort of circularity is universal in robust, live conversations of serious merit, particularly in the Judeo-Christian tradition where it speaks about God: "It is the great maxim of pre-Jewish, pre-Christian religion (and now, of post-Christian religion) that though it is nice to tell stories about God or the gods, such stories are not to be taken with final seriousness. . . . Not so with the god of Israel! In this case, there is an actual, particular people, about whom stories can be told; and their God is so involved with this people—so taken up in conversation with them—that their stories are his stories too. . . . Abraham's descendants saw God this way because they believed he had in fact called Abraham and had gone adventuring with him. Now, that is of course a circle. They saw God this way because they believed that he called Abraham and went adventuring out with him, and they talked about Abraham that way because they see God that way. That is a circle, but not a vicious one. It is called a hermeneutical circle, and it develops in every serious intellectual enterprise." *A Theology in Outline: Can These Bones Live*, ed. Adam Eitel (New York: Oxford University Press, 2016), 16.

had (and plausibly has) implications for its continued, living use. However, before proceeding, we should note that Legaspi is not arguing that continued, living use of scripture occurred robustly in the changed context (although he will turn out nostalgically sympathetic to that aim). He is arguing that the change in context constituted a rupture between the old, now bygone state of affairs and a new one, with radical discontinuity. That claim has large implications for any project of renewed engagement with ruled reading and deserves closer examination.

Having contended that the scriptural Bible died in the Reformation era, Legaspi now turns from obituary to birth announcement, the "Rise of Biblical Studies." In telling this portion of his tale, Legaspi narrows his genre from that of broad-strokes historical background to that of "intellectual biography,"[32] taking several chapters to highlight the life and career of the eighteenth-century biblical scholar Johann David Michaelis (1717–1791 C.E.) in its setting at the Georg-August-Universität in Göttingen. Michaelis's work as described by Legaspi is marked by (yet another) paradox: what Michaelis explicitly set out to do tarnished very quickly, even within his own lifetime, and would be held up to scorn by his academic successors. This was "the recovery of a classical Israel" analogous to the civilizations of Greece and Rome. However, in the process this failed recovery re-animated the scriptural Bible's textual corpse into the academic Bible with its associated field of systematic research. His project aimed particularly for the Old Testament to be re-appropriated "as part of a cultural Bible, a scriptural Bible,[33] and, finally, the academic Bible" that is the main subject of Legaspi's treatment.[34]

The success and radical distinction of this academic Bible from its predecessor could be seen in part precisely by the antagonism Michaelis generated among the old guard. One such figure was Johann Georg Hamann. His rivalry with Michaelis took a very specifically religious and hermeneutical spin:

---

32. Legaspi, *Death of Scripture*, 6. It is important to note that Legaspi never intends, to use his own words, "simply an intellectual biography." (Ibid.) The biographical chapters of his book, which take up the majority of its pages, are designed to illustrate and defend his thesis.

33. Legaspi does not explain what he means by this sudden mention of Michaelis as partisan of a (renewed?) "scriptural Bible," nor address the obvious question this raises for the reader. Perhaps, for him the old scriptural Bible died only to be reincarnated for, say, ecumenical and proto-ecumenical cause amongst the feuding daughters of the medieval Catholic Church. Michaelis was, after all, "a lifelong Lutheran" (155) and never associated with "aggressive heterodoxy" (ix). The curiosity of a scriptural Bible after the reported death of the same, however, together with the other paradoxes and counter-intuitive elements of Legaspi's thesis, should perhaps incline us to a less starkly drawn and more nuanced hypothesis about the relationship between academic biblical studies and the Bible of Christianity.

34. Ibid., 159.

The most fundamental question that one can address to Michaelis's biblical project is whether the Bible—given its particular shape, contents, and afterlife—can be fully comprehended
in cultural categories. . . . In Hamann's view, Michaelis embodied a mode of criticism that was predicated on a fundamental
misunderstanding of what the Bible is. For Hamann, biblical
interpretation derived its importance from the divine origin
of the Bible. . . . The cultural overlay of the Bible, when scruti-
nized by scholarship, shows the human character of the scriptures to be deliberately low and base. It is like the dirty rags
used to pull Jeremiah from the well (Jer. 38:11–13), the spittle
formed by Jesus to heal the blind man (John 9:6), and David's
pretended insanity in Gath (1 Sam. 21:13–15). The fact that
these things served useful purposes, rather than transforming
their lowliness, only highlights the extraordinary nature of
the uses to which they were put. So it is with the Bible. One
must not attend to historical and linguistic minutiae in these
passages but rather cultivate perception of the divine truths
to which they paradoxically point.[35]

So, Hamann held to a particular ontology of scripture, one that recognized
relationship to certain kind of reader, namely one initiated to and in pursuit of
divine meaning—the soul or the Church pursuing salvation?—as irreducibly
constituent of what the Bible was. That meaning, while it involved an economic
accommodation of the inspiring Spirit to the creature, could not be identified
with the creaturely dimensions of the Bible because that dimension's witness to
the Spirit's meaning was, in Legaspi's reading of Hamann, a paradox. Michaelis's
apparent rejection or qualification of this understanding of the Bible, or perhaps his never having seen it in the first place, occasioned a bit of *odium theolog-
icum* in the other scholar. Ultimately, that frustration expressed an underlying
theological or ideological rivalry:

Hamann saw many things clearly and accurately. With mor-
dant wit, he showed that Michaelis's approach to the Bible was
not consistent with a scriptural hermeneutic based, above all,
on the authorial role of God. What he perhaps did not see was
that this inconsistency was intentional. There is too much ar-
rogance, too much condescension in Hamann's sarcasm to
permit the conclusion that Hamann understood Michaelis's
interpretive mode to be the serious, clear-eyed, and deliberate

---

35. Ibid., 160–61, emphasis Legaspi's. As an important side observation, I would note
that, if Legaspi's reading of Hamann is on target per the call "not to attend to historical
and linguistic minutiae," then Hamann's ontology of Scripture and related hermeneutic
is not exactly a species of ruled reading as I have tried to describe it. Early fathers actually
often were minutely attentive, in large part because they believed even seemingly low
or base qualities in Scripture were actually by the Holy Spirit's revelatory designs. They
also tended to praise, not demean, Scripture's literary form.

circumvention of confessional interpretation that it, in fact,
was. For Hamann, the most troubling feature of Michaelis's
project was not simply its profane, rationalistic bent but rather its growing cultural authority. . . . Hamann, from his decidedly nonacademic vantage point, discerned that the new
irenic mode of reading, despite what he thought were its foolish pretensions, was becoming a dominant one.[36]

Crucially for Legaspi's thesis, Michaelis had not only a different vision of
what the Bible was and for what purposes it ought to be read but also had successfully raised this vision to be the rising star on the scene of study of the Bible
in Germany. Whereas for Hamann and those like him in the old guard the Bible
was scripture to be read for discerning God, for Michaelis and the developing
consensus the most intellectually interesting and culturally valuable use of the
Bible was the reconstruction and critical investigation of the human past construed apart from the question of God. In Legaspi's words, "In the future that
Michaelis envisioned, it is the academic Bible, and not the scriptural one, that
shapes culture."[37] The abiding, especially theological and philosophical, consequence of his star's ascent would be just as stark as this divide. Legaspi concludes his book in that sentiment:

What, finally, of the scriptural Bible? . . . Though perhaps only
a shade, it has lived on in religious communities as long as
men and women have revered its authority. A full account of
the relationship between the scriptural Bible and its counter-
parts is beyond the scope of this work. In concluding this
study, though, I would like to offer a brief reflection. I believe
that the scriptural Bible and the academic Bible are fundamentally different creations oriented toward rival interpretive communities. Though in some ways homologous, they
can and should function independently if each is to retain its
integrity. While it is true that the scriptural reader and the
academic interpreter can offer information and insights that
the other finds useful or interesting, they remain, in the end,
loyal to separate authorities.[38]

It is perhaps with some irony that, with these words, Legaspi sets himself
in surprisingly close agreement with an interlocutor against whose apparent
sympathies he seems otherwise in contest: the biblical critic John Barton.[39]

---

36. Ibid., 163–64.
37. Ibid., 164.
38. Ibid., 169, emphasis mine.
39. As we will see, in appraising the divorce between the critical reading task and
the devotional one, Barton is far more positive than Legaspi about the moral and even
religious value of critical reading. Ultimately, Legaspi applauds the devoted reader, sym-
bolized for him by the scriptural Bible, and holds back such approbation from the academic: "I grant the moral seriousness of the modern critical project and, to a modest

Partly to anticipate the argument I will advance in the next section, I will note here that Barton, while attempting an irenic stance toward biblical criticism's critics, ventures some sharp claims against Augustine and Origen, claims that then reverberate in polemical tones against present-day theological interpreters whose paradigms Barton thinks are incompatible with the biblical critic's enterprise. This incompatibility will lie in how confessional approaches ostensibly force the biblical text to match their presuppositions. Like Barton in this regard, Legaspi has asserted a radical opposition, likely irreconcilable, between what I have termed classical Christianity's project of ruled reading and the modern academy's project, "rival interpretive communities" being Legaspi's category.

Before proceeding to Barton, some summary evaluation of Legaspi, coordinated with my larger argument, is due. Much is positive and helpful. Legaspi's historical analysis and vivid storytelling commands attention and fairly clearly, even if with a caricature's distortion, locates an origin for the anxiety explored by this book's introduction. Also valuable seems his observation that modern biblical criticism was carried forward with only partially acknowledged social and ideological motivations. Related to this, his recognition that the contexts for interpretation changed with the Reformations period helps motivate why postmodern readers might need to engage in some critical *ressourcement* in order truly to explore ruled reading after modernity; simply reading the Bible as if the ancient and medieval world continued is impossibly naïve. Legaspi's two-Bibles hypothesis gives a name and an explanation to the frustration often experienced by those whose calling it is to interpret the Bible as scripture but whose formal training is to treat the biblical anthology as an artifact of alien cultures and long past states of affairs.

Negatively, however the over-thick lines Legaspi draws, the implausibly radical discontinuities he posits, suggest that the incompatibility or rivalry between confessional and critical reading he and others argue for deserves to be called into question. Along those lines, and again somewhat in anticipation of the argument of my succeeding section, it is perhaps telling that, where Michaelis is for Legaspi the original critical reader, his rival Hamann is the old-guard classical one. Yet, Hamann, according to Legaspi's description, deliberately called for methodological inattentiveness to the rub of scripture's details. The reading practices commended by the fathers interviewed in this book's first two chapters are not this way; they tended to praise even scriptures' lowliness as a

---

degree, the social and political utility of the academic Bible. . . . There is value in the social and moral by-products of academic criticism, in things like tolerance, reasonableness, and self-awareness. The problem is that these rather thin, pale virtues seem only thinner and paler when compared to the classic virtues associated with the scriptural Bible: instead of bland tolerance, love that sacrifices self; instead of an agreeable reasonability, hope that opens the mind to goodness and greatness that it has not yet fully imagined; and instead of critical self-awareness, faith that inspires and animates the human heart." (Ibid., emphasis Legaspi's.)

sublime feature of the Holy Spirit's artistry and called for careful attention to even the slightest detail. This is an observation that deserves to be kept in mind as we turn to Legaspi's and Barton's anticipated agreement on the ostensible incompatibility of biblical criticism and ruled reading—and, indeed, that is what I will contend.

John Barton and the Nature of Biblical Criticism

Unlike Legaspi's work, Barton's *The Nature of Biblical Criticism* is not a history of its subject, and even when Barton does turn to history his approach is not what I would term historiographical. His genre is primarily one of second-order reflection on what he and his colleagues in the biblical studies guild do, at least ideally and on their better days. This makes his entry into consideration of biblical studies distinct from Legaspi's. If I may speak by way of analogy to spiritual theology, his approach is somewhat apophatic in the sense that much of what he does is tell us what biblical criticism is not, especially where the discipline has been perceived as such. In Barton's telling, many things traditionally, even definitionally, identify the critical mode, yet these turn out on close inspection to be only contingently characteristic of criticism in specific instances, not essential to criticism *per se*. The thing to do is to raise and dismiss serially various claimants to the title. Additionally, there is a crucial secondary genre to Barton's text, one akin to apologetic. In his own words, "There are many voices at present urging that biblical criticism has had its day. . . . I do not believe this, and in that sense the present book has as one of its many aims to argue that biblical criticism is not dead yet."[40] Consistent with both these genres, the overall tone of the work is deliberately and, to my ear, successfully irenic.[41] However, the apologetic side of his work occasions some sharp polemics which will deserve analysis and evaluation in their own right when we come to them.

Through the method outlined above Barton develops a series of theses about what is essential to critical reading. He does his readers an excellent service in listing these theses for us in advance in his introductory chapter. Not all of these are equally relevant for comparison with Legaspi or with the larger aims of this chapter and book, yet fair analysis requires we supply a précis for the whole, and listing all ten of his theses provides the most obvious route for doing so. Largely in his own words these are:[42]

1. "Biblical criticism is essentially a literary operation, concerned with the recognition of genre in texts and with what follows from this about their possible meaning."

---

40. Barton, *Nature of Biblical Criticism*, 7.

41. Ibid., 8.

42. Barton's original statement of his theses, which I will summarize in the list following this footnote, can be found on his 5–7.

2. "Biblical criticism is only accidentally concerned with questions of 'Introduction' or history. . . . Historical reconstruction has often rested on the application of biblical criticism to the texts, but such reconstruction is not of the essence of the critical approach, whose aim, rather, is understanding."

3. "Biblical criticism is . . . partly the product of the Enlightenment emphasis on reason in the study of texts. But it also inherits the Renaissance turn *ad fontes* and the Reformation emphasis on freedom in reading Scripture. . . . The contrast between critical and precritical interpretation is flawed in suggesting that the difference can be plotted on a timeline."

4. "Biblical criticism is not reductive or skeptical in essence. . . . It does not of itself produce 'thin' or positivistic readings of texts, but requires sensitivity to deep meaning and to the possibility of many meanings in certain texts. Reading texts well is similar to understanding other people, not a matter of applying bloodless methods or techniques."

5. "Biblical criticism is not the application of 'scientific' methods to the Bible."

6. Crucially, for he returns to this thesis repeatedly, "Biblical criticism requires the reader not to foreclose the question of the truth of a text before reading it, but to attend to its semantic possibilities before . . . asking whether what it asserts is or is not true."

7. "Biblical criticism is not . . . the only worthwhile way of reading biblical texts . . . nor is it inimical to the liturgical or devotional use of the Bible."

8. "Biblical criticism . . . is not necessarily linked to theological 'liberalism.'"

9. "Biblical criticism . . . does not claim a degree of objectivity higher than is possible in humanistic study generally."

10. Finally, "Biblical criticism is concerned with the 'plain' sense," which, Barton is at pains to note, is neither the literal nor the original sense as these are often construed.

Of these ten theses, those numbered three, six, and seven suggest themselves as of importance for our discussions here. In order, we will first briefly discuss his third thesis because of its importance for relating his arguments to those of Legaspi and this book. Then, we will move to a more detailed analysis and critique of Barton's sixth and seventh theses, as to my eye these two claims are closely integrated in his argument and vital for understanding his overall outlook and, most crucially, where that picture is open to critical resistance.

On its face, Barton's third thesis offers welcome, if tangential, support for the arguments I have been making. Whereas for Legaspi the rise of the academic Bible and related discipline of biblical studies represent a radical discontinuity from ancient and medieval biblical hermeneutics and are (in a qualified sense) positive, creative contributions of the Enlightenment following upon crisis developments of the Reformation, Barton, while acknowledging historical advances, views criticism as essentially a matter of "literary perception"[43] on

---

43. Ibid., 20.

which, at least in principle, no time period or historical movement has a monopoly. The Enlightenment, together with the Renaissance and Reformation, primarily freed critics to pursue their art more aggressively. Thus, what Legaspi termed "the rise of biblical studies" involves, for Barton, more overlap and less dichotomy. On the one hand, biblical interpretation has undergone development and advance; on the other, that development has not proceeded, as it were, *de novo*, producing entirely new species or paradigms of interpretation.

However, although Barton does not assert a historical, temporal discontinuity, he actually is developing a subtle case for incompatibility between what I have termed ruled, and what he terms critical, reading. One prominent place where Barton pursues this argument with sophisticated nuance is where he dismisses "awareness of problems in the [biblical] text" as of the essence of biblical criticism.[44] Augustine's *City of God*, for example, shows amply how premodern readers were often fully aware of the features that also trouble modern readers.[45] Barton wields this observation like a two-edged sword, disarming both those who abhor criticism's ostensibly skeptical stance and well-meaning partisans who want to turn it into a victory over an (also ostensibly) superstitious dark age preceding our own. An extended quote is overdue:

> On the one hand, biblical conservatives need to be reminded that it is not the rationalism of the enlightenment, or the materialism of the nineteenth century, or the supposed skepticism of modern German theology, that have discovered the inconsistencies and historical difficulties in the biblical text and have led to "critical" theories about it. Careful readers have always noticed such things. Far from being an invention of modern scholars who are trying to detract from the authority of the Bible, they are features of the text that have always cried out for explanation and have always been felt to do so. . . .
>
> On the other hand, there can be a kind of rhetoric of biblical criticism, perhaps less heard now than it once was, which goes to the other extreme and exaggerates the contribution of modern biblical study in order to commend rather than to condemn it. One sees this, for example, in Kraus's work, which represents the growth of biblical criticism as a triumph of light over darkness. A student taught in this way can easily get the impression that all "precritical" scholarship was naïve, dogmatic and blind. . . . The traditional organization of handbooks on biblical study, in which the patristic and medieval periods are credited with only occasional glimpses into the historical problems of the text, does need to be countered. . . . The impression that results if the rhetoric I have described is

---

44. Ibid., 10.
45. Ibid.

left unchallenged is, paradoxically, rather similar to the conservative perception of biblical criticism as a modern, secular
procedure; the difference lies only in the value judgment expressed about this.[46]

A significant goal for Barton is to deconstruct commonly held prejudices
that set opposite each other the methods of premodern and later interpreters
and plot them "on a timeline,"[47] in turn inflaming debates over criticism's value
by making it out to be the bane of biblical authority. Already, Barton's irenicism
is in view. Additionally—and crucially for my review of Barton, here—it also constitutes an observation, cognate to one facet of this book's thesis, that premodern Christian reading has often been misunderstood and caricatured by late
modern readers when they radically oppose it to biblical studies of today.

It would be a mistake, however, to see in this irenic move the opinion that
the biblical critic's stance was common in, let alone essential to, the premodern
Christian tradition, or that Barton offers a positive appraisal of what we have
been calling ruled reading. It would also be a mistake to see in his irenicism an
olive branch extended to "conservative" or "confessional" readers, against
whom he actually is developing a subtle and nuanced polemic. Barton's goal is
not to create space for critically re-engaging classical hermeneutics but arguably the opposite: to fortify biblical criticism (under a certain construction of
such) against calls for reform. Towards this end Barton critiques particular early
Christian readers beginning with Augustine apparently in order to assimilate
them to a larger class of "confessional" readers that also includes various present day "theological interpreters" following in the wake of Karl Barth and Brevard Childs. This school of postmodern theological interpretation, if I may call
it such, seems to be the real object of Barton's concern.

Augustine is his target, for a first example when the bishop aims to harmo-
nize the gospels. Here is a set of texts that present obvious difficulties to modern
and ancient readers alike: their versions of the career of Jesus simply are different. To Augustine the ex-Manichean, this constitutes a pastoral crisis the clear-
est solution to which is apologetic moves that show how the differences do not
amount to a legitimate intellectual stumbling block to Christian faith. If two gospels present two versions of what appears to be one story, either the details do
not matter or, if they do, the stories in fact either relate separate events both of
which happened or differ because of selective omission. The differences between Matthew and Luke on the order of Jesus's wilderness temptations show
only that order does not matter; when John and the synoptics record different
occasions wherein Simon was named Peter that only means this event happened twice; when Matthew lists two blind men healed on the road and Mark
names one, Mark has simply omitted blind man number two because the one he

---

46. Ibid., 11–12.
47. Ibid., 6.

names (Bartimaeus) must have been known to Mark's readers.[48] These techniques come to be deployed more extremely in the Lutheran tradition by Andreas Osiander, who in his 1537 *Harmonia evangelica* rejects even Augustine's admission as to the possible historical insignificance of order in narrative sequence to "comic" results: "Jesus heals the servants of two different centurions, cleanses the temple three times, and cures four blind men in Jericho. His ministry includes four Passovers, for only so can all the events of the Gospels be accommodated."[49] The problem in this approach for modern readers lies not in the ofttimes amusing quality of its solutions—to say that would be merely to name the issue, not explain it. More serious is the literary perception that forces itself to the forefront of our consciousness but appears not to have so occupied Augustine and Osiander: the Gospels have a genre, and this has certain implications. In Barton's words:

> There is no sense in any of the harmonists that each Gospel tells a separate story. . . . To say that Jesus healed one blind man really is to say that he did not, on the same occasion, heal two; to say that there was an angel inside the tomb really is to say that there was not one outside. This is because we think that a writer who went to the trouble of recording the presence of the one angel would not have simply overlooked the presence of the other; and that one who wrote that one blind man was healed meant not at least, but precisely one—that being part of the convention of telling stories. To our perception, the harmonistic attempt to combine the stories simply produces a fifth story that is incompatible with all the other four.[50] This is because we have a clear sense of how the telling of a story works; we have a sense for genre. Even though we do not know exactly how to classify the Gospels generically, we know that they are not simply files containing facts, but constructed accounts of the life of Jesus with a plot and shape.[51]

It may be worth pausing in our summary of Barton's points, here, in order to engage with and offer preliminary evaluation of them. First, Barton helpfully identifies a feature of approaches like those taken here by Augustine and Osiander and, I would add, any other use of the Gospels. Whether (as here) the goal is to build an apologetic for Christian truth claims or to develop another account of the career and significance of Jesus, the account thus constructed is neces-

---

48. Ibid., 15, citing *De consensu evangelistarum* 2:12, 2:17 and 2:65 respectively.

49. *Nature of Biblical Criticism*, 17.

50. It is telling in this regard, for assessing where and how ancient ruled reading was or was not (compatible with) biblical criticism, that early Christianity canonized none of the gospel harmonies, not even Tatian's *Diatessaron*, but four unharmonized accounts.

51. *Nature of Biblical Criticism*, 19, emphasis mine.

sarily other than that of the Gospels themselves. It occupies a different, if re-lated, *Sitz im Leben*, and proceeds with distinct (again, even if related) goals. With regard to gospel harmonies—or, *mutatis mutandis*, passion plays and even recon-structions of the historical Jesus—these should be regarded at most as supplying heuristics for returning to the analytical, literary critical task later and not im-mediately as getting at the meaning of the Gospels themselves. The *Gospel According to Matthew* should be regarded in its own right and not simply assimilated to (variously) Augustine, Bach,[52] Stephen Schwartz,[53] or even Marcus Borg and N.T. Wright.[54] Second, to acknowledge this is not to pass any sweeping judg-ment either positive or negative on such interpretations or on such interpreta-tion *per se*. It simply marks off the sort of reading that concerns itself primarily with summary and analysis from reading that aims towards synthesis and eval-uation. That Barton, too, acknowledges this in principle is evident from his sev-enth thesis, which, as we have seen, states that the interpretive discipline of biblical criticism is worthwhile as are other approaches. However, Barton does not seem here entirely sensitive to this point. For him, Augustine was simply being a noncritical reader when he composed gospel harmonies, and his being so is treated as somehow or other inimical to the pursuit of literary critical aims—and thus, in this instance, negative in important respects.

The reason why apparently has to do with Barton's larger, polemical agenda and his advancing his sixth thesis: "Biblical criticism requires the reader not to foreclose the question of the truth of a text before reading it, but to attend to its semantic possibilities before . . . asking whether what it asserts is or is not true."[55] It turns out that this thesis has significance for evaluating "the harmo-nizers":

> In the harmonizers, a premature concern for the truth of the
> Gospel stories is in many ways the factor that gets in the way
> of a due literary understanding of them. Augustine wants to
> know what Jesus actually did and said, before he has stopped
> to ask what sorts of stories he is dealing with. He already
> "knows" that the different and discordant accounts in the four
> Gospels must be reducible to a single concordant one before
> he has examined them, and so he forces them into a frame-
> work that derives from none of them. He approaches the bib-
> lical texts from what is now sometimes called a confessional
> or confessing point of view, already convinced that they con-
> vey absolute truth; his task is then simply to demonstrate that
> truth by reading them in a way adapted to produce it. Biblical
> criticism is the opposite of this. It studies the text in a value-
> neutral manner, trying to understand it before passing judg-

---

52. Who composed St. Matthew's *Passion*.
53. Playwright for *Godspell*.
54. Co-authors of *The Meaning of Jesus: Two Visions* (New York: HarperCollins, 1999).
55. *Nature of Biblical Criticism*, 6.

ment on matters of truth and falsehood, relevance or irrelevance. . . . I shall argue later that the neutral, bracketing-out
approach proper to biblical criticism not only is essential, but
actually expresses more respect for the text than a so-called
theological hermeneutic.[56]

Thus, Augustine is taken to be an exemplar of an approach today associated
with partisans of a "theological hermeneutic" to whom Barton is opposed. The
apologetic side of his agenda has come into view. Partly as preview of the arguments I anticipate making later in this chapter, when reviewing Barton's as-
saults on the theological interpreters, I note that, while I can partly sympathize
with Barton's concerns, the way in which they are argued in these paragraphs
strikes me as peculiarly unsatisfying. Tin-eared as Augustine might have been
at times, including this occasion, this attack on him seems itself lacking in literary perception and historical consciousness. The bishop of Hippo may well not
have taken the right and proper step of asking what sorts of texts the gospels
are, and he certainly does presuppose that they are each faithful accounts of the
career of Jesus and so useful for getting at "what Jesus actually did and said."[57]
With certain qualifications it can also be said that Augustine believes the biblical
texts convey truth and is determined to read them so as to discover that truth,
in his case in homiletic presentation, Spirit-empowered presence in worship,
pastoral efficacy, and Christian faithfulness. However, to get from there to a
negative evaluation of him as one who, along with obliquely referred to practitioners of a "theological hermeneutic," shows disrespect to the Bible and fore-
closes upon pursuit of literary meaning seems something of a leap. Augustine's
goal in De consensu evangelistarum is itself apologetic. He probably has a younger
version of himself, from his Manichean phase, in mind. If he can get people out
of that phase, he stands a chance at getting them to take the Christian scriptures
seriously—a necessary first step, apart from which it is doubtful they would read
the gospels at all. In other words, biblical and literary criticism is a species of
critical thinking of which there are also other species. Augustine's focus here is
on one such other species. Augustine is showing pastoral concern for a particular audience, one that wants to know what Jesus did and whether what Jesus did
can be known to an epistemically robust degree from the gospels, both questions manifestly cognate to that of today's quests for the historical Jesus. Augustine is trying mostly to address the second, epistemological question by way of
seeking plausible answers to the primary, historical one; in addressing such
questions, some textual details and reading operations seemed more useful to
him in his context than others. We might critique Augustine for pursuing what
we now believe to be methodological dead ends, but his activity does not seem

---

56. Ibid., 27.
57. Interestingly, Barton's occasional opponent R.W.L. Moberly negatively evaluates
Augustine on what seems a related charge when the father interprets Genesis, see *The
Theology of the Book of Genesis* (New York: Cambridge University Press, 2009), 23–27.

noncritical in the sense of precluding reading the gospels from other, more literary, angles. Indeed, on its face Barton's seventh thesis—that species of reading other than the literary critical one are also valid—suggests openness to this observation. Why, then, does Barton not consider this possibility?

To continue to consider why, we turn to Barton's praise for the third century's Julius Africanus for having represented the spirit of criticism in his approach to the Book of Daniel. Different textual and canonical traditions diverge significantly on Daniel's literary contours. Depending on which Daniel you pick, you either will or will not be presented with the tale of Susanna. Various features of the tale indicate to Africanus that it cannot have been a part of the original. Barton adduces these reasons in summary as:

- Daniel is there presented as an inspired prophet, receiving direct revelations from God, whereas in the rest of the book he is informed through visions.

- The style is different in the two cases [i.e., in "Susanna" and in the rest of Daniel].

- The puns in the story work in Greek but not in Hebrew, which implies that the book is not a translation from the Hebrew (or Aramaic), as is the rest of Daniel.

- The work is not present in the Bibles of Jews, who accept only the Hebrew and Aramaic portions of Daniel.

- The story is historically implausible because it attributes to the exiles in Babylonia conditions that cannot have applied—possession of grand gardens, for example.... He also argues that Jewish courts would not have had the authority to pass the death sentence.

- The story is ridiculous and thus unworthy of a place in Scripture.[58]

Barton goes on to add that, "The arguments adduced by Africanus are a mixture of literary and historical points . . . All are just the kinds of argument employed by modern biblical critics."[59] The larger chapter in which Barton observes this is designed to develop his first thesis—the thesis that biblical criticism is misrepresented by narratives of evolution by punctuated equilibrium. When Barton turns to Africanus's correspondent Origen, however, his analyses raise questions about what precisely he means by his *sixth* thesis. He writes:

---

58. *Nature of Biblical Criticism*, 131, bulleted organization and presentation Barton's. As an aside, I do not know what Barton means by saying, apparently, that assessing whether a writing is or is not ridiculous and (un)worthy of canonization is the sort of argument that a biblical critic properly makes. It otherwise seems to me that such evaluative judgments must be subsequent to critical reading as Barton is defining it.

59. Ibid., 131.

However, criticism was often neutralized, and its insights ignored or discouraged, because of a commitment to the religious authority of the biblical text. Thus Origen does not for
the most part counter Africanus's objections to Susanna on
their merits, but argues that the acceptance of the work by the
church overrules them—even though elsewhere he accepts
the validity at least of the argument from style as valid in de-
ciding whether or not Hebrews is by Paul. He also accepts that
the literary point about the inherent merit of the story is potentially valid, though he tries to show that it is in fact no
more ridiculous than the story of Solomon and the two pros-
titutes, and therefore may well stand in Scripture.[60]

This description is by now familiar to us. Origen points Africanus back to
the Rule of Faith, here in the form of the authority of the Church—which, interestingly enough, is basically to say that Susanna, as Origen knows it, is being
used effectively in pastoral and liturgical situations such as oral performance in
worship, in supporting catechetical dialogues, and in inspiring homilies. However, to Barton, this serves primarily to discourage biblical criticism. This seems
a singularly odd claim in view of the fact that Origen's judgments here have little
or nothing at all to do with literary critical assessment of Susanna's meaning
but only with its canonicity. It seems even more odd in view of Barton's own
seventh thesis—amounting to the assertion that concerns merely distinct from
criticism are actually anti-critical. Barton might respond that he is not accusing
Origen of being anti-critical but only of contributing, by way of his appeal to the
authority of the Church, to an ethos wherein critical judgment has become
stunted. However, is the conversation between Africanus and Origen really a
solid example of what has caused such stunting? Is it really necessary, in order
to engage in biblical criticism, to bracket out not only questions of (propositional?) truth but even whether the text at issue can or should be read as part
of the Bible?—which is to say, in Origen's and Africanus's day when there was
no published Bible, that they were concerned with "Susanna" because early
Christian leaders were committed by the discourse tradition in which they
stood to read it in connection to the liturgy, catechesis, and homiletic reflection?

I have already suggested that Barton's critique of ancient ruled readers is
coordinated with his criticism of present-day theological interpreters, and it
now seems appropriate to turn to reviewing where he directly engages that
task. He devotes the most space to this topic in his chapter entitled "Biblical
Criticism and Religious Belief" which, also interestingly, is his longest chapter.[61]
Its opening words read in the light of its title indicate his goal:

To anyone uninitiated in the jargon of biblical studies, biblical
criticism sounds like an attack on the Bible. There has been a

---

60. Ibid., 132.
61. Ibid., 137–87.

persistent tendency among those who are initiated to think that this is not so far from the truth. The contention may be that any critical approach to the Bible must reflect an underlying hostility to the Bible, or perhaps to the religions (Judaism and Christianity) whose Scriptures it is. Or it may be, more subtly, that biblical critics damage the Bible even when their intentions are not hostile. A common complaint is that the critics have "taken the Bible away from the church" and that some means needs to be found of reconnecting them. In this chapter we shall examine a range of opinions that share this general sense of wariness or hostility toward the work of "the critics."[62]

This chapter abstract is followed by a short reflection on the historical roots of this mood. Although initially designed to bolster Roman Catholicism against Protestant attacks, Richard Simon's *Histoire critique du Vieux Testament* of 1678 received wide condemnation from Catholic readers and was suppressed as its approach seemed to belittle scriptural authority.[63] Against the backdrop of that troubled age, such conservative backlash ironically promoted a mood of counter-revolution from a more radical wing, and in the words of Patrick Lambe, who Barton quotes in this regard, "biblical criticism came to be seen by the world as a glamorous and revolutionary enterprise" against oppressive "ecclesiastical authorities."[64] Time calms all things, even revolutions, but the fault lines of that debate nonetheless trouble the landscape of biblical studies for all subsequent centuries with variously Kierkegaard, Wellhausen, William Robertson Smith, Edward Bouverie Pusey, Bultmann and many others plotted on a timeline of epicenters in subsequent aftershocks.[65] More true to his own literary device than my earthquake allegory, however, is how Barton has now laid out his subject in terms of two sides or moods, one critical and the other ostensibly anti-critical, with anti-critical readers historically motivated by ecclesiastical loyalties and critical readers misunderstood and abused both by opponents and partisans.

At this point Barton introduces a new subheading to focus his topic: "The Need For a Theological Hermeneutic."[66] He describes the community that claims this need as a "powerful lobby" with "nuanced" views:

> The world of academic theology today contains few figures who are simply hostile to biblical criticism.... Attitudes are more nuanced than that. At the same time, there is a powerful lobby that canvasses the view that biblical criticism has been

---

62. Ibid., 137.
63. Ibid., 138.
64. Ibid., 139, quoting Patrick J. Lambe, "Biblical Criticism and Censorship in Ancien Régime France: The Case of Richard Simon," *Harvard Theological Review* 78 (1985): 149–77, with the quotation taken from 175.
65. *Nature of Biblical Criticism*, 139–41.
66. Ibid., 141.

an extremely mixed blessing—distancing the Bible from the churches and from religious believers. What is needed, it is argued, is a more theological style of biblical study, starting from an overtly confessional position and acknowledging that these books are the church's Scriptures, not a playground for scholars. Biblical criticism, so it is said, may be legitimate as far as it goes . . . but it is hopelessly inadequate as a total approach to the Bible. It has a false self-image as an objective and unprejudiced approach, wholly at variance with its actual practice, which betrays a deep commitment to "the Enlightenment project" of rationalism and religious skepticism, and is often rooted in white, Western, middle-class values. It fragments the text in order to get back to its supposed original sources, rather than interpreting what lies before us—which, after all, is the text that church and synagogue have committed to us to interpret. In short, biblical criticism as we have known it is bankrupt and marked by hostility to the very text—the Bible—that it should be serving, for the sake of the church's faith.[67]

This paragraph reads as if describing in one litany a hodgepodge of distinct positions loosely aligned in the common cause of criticizing criticism, no pun intended—and, indeed it is, as Barton admits in his next sentence: "This charge is obviously a complex one, in which one may detect several strands."[68] In his evaluative summary that follows this point I detect possibly three, although Barton apparently sees primarily two, given that he further subdivides this section with the headings "Reclaiming the Bible for the Church"[69] and "'Advocacy' Interpretation."[70] Although I demur whether the scholars described in the first of those two sections really deserve to be lumped together,[71] to do justice to Barton's treatment I will restrict myself to his two-strand discussion here. Also, I will invert his discussion, treating advocacy interpretation first, as Barton engages it with apparently more sympathy and, as it turns out, those who want to "reclaim the Bible" have offered the critique that both more explicitly shows

---

67. Ibid.

68. Ibid.

69. Ibid., 142–50.

70. Ibid., 150–51.

71. Two clusters seem to me to occupy just this sub-heading: scholars whose methodologies are located in systematic, historical or pastoral theology, or ethics and who are more likely to view themselves as aggrieved outsiders to the biblical scholar's discipline (Carl Braaten, Robert Jenson, and Karl Barth are Barton's examples; I think I can add to that list R.R. Reno, David Steinmetz, Brian Daley and many others), and biblical specialists who are more likely to see themselves as offering a sympathetic insider's critique (examples including Brevard Childs, Christopher Seitz, R.W.L. Moberly, and Francis Watson with, again, others).

points of connection with ancient ruled reading and pose a challenge to biblical criticism as Barton wants to define it.

The heart of the advocacy interpreters' objections to biblical criticism as practiced in modernity is the observation that claims to objectivity are also rhetorical acts designed to wield power. Power invariably liberates its possessor, goes the advocate, yet too often does so by disempowering others. Barton quotes R.S. Sugirtharajah to this effect:

> I would like to make it clear that my attitude toward historical criticism is one of an ambivalence. On the one hand, I would like to affirm the historical method, and I can see its benefits, but on the other, I can see its damaging effects when it is transferred to other parts of the world and especially when it is used to conquer and subjugate other people's texts and stories and cultures.... Though historical criticism was liberative particularly to the Western, white and middle classes, it had a shackling and enslaving impact on women, blacks and people of other cultures, as the recent exegetical works of these groups have manifestly demonstrated.[72]

When Barton turns from summary and analysis to evaluation and apologetic response, first he empathizes with the advocacy critics and rebukes any attempt simply to dismiss their charges against status quo biblical criticism: "The charge is a grave one.... This attack on biblical criticism as the academic world of biblical scholarship has received it is not to be ignored with a superior smile."[73] Second, he points out that, for the advocacy interpreters' charge to work, it cannot be read simply as a rejection of the possibility or ideal of objectivity.[74] For example, he considers sub-charges of misogyny. If the biblical critic's crime was that he failed to observe that some pericope really could function misogynistically, and the accuser has detected this, then, ironically, she actually has attained to a degree or quality of objectivity the critic lacked. On the other hand, if a critic has read a text in such a way as to produce misogyny where the text's own potential pointed elsewhere, and the advocacy interpreter is able to detect and call the critic on this, then, again, she was able to do so because she was more objective, not less. Ergo, objectivity, which turns out to be something approaching the desideratum of biblical criticism, was not to blame, only the tin-ears of the critic, and a Stradivarius should not be blamed for the failings of a deaf musician. The same holds for biblical criticism. The problem is not with the discipline but with its practitioners.

Barton's tone thus remains irenic in his reply to biblical criticism's cultured despisers on this point. Nonetheless, it concerns me that the phraseology that

---

72. *Nature of Biblical Criticism*, 151, quoting "Critics, Tools and the Global Arena," in *Reading the Bible in the Global Village: Helsinki*, ed. Heikki Räisäanen et al. (Atlanta: Society for Biblical Literature, 2000), 49–60.

73. *Nature of Biblical Criticism*, 151.

74. I will be summarizing Barton's discussion from ibid., 158–62.

texts have function and potential—by which I mean that texts are tools for the negotiation or discovery of meaning, and that any given text may serve some goals more than others—is my interpretation of Barton and not his own wording. It is also possible that Barton's outlook lies nearer the thesis that texts have meaning, and in that case it seems doubtful the advocacy or postmodern critic will be mollified. The advocacy critic's point is that texts are dynamic. Texts do things, or, rather, people do things with them. By itself, concern for objectivity does not complete the ethical formation wherein a person can discern the difference between text-mediated communication that heals from those that injure. Just so, the advocacy interpreter is not so much damning biblical criticism—the quote from Sugirtharajah in this chapter notably acknowledges criticism's past usefulness—as she is identifying what the paradigm cannot, by itself, do, but which needs to be accounted for in any complete theory of biblical interpretation.

If Barton has missed this point, then he actually has not grasped the advocacy critic's core concern; more importantly for my argument at present, we might also be perceiving where his eye is biased not to see what early Christian readers sought to do, which shows marked similarity to the concern of the advocacy critics along one crucial dimension. As we have already seen, early Christian ruled reading was concerned not just with discerning what texts could possibly "mean" to their readers but more importantly with what the Holy Spirit was doing in the Church to save and sanctify her children—to initiate them to discovering identity and vocation in God's story with and as God's people. Their ontology of scripture understood the scriptures to be the written form of God's living and dynamic Word, the paradigmatic form and right interpretation of which was performance of the Church's Rule of Faith. Thus objectively given, transcendent meaning had to be united to intersubjectively discerned and enacted existential engagement. Neither objective nor subjective pole were complete without the other. Setting early Christian "confessional" readers (as Barton calls them) alongside postmodern advocacy interpreters thus fleshes out the latter's criticism of modern biblical studies—criticism to which Barton seems partly deaf. More importantly, it might motivate calls for revisiting early Christian ruled reading with sympathy, not as a rival to biblical studies but as a larger project within which the modern, philologically and literary critically focused paradigm might discover renewal and reinvigoration. Setting this point momentarily to the side, when we turn from the advocacy critics to the theological interpreters Barton's reading of them, much as his readings of Augustine and Origen, seems more clearly off target. He initially attempts to remain irenic and to empathize with them (particularly with the rhetoric of Braaten and Jenson) but ends by charging particularly Childs and the trio of Seitz, Watson, and Moberly either with intentionally predetermining the meaning of the Bible by foisting doctrinal strictures upon it or with otherwise approbating strategies that necessarily do so. Regarding Childs he writes:

Thus for Childs the interpretive process does not consist of two stages—first ask what the text means or how it came to be, and then ask what it has to say to the modern believer—but only one. This single, unitary approach asks what the text means in the context of the whole canon, that is, what it has to say to the theologically attuned reader. As soon as we concede that questions of meaning are to be settled before asking about what traditional terminology calls application, we have already sold the pass.[75]

This method finds natural extension in the hermeneutics of the aforementioned trio with the result that "the meaning discovered in Scripture should be . . . 'confessing,' as Moberly calls it."[76] The resulting paradigm is incompatible with biblical criticism:

It could be thought that this [i.e., Seitz's, Watson's and Moberly's paradigm] does not conflict with biblical criticism. One might argue that criticism delivers the plain sense, but that readers are entirely free then to go on and use the text in other ways, including a confessional use to illustrate or commend the Christian faith. . . .But, clearly both Seitz and Moberly mean more than this. They argue that the "ruled" reading of Scripture provides access to its true meaning, the meaning that a responsible interpreter should feel constrained to adopt. Their position is not compatible with a pluralistic approach in which one may use the Bible for any purposes one likes, including critical ones, but rather makes claims to normativity. And in that respect it comes into genuine conflict with a critical approach, if a critical approach is as I have proposed.[77]

Later and in more condensed fashion Barton has this to say about his targets' methods: "One cannot establish what the Bible means if one insists on reading it as necessarily conforming to what one already believes to be true—which is what a theological reading amounts to."[78] The theological interpreters thus turn out to have been intellectually dishonest because their approach hyper-determines meaning, guaranteeing they will see only what they want to see and learn what they already know. We are reminded of the opposite of Hilary of Poitier's ideal reader, at the same time as Barton's terms allude to his sixth thesis.

Here is not the place to mount a defense of Childs and those who have (actually or ostensibly) taken up his intellectual mantle. Moberly has, in any

---

75. Ibid., 145.

76. Ibid., 146.

77. Ibid., 147, emphasis original.

78. Ibid., 164, emphasis mine.

event, published his own reply to the charges.[79] Since those charges bring us full-swing back to Barton's thesis that questions of the truth of texts must be bracketed out while interpreting them, I will restrict myself to critiquing Barton's calls for this bracketing activity. First, theological interpretation, at least as Moberly practices it, is not designed to pre-determine meaning:

> The rule of faith was formulated in the early Church concurrently with the process of canonical recognition and compilation. The purpose of the rule of faith, which was in due course summarized in the creeds, is to guide readers so that they may discern the truth of God in Christ to which the Church, through its scriptures, bears witness. In an historic Christian understanding, formation of canon, rule of faith, and creeds are mutually related and integral to the quest of recognizing truth about God. In general terms, guidelines such as a rule of faith embodies are obviously integral to the health of the never-ending dialectic between an authoritative text and a community which seeks to conduct itself in the light of that text.
>
> How then might a rule of faith be understood? It sets the biblical text within the context of the continuing life of the Christian Church where the one God and humanity are definitively understood in relation to Jesus Christ. In this context there is a constant interplay between the biblical text and those doctrinal, ethical and spiritual formulations which seek to spell out its implications. The concerns in this are at least twofold. On the one hand, the initial concern is not so much to explain the Bible at all (in senses familiar to philologist or historian) as to preserve its reality as authoritative and canonical for subsequent generations, so that engagement with the God of whom it speaks, and the transformation of human life which it envisages, remain enduring possibilities; that is, to say 'God is here'. On the other hand, the interest is not so much the history of ideas and religious practices (though this remains an important critical control) as the necessities of hermeneutics and theology proper, that is, the question of what is necessary to enable succeeding generations of faithful, or would-be faithful, readers to penetrate and grasp the meaning and significance of the biblical text; that is, to say 'God is here' in such a way that the words can be rightly understood without lapse into idolatry, literalism, bad history, manipulation, or the numerous other pitfalls into which faith may stumble. It is when the Christian community fails sufficiently to grasp the

---

79. See "Biblical Criticism and Religious Belief," *Journal of Theological Interpretation* 2.1 (2008): 71–100.

implications of its own foundational texts that a rule of faith changes role from guide to inquisitor.[80]

Dialectical engagement of texts that conscientiously keeps philological, historical, and literary critical controls in mind does not imply a theological straitjacket. If anything, it sounds, especially in Moberly's closing sentences, as if what he is calling a rule of faith is designed to preserve a respect for scripture that, at its best, forswears censuring scripture's capacity to challenge the reader's prior assumptions. That is to say, readers always approach texts with preunderstandings. If they did not, it would be impossible even to begin reading. The question becomes whether and how I can shape those preunderstandings so as to meet the preconditions for a fruitful, conversational encounter. This is a far cry from gagging texts' semantic potential. Thus, if the theological interpreters as exemplified by Moberly really are violating the sixth thesis, that would suggest that Barton's call to bracket out questions of truth, and his cordial dislike for some features of Augustine's and Origin's approaches, may indicate something more or other than simple concern not to foist meanings on texts.

To see what that something more or other might be, we might start by turning to a few places where Barton spells out specifically his sixth thesis in greater detail. Although he returns to it repeatedly throughout his book, he does so fairly clearly in the paragraphs following his attacks on the theological interpreters:

> The heart of the matter is this. Assimilating any text, the Bible included, is a two-stage operation. The first stage is a perception of the text's meaning; the second, an evaluation of that meaning in relation to what one already believes to be the case. (This may or may not lead to a third stage in which one's beliefs about what is the case are changed, but that is not the point at the moment.) This operation cannot be collapsed into a single process, in which meaning is perceived and evaluated at one and the same time and by the same operation.[81]

Although the sixth thesis is not directly mentioned here, there are evident points of contact between this section and his statement of his sixth thesis from the book's introduction. When Barton calls upon the reader to bracket out questions of truth, he does so out of his conviction that literary perception ("assimilating any text") must entirely precede evaluation and application in order truly to be perception of the text rather than of one's own prior convictions masquerading before one's mind as the text. This becomes even more clearly

---

80. This entire quote comes from R.W.L. Moberly, *The Bible, Theology, and Faith: A Study of Abraham and Jesus* (Cambridge: Cambridge University Press, 2000), 42–43. Barton's quotation of Moberly occurs in Barton's *Nature of Biblical Criticism*, 146.

81. *Nature of Biblical Criticism*, 159.

his meaning when, later in the same chapter and continuous with his larger argument he writes, in a section provocatively titled "Bracketing Out":

> The case I am trying to make argues, as I put it above, that there are two stages involved in understanding a text. One must establish what it means; one may then ask whether what it means is true. This is an elementary point, which in reading texts other than the Bible almost everyone takes for granted. . . . The bracketing out of the question of truth while one tries to make sense of the text is not the result of some kind of skepticism or unwillingness to believe that the text is right; it is simply a procedure without which we have no meaning whose truth value we can even begin to assess.[82]

Hence, Barton is concerned that a reader might approach the Bible with one particular prior conviction regarding its meaning, namely that that meaning is true. Perhaps he is anxious over that sort of reader who approaches the Bible with the belief that it is somehow a mine for logical, propositional statements and that the theological task is primarily a matter of extracting those propositions under the assumption that every one of them is factually correct—an anxiety that is not entirely out of place, as much use of the Bible has taken that form. This takes us a little further towards understanding him, however not as far as we might have hoped, for it is difficult to see how one could conclude that Childs and company are guilty of holding this view. The excerpts from Moberly, for example, mention truth only once: "The purpose of the rule of faith, which was in due course summarized in the creeds, is to guide readers so that they may discern the truth of God in Christ to which the Church, through its scriptures, bears witness."[83] Moberly nowhere in this quote, or in its surrounding context, subscribes to a propositional view of the Bible's truth. Indeed, he does not even say the Bible is true at all—only that "God in Christ" is true and that the "Church, through its scriptures" bears witness to this God. As we have already seen extensively in Origen, the Christian tradition has contemplated the possibility of biblical texts being false or even logically impossible, that falsehood serving to provoke the reader to join the Holy Spirit's all-searching activity, and, in this sense, canonical scripture occasioning the inculcation of wisdom or, if one wants to put it this way, discovery of truth. Given Moberly is calling for dialectical, heuristic application of the rule of faith, and the pedigree for this application are fathers such as Origen, it seems Moberly has this notion of truth, and not the banally propositional one, in mind.

This leads to the question, just how far must the question (or conviction?) of truth be bracketed out?—or, in other terms, what does Barton mean by the word true? On this point, Barton seems less clear than we might want yet focused enough to confirm a growing suspicion:

---

82. Ibid., 171.
83. Moberly, *Bible, Theology, and Faith*, 42.

> A prior conviction that anything that is in the Bible must be true (in some sense or other) blocks the normal way of reading a text and convinces people that reading is a one-stage process in which meaning is understood and truth assessed in a single, undifferentiated act.[84]

Our question about just what Barton means by true remains unanswered, unless by his parenthetical "in some sense or other," he means any and all possible senses of the term. However, from what we have seen earlier, there is perhaps good reason to believe that this is precisely what Barton does mean. We have already seen in the example of Origen's reply to Julius Africanus that, for Barton, not just judgments about the contents of the text but also judgments about the canonicity of texts must be excluded. De facto, and somewhat ironically, for Barton, in order to read the Bible critically one must first enter into a state of mind wherein even its being the Bible is ignored by the reader. It also of necessity means that liturgical and devotional reading may only occur separately from critical reading, with the latter hermetically sealed away from the other two and not motivated by questions or concerns originating in them, for both those other approaches presuppose the canonicity of the text being read. It turns out that, the seventh thesis's apparent commendation of devotional and liturgical patterns aside, Barton's sixth and seventh theses are together designed in at least somewhat conscious rejection of ruled reading, for tacit in his seventh thesis is that critical and other modes of reading bear no clear, or at least only coincidental, relation to each other.

Two reactions come to mind. I will treat them in increasing order of importance. First, Barton's sixth thesis as spelled out seems obviously to say too much. If circumscribed to proscribe straitjacketing the biblical text in dogmatic strictures rather than allowing the biblical text to fill out and even outgrow currently held doctrine in the course of a reader or reader-community's engagement with it, then the thesis is intuitively right. However, Barton apparently has in mind a complete suspension of reverence for the text as sacred and canonical and not simply suspension of prior convictions about meaning. The effect of this would seem necessarily to be, as hinted at earlier, a near complete disrelating of critical and other modes of reading the Bible. Second, if by Barton's two-stage operation model for "assimilation of texts" he means that texts ought to be allowed to speak before we decide a) what they mean and b) whether and how what they mean is true (propositionally, historically, or logically), then I can admire his model as heuristically valuable. However, the model of truth and meaning he seems to apply here is one wherein the reader must suspend not only judgments about the contents of the text, but also judgments about the text itself—about what it is and what larger conversation it serves, and this, surely, is counter-intuitive, as we have already seen from engaging his counter to the postmodern advocacy critics.

---

84. *Nature of Biblical Criticism*, 172, emphasis mine.

A metaphor from the applied sciences comes to mind as relevant along these lines. Engineers and architects read designs with a real respect for objectivity; if they did not, we would question the soundness of their judgments. Yet, builders also read with expectations about how to interpret designs fruitfully. In this respect, builders and engineers approach their texts with sets of prior judgments not unlike the Christian's baptismal Rule: they are initiated through their disciplines to expect meanings of a certain kind and to engage those meanings with critical imagination. The reason has to do with what it means to mean when designs are in view: their genre envisions conversation towards realizing in the world the object perceived along their semiotic horizon. In much this way, for a person or a community that reads the Bible as Holy Scripture, the Bible bears many similarities to a set of designs because it is constructed not as a static set of texts but as sacrament of the Word of God who has said, "I will build my Church."[85] Now, it is true that this analogy only goes so far. Should the engineer in my example discover an anomaly in the designs that no amount of critical imagination can resolve, she or he is likely to conclude that anomaly is an error and go back to the proverbial drawing board. The religious reader—if we are to take, say, Origen's or Hilary's examples as typical—by contrast will assume that that anomaly is indeed anomalous in God's pedagogical and economic purpose and allow the paradox to provoke *metanoia*. If anything, however, the reader with this hermeneutic of faith is showing even greater respect for the objectivity of the Church's scriptures than the engineer in my allegory shows her designs, for it is precisely the anomaly *qua* anomaly to which the believer submits. In this example, it is ironically the religiously devoted reader who is allowing the text to stand as it is, as an enduring ground of provocation; the reader who approaches his or her text with objective scientific or technical aims must instead fix the text upon discovering something outside the possibilities of expectation.[86]

In this sense, Barton's sixth and seventh theses seem helpful when restricted to calling for the bracketing out questions of truth under appropriately narrowed construal of what that might mean. Ironically, ancient readers to whom he bears something of a cordial dislike agree with him on the point. His opinion, however, that the sorts of expectations brought to bear by the theological interpreters and certain early fathers such as Origen violate texts—that they prevent readers from approaching the Bible afresh for the sake of learning something new—is simply false. He regards the intellectually serious devotion these species of interpretation bring to the Bible as incapable of what he terms "objectivity," by which he means regard for the text's givenness. The opposite

---

85. Mt. 16:18.

86. Barton does seem to appreciate this point to an extent—but only to such an extent as is necessary to defend his discipline from its religious despisers. (*Nature of Biblical Criticism*, 173–86.) He does not finally admit that there is, even for the biblical critic, something of a dialectical relationship between the attitudes and expectations of the reader, on the one hand, and discernment of meaning on the other.

is actually the case; the religiously devoted reader is, ideally, committed to engage the text via a dialectic the goal of which is personal conversion. Likewise, while Barton is more sympathetic to the advocacy critic than he is to theological interpretation and ruled reading, he seems to miss the advocacy interpreter's insight that, desirable as objectivity is, it does not constitute the be-all-end-all of the insightful interpreter who must also be able to relate to texts in ways that involve wrestling with them and acknowledging the larger contexts in which those texts function. The advocacy critic and the ancient ruled reader differ in their devotion to the Bible in this regard but come surprisingly close to each other precisely at the desideratum of wrestling. As exemplified by ancient personalities such as Origen, ancient ruled readers most valued precisely those textual features that provoked and thereby occasioned deep intellectual and moral struggle. Along these lines we might expect ruled reading in postmodern recontextualization not to disengage from critical reading strategies but to embrace them precisely as a means of experiencing holy disorientation, paradoxically marrying radical, unswerving devotion to techniques designed to produce objective distance.

Conclusions

We have spent this chapter in review of Legaspi's thesis, concerning the origin of biblical studies as a field, and Barton's objections to ancient ruled reading (*mutatis mutandis* postmodern, theological interpretation). The two scholars stand opposite each other in their ultimate sympathies. Legaspi mourns the passing of the Church's "scriptural Bible" along with the hermeneutical ends devotion to it served; Barton remonstrates against theological interpretation both ancient and modern for the lack of objectivity its devotion ostensibly smuggles into the interpretive task. Yet, precisely through these cross-ends, the two scholars manifest one point of surprising agreement. Each, in distinct ways, regards the ontology of scripture and concomitant reading practices brought to the Bible by ruled or confessional reading to be intrinsically incompatible with biblical criticism of the sort the post-Reformation, post-Enlightenment world has valued. For Legaspi, this incompatibility is a pattern of social or ideological rivalry whereas for Barton it is more a matter of the psychological impossibility of holding together conviction of truth and objective distance. However, for each scholar the end result is the same: the permanently irreconcilable divorce of ruled reading from modern biblical studies and split custody of their shared children, the texts that in the ancient construal hold together as the Bible.

However, if ancient and medieval ruled reading was as I have explored it in my first two chapters, this is a misreading of the classic tradition. While Legaspi is surely and importantly correct that the contexts for interpretation changed after the Reformation and in the early modern period, and his related sense is also helpful that much biblical criticism and theological interpretation have had rival interpretive communities as their respective partisans, these historical developments do not plausibly constitute grounds for writing Scripture's obituary. Much less do they do so on the sorts of grounds that cohere with Legaspi's reading of Hamann, who, in that reading, called for a low view of the Bible's literary forms and related inattentiveness to textual detail. Ancient ruled reading held to a high, sacramental view of scripture, perhaps corresponding to the Nicene trajectory towards high Christology and soteriology, a stance that dialectically generated profound attentiveness to textual details especially where those details were provocative, as when they seemed somehow base, low, or offensive. Observation of this point becomes even more important when engaging Barton's attack on today's theological interpreters and ancient ruled readers. Barton apparently believes that the sorts of expectations the Rule of Faith involves so constrain interpretation as to prevent objectivity. However, it is better to say that they call for unifying objectivity with (inter)subjective, living engagement with the Bible as sacrament of the Word of God. In this sense ruled reading is not a rival to criticism but a larger project in which philological and literary critical awareness can (but do not have to) operate with a greater raison d'etre. It should immediately be granted that observing this does not solve hermeneutical problems but, rather, makes room for the possibility of honestly discovering them—which is partially the actual point. However, the possibility of such an honesty underscores that ruled reading is not, in Legaspi's terms, an adjacent hermeneutical territory, but a (perhaps partially) overlapping one. With this consideration in mind, we can turn in the next chapter to considering two postmodern theological interpreters who wish to explore that overlapping space.

Chapter 4
A Case Study in "Postmodern" Ruled Reading

The previous chapter ended on a perhaps surprising note. Two substantially different scholars, each reflecting from his own perspective on the discipline of biblical studies as practiced in modernity, concluded that characteristics associated with premodern, Christian hermeneutics and explicitly reprised by some present-day theological interpreters are incompatible with modern biblical criticism. However, in reviewing Legaspi and Barton I observed that, despite their respective, illuminating discussions of biblical studies / criticism and its origins, each seems not entirely to have understood the ancient and medieval paradigm thereby declared incompatible with the modern, critical art, at least as ruled reading took form in Origen and Hilary and now more recently in the work of R.W.L. Moberly. If this observation is on target, then perhaps what I have been calling ruled reading is not as incompatible with biblical studies as has been believed.

If my last sentence were a hypothesis, then the goal in this chapter will be to test it by reviewing two more present-day scholarly works that expressly attempt to revisit reading with the Rule of Faith while yet keeping the modern discipline somehow in view and critically engaged. For that closer look we will examine R.R. Reno's commentary on Genesis in the Brazos commentary series[1] and R.W.L. Moberly's *Theology of Genesis*,[2] emphasizing where possible their treatments of the early chapters of Genesis with glances to their larger visions as needed. Reno's and Moberly's respective works on Genesis stand out for our purposes as each author is explicitly concerned with biblical interpretation (to use Moberly's phrase) "downwind of modernity,"[3] is engaged in the practice of

---

1. R.R. Reno, *Genesis*, Brazos Theological Commentary on the Bible (Grand Rapids, MI: Brazos, 2010).

2. R.W.L. Moberly, *Theology of Genesis*, Old Testament Theology (Cambridge: Cambridge University Press, 2009).

3. Moberly, *Prophecy and Discernment* (Cambridge: Cambridge University Press, 2006), 36. In context, Moberly is rehearsing the thesis of Nicholas Lash, *The Beginning and End of 'Religion'* (Cambridge: Cambridge University Press, 1996).

interpretation rather than its theoretical description merely, and, at points, sympathetically and imaginatively re-engages the premodern world. Comparing these two scholars is interesting also because of the ways in which they, like Legaspi and Barton, approach their subject from significantly different angles from each other. Although both are sympathetic to reprising explicitly theological reading in a postmodern world, their proposals are rooted in different social locations. Moberly is an Old Testament scholar laboring in a secular context, while Reno, at the time he composed his commentary, was a professor of systematic theology at a Jesuit university. This suggests from the outset that a conversation with them stands to flush out different concerns and emphases or, alternately (and as with Legaspi and Barton), to highlight factors more universal within current frames of reference. Finally, I will look specifically to their treatments of Gen. 1–4 because these chapters have identified, over the history of interpretation and for Christians particularly, both the origin of the world and the fundamental conflict (the Satanically provoked fallen state) in which they discover themselves and the Church as central and beloved characters.

Theological Interpretation in a "Postmodern" Age: A Detailed Consideration of Russell Reno

Russell Reno on Theological Commentary

    I will begin my treatment of Reno's *Genesis* with a brief but perhaps important observation before going into a discussion of his stated theory of theological commentary. While Reno acknowledges the widely recognized redactional seam at 2:4 and ascribes the passages before and after to different hands, he chooses to combine discussion of 1:1–2:3 and 2:4–25 into one chapter entitled "Creation" and construe the contents of both narratives accordingly. In his own words:

> Readers quickly notice the odd way in which Genesis gives a double account of creation. I read these two accounts as complimentary [sic] portrayals of the same, stage-setting divine act. The architecture of the six days of creation is made plastic and mobile by the possibility of the seventh day, a literary effect that, I argue, reveals the goal of the divine plan "in the beginning." God creates in order to consummate; nature is for the sake of grace; everything leans toward something more. The dynamic, forward-reaching structure of creation is even clearer in the second, more human-focused account of creation. It ends with the aching desire of the first man for companionship. This poignant moment of human subjectivity illustrates the way in which all creation groans for fulfillment.

It is a yearning taken up and intensified in the nuptial fulfill-
ments that echo throughout scripture.[4]

His decision, then, is not naïve—say, reflecting an ignorance of the text's
literary shape. Rather, Reno intentionally reads the narrative starting at 2:4
through (or with?) the account that begins at 1:1, the second narrative typologically recapitulating the first. The effect, to my eye, downplays the distinctive
literary characteristics of the two passages, instead treating them like two
lenses of a pair of binoculars where each lens provides a distinct but coordinated
angle on a common object of reflection—in this case the doctrine of creation—
to be followed by reflection on the doctrine of the fall using chapters 3–4. In the
process, a literary break has been added at 3:1.[5]

The reason I begin with this observation, which to some may seem simply
obvious given the long tradition (especially) of treating Gen. 3 separately from
2:4–25, is because it raises a question for me on precisely how ruled reading's
hermeneutical spiral might be acknowledged in Reno's larger approach. Intuitively speaking, the medieval chapter breaks (e.g., the one at 3:1) are an artifact
of the Church's liturgy and catechesis; the actual grammar and lexico-semantics
of the underlying passages constitutes, by contrast, the warp and woof of the
text by which something like its "plain sense" might be discerned. The argument I have been making in this book is that *both* these factors are significant
for ruled reading as the early fathers practiced it. How might the plain sense—
acknowledging that the construction and discovery of such is nontrivial and involved—relate to doctrine for Reno's approach? Put in other words, for him,
what is theological commentary? Is it commentary *on doctrine* that uses the Bible
(say, to illustrate or prove or teach doctrine) or is it commentary *on the Bible* that
uses doctrine (to orient to the sacred page)? Or, is it, again, somehow both? The

---

4. Reno, *Genesis*, 22.

5. I note that his association of 1–2:3 with 2:4–25 results in his putting a break just
before chapter 3, and this does seem to weight the theological judgment that 1:1--2:4 is
about Creation and chapter 3 is about the Fall more heavily than various literary cues
that link 2:4–4:26 while putting a sharper break at chapter 5. 2:4 begins with what reads
almost like a stock phrase, (in the NRSV) "These are the generations of. . . . " (MT: *eleh
toledot*, LXX: *haute he biblos geneseos*), and this phrase will be repeated at various points in
the primaeval history, the next repetition after 2:4 occurring at 5:1. Further, 3:1 arguably
continues the narrative from chapter 2 with the word "now." The MT has a simple *waw*
and the LXX the conjunction *de*. This may indicate a break, yet here, to my eye, does not
introduce a strong one. The main topic of the immediately preceding passage—the
woman, Eve—remains in focus throughout chapter 3, as the otherwise seemingly dis-
placed 3:20 underscores. Does this signify that, on a literary level, 2:4–4:26 is, to some
degree, one literary unit, the stated genre of which is something like family history? The
question goes far beyond the scope of this chapter. However, my main point is simply to
note that Reno shows no interest in the question but rather allows prior theological questions and concerns to set the pericope boundaries.

possibility that the answer actually is both highlights a related, critical observation standing tacitly to the side. By reifying *doctrine* and *Bible* and relating them to one another as separate things, I have already betrayed my context's particular construal of the Bible and the doctrinal tradition. However, as touched on in my first chapter, *Rule* (tradition?) and *scripture* were not so clearly separated in the context of early Christianity. One of the challenges facing Reno is whether and how to be informed by the classical ontology of doctrine (as something intrinsically related to scripture and even, in a crucial sense, identifiable with it) in *our* context.

To begin to consider these issues, we might, first, note that Reno is the general editor for the series in which his *Genesis* is published, and so the series preface, written by his hand, is a possible source for obtaining at least partial answers. At points, his words suggest that theological commentary should use doctrine to orient readers to the scriptures. For example, restating the classic dictum that the keys of doctrine unlock the scriptures, Reno tells us:

> God the Father Almighty, who sends his only begotten Son to die for us and for our salvation and who raises the crucified Son in the power of the Holy Spirit so that the baptized may be joined in one body—faith in this God with this vocation of love for the world is the lens through which to view the heterogeneity and particularity of the biblical texts. Doctrine, then, is not a moldering scrim of antique prejudice obscuring the meaning of the Bible. It is a crucial aspect of the divine pedagogy, a clarifying agent for our minds fogged by self-deceptions, a challenge to our languid intellectual apathy that will too often rest in false truisms and the easy spiritual nostrums of the present age rather than search more deeply and widely for the dispersed keys to the many doors of Scripture.[6]

Our question is now partially answered, although much remains to be fleshed out. Theological commentary, according to Reno, is a genre that uses dogma to orient readers so that they might encounter the scriptures in all their "heterogeneity and particularity." Importantly along these lines, the Rule of Faith as Reno promises to engage it is not a narrow list of discrete propositions, but something more organic, "the animating culture of the church," long-developed over the course of receiving scripture's challenge:

> The Nicene tradition does not provide a set formula for the solution of exegetical problems. The great tradition of Christian doctrine was not transcribed, bound in folio, and issued in an official, critical edition. We have the Niceno-Constantinopolitan Creed, used for centuries in many traditions of Christian worship. We have ancient baptismal affirmations of faith. The Chalcedonian definition and the creeds and canons of

6. Reno, *Genesis*, 11–12.

other church councils have their places in official church documents. Yet the rule of faith cannot be limited to a specific set of words, sentences, and creeds. It is instead a pervasive habit of thought, the animating culture of the church in its intellectual aspect.[7]

Further, theological commentary in Reno's outlook does not simply engage scripture starting from the questions and categories of the Nicene tradition *as it has developed in the past*. It also re-engages the Rule for the purpose of revolution against the perceived tyranny of "modern historical-critical scholarship," with its perceived claim of an interpretive monopoly. Most clear are Reno's words from his own author's "Introduction":

> *I want to identify my polemical interest and argumentative agenda.* I have pointed things to say about modern historical-critical study of the Bible. No doubt thin-skinned biblical scholars will image me preoccupied with an antimodern campaign against critical scholarship. In the main, I find modern historical-critical scholarship sometimes helpful, sometimes maddeningly myopic, and sometimes irrelevant to the sorts of questions I find myself asking about Genesis. So, in this commentary I do not reject historical-critical exegesis. I am happy to consult it when helpful. I am only irritated by its unsustainable claims to an exclusive interpretive authority. As a tradition of scholarship, historical-critical [*sic*] cannot provide us with all the resources necessary to interpret the Bible as the living source for Christian faith.[8]

Reno follows this paragraph with a lengthy, almost homiletic, description of the questions he wants to privilege in interpreting scripture. Our age, he tells us, is pervasively "gnostic" in its desire to transcend and escape historical and cultural particularity.[9] Biblical criticism of the historical-critical sort is rarely useful for addressing that pastoral crisis, and, yet, claims an interpretive monopoly. The solution is to revolt against it and insist upon the *a priori* validity of an approach to scripture that opposes this postmodern gnosticism with the resources of doctrine. To return to the question with which I opened this section,

---

7. Ibid., 12.

8. Ibid., 26, emphasis mine. As an aside, it would be perhaps interesting and valuable to compare Karl Barth's second preface to his commentary on Romans. He, likewise, was accused of being anti-critical in the historical sense and, also likewise, countered that he was not but that he was opposed to stopping with "historical-critical" matters and calling it a day, proverbially speaking. Rather, he said, historical criticism also being done and taken into account, the objective was then so to wrestle with the subject matter of the scriptures that the "walls" separating the *Sitz im Leben* of the original and our own day, so to speak, vanish. Calvin, for him, is exemplary. (*The Epistle to the Romans*, trans. Edwyn Hoskins [Oxford: Oxford University Press, 1968], 2–15 and esp. 7.)

9. Reno, *Genesis*, 26.

is theological commentary now turning out to be also the inverse of using doctrine to orient to the scriptures? That is, does it use the Bible to illustrate doctrine? If it is both orientation to the Bible and development from encountering the Bible, then we have rediscovered, with Reno, something like the dialectical spiral outlined in this book's first chapters. As a not unimportant side observation, Reno's decision here, to privilege not simply a contemporary pastoral crisis but to categorize that crisis by way of analogy to a great heresy of Christian antiquity, effectively locates him and any who accept his categorization inside that living "Christian doctrinal tradition."[10]

Reno's polemic against the modern biblical critic will come up again at various points throughout his commentary, in the process further demonstrating how central this commitment—to use the Bible to answer the questions of "the Christian doctrinal tradition" conceived as a living present and not a past state of mind—is to Reno's understanding of theological commentary. For example, and to get ahead of ourselves slightly, in an extended section discussing and defending the traditional interpretation of Gen. 1:1 (as proclaiming creation from nothing) from a putative modern historical-critical judgment that the verse merely names the occasion on which God began to create, Reno says:

> The immediate reasons in support of a traditional interpretation and translation are strong, but we should broaden the argument, not only because further reasons are important in their own right, but also because we need to be clearminded about the expansive scope of interpretation. A theological reading needs to approach scripture in such a way as to sustain a coherent, overall view of God's plan and purpose. What is entailed in sustaining such a view is complex and opaque. No one can set criteria ahead of time, and there are no particular methods that will guarantee good results. Sound interpretive arguments are always varied and cumulative. In this case, three broad considerations speak in favor of the traditional translation. A substantive interpretation of "beginning" will allow us to approach the larger question of creation in a way that (1) helps us avoid a false conflict between creation and science, (2) facilitates a fruitful engagement of faith with reason, and (3) gives a proper spiritual focus to our interpretive concerns.[11]

---

10. Ibid., 12. It is important to note that Reno's reference to "the Christian doctrinal tradition" does not give interpretive monopoly to past great readers of Christian history, as, for him, this Tradition is alive—it includes any modern or postmodern reader who consciously participates in it. Excluded are not new questions, or modern or postmodern ones, but stances that dismiss the Tradition as irrelevant.

11. Ibid., 35.

The point of this paragraph is not that there are no textual or literary reasons for preferring the reading "In the beginning God created . . . " over something like "In the beginning when God created . . . " Earlier in his discussion Reno adduces such examples. The point is to push towards a mode of interpretation wherein questions and concerns formed from within the Tradition, such as the three he lists in the paragraph above, motivate the interpreter.

Features such as these already invite comparison between Reno's interpretation of ruled reading and the description my first two chapters give to the paradigm as it developed through Irenaeus, Origen, Hilary, and Augustine. Grappling with the situations of readers and using scripture to instruct in doctrine takes seriously scripture's origin in and existence for the economy of salvation and its pedagogical role in the service of the Word and Spirit of God. In this respect the correlation is positive. We have, also, already seen some promise that Reno intends to dive into what my early chapters described as ruled reading's dialectical spiral insofar as he intends theological commentary *both* to orient to the scriptures *and* to use those scriptures to doctrinal ends.

However, this spiral as my early chapters described it involved more than simply two-way traffic between doctrine and scripture. Doctrine (the Rule) was initiation to scripture's subject matter such that scripture could, in turn, flesh out what doctrine truly meant. Ruled reading neither sought to force scripture to answer questions that cut against the grain of scripture's own internal categories and priorities, nor did it suspend minute, attentive devotion to its jot-and-tittle details—e.g., the literary breaks of Genesis's early chapters. So far, Reno's approach clearly resembles ruled reading in its application of questions and concerns formed in the development of Christian faith, but will he recognize points where the text provokes re-prioritization of concerns through careful, detailed, critical attentiveness? To reuse his own application of the patristic adage that the keys of doctrine unlock the scriptures, how can one tell when a key does not quite fit? Reno's approach to 1:1–3:24, to my eye, seems mixed in this regard, with some perhaps substantial fumbling at the lock with respect to the sharp dichotomies he draws between traditional and historical-critical (philological?) factors in interpretation, as, for example, in the case where Reno minimizes the literary break at 2:4 and inserts one at 3:1. Concern for features such as this one is central to the historical-critical paradigm that is the target of Reno's polemics. We have already seen that Reno hopes, in his own words, to "consult it [i.e., historical criticism] where helpful."[12] Is his (dis)regard for the literary shape of Genesis's early chapters indicative of some of the ways in which he distinguishes between helpful and unhelpful uses of biblical criticism? Will Reno consult modern criticism where it supplies observations or raises critical questions for the doctrinal Tradition to engage dialectically, perhaps aiding the exegete in selecting the right key from the doctrinal keychain, or are his

---

12. Ibid., 26.

polemics arranged against modern biblical criticism in such a way as to discourage their use for that purpose?

Reno's pervasive polemic against criticism, and, as we shall see, his preference for traditional interpretations, hint already that the "plain" sense, at least as construed in modernity, might be little used to discern which of doctrine's many keys should be used at any given time. The sharp note sounded by his pervasive polemic (e.g., that the interpretive status-quo has produced a debilitated condition, "like stroke victims"[13]) indicates that modern interpretation has been something of a serious interpretive misstep for him—perhaps too serious of a misstep for it or its preference for a plain sense to be helpful all that often. Regarding one figure, Benjamin Jowett, whom he takes as representative of modernity, Reno writes:

> If self-consciousness about the role of history in shaping human consciousness makes modern historical-critical study critical, then what makes modern study of the Bible modern is the consensus that classical Christian doctrine distorts interpretive understanding. Benjamin Jowett, the influential nineteenth-century English classical scholar, is representative. In his programmatic essay "On the Interpretation of Scripture," he exhorts the biblical reader to disengage from doctrine and break its hold over the interpretive imagination. "The simple words of that book," writes Jowett of the modern reader, "he tries to preserve absolutely pure from the refinements or distinctions of later times." The modern interpreter wishes to "clear away the remains of dogmas, systems, controversies, which are encrusted upon" the words of Scripture. The disciplines of close philological analysis "would enable us to separate the elements of doctrine and tradition with which the meaning of Scripture is encumbered in our own day."[14] The lens of understanding must be wiped clear of the hazy and distorting film of doctrine.[15]

What makes modern criticism modern, for Reno, is precisely this attitude of which he accuses Jowett.[16] Criticism as a paradigm, in this sense, he sees not

---

13. Ibid.

14. He quotes from Benjamin Jowett, "On the Interpretation of Scripture," in *Essays and Reviews* (London: Parker, 1860), 338–39.

15. Reno, *Genesis*, 10.

16. It is beyond the scope of this book to evaluate Reno's reading of Jowett and yet further beyond it to evaluate Jowett's sprawling essay. Nonetheless, it is worth mentioning that Reno's interpretation of Jowett, while not entirely unproductive when viewed as one rhetorical element of his polemic, arguably oversimplifies the latter's motivations and method alike. The main thrust of Jowett's own polemics was directed not against Reno's doctrinal tradition but against the sectarian divisions and construals of doctrine that occupy Jowett's own historical neighborhood and were infamously responsible for the wars of religion of the immediately preceding centuries, and also against construals

just as a limited set of methods that have claimed for themselves an undue interpretive monopoly. For him, criticism is anti-doctrine at its heart, and this makes the discipline of using it, even where helpful, not unlike, to use another ancient patristic allegory, spoiling Egypt—using an enemy's tools against his interests.[17] The situation is not changed for the better after modernity. Reno goes on to describe how it persists in postmodernity, albeit in mutant form, and finally fires several rhetorical questions to the critic: "Are readers naturally perceptive? Do we have an unblemished, reliable aptitude for the divine? Have we no need for disciplines of vision? Do our attention and judgment need to be trained, especially as we seek to read Scripture as the living word of God?"[18] Finally, he adds:

> According to Augustine, we all struggle to journey toward God, who is our rest and peace. Yet our vision is darkened and the fetters of worldly habit corrupt our judgment. We need training and instruction in order to cleanse our minds so that we might find our way toward God. To this end, "the whole temporal dispensation was made by divine Providence for our salvation."[19] . . . In Augustine's view, the reading of Scripture both contributes to and benefits from this divine pedagogy. With countless variations in both exegetical conclusions and theological frameworks, the same pedagogy of a doctrinally ruled reading of Scripture characterizes the broad sweep of the Christian tradition from Gregory the Great through Bernard and Bonaventure, continuing across Reformation differences in both John Calvin and Cornelius Lapide, Patrick Henry

---

of biblical interpretation and authority that were irreconcilable to science along that horizon that has since become theories of anthropological and geological protology, i.e., what we, in our day, sometimes obliquely term theories of evolution. By contrast, Jowett's attitude towards application of scripture—what he deems to be the early Fathers', medieval interpreters', and the Reformers' main contribution and mode—is positive on balance, their spiritual and theological legacies more an object of praise than of criticism. To Jowett's eye, the way to reform theological science with respect to biblical interpretation, given the exigencies of his day, was literary criticism of Christianity's sacred deposit paired with a theory of progressive revelation, which, he believed, would allow readers to distinguish between the "accidents" and "essence" of religion; this step taken, presumably, interpreters would be freed to "apply" scripture in their own contexts much as the Fathers and Reformers "applied" it in theirs. See Benjamin Jowett, "On the Interpretation of Scripture." Also, for two recent analyses and (partial) evaluations of Jowett's contribution see R.W.L. Moberly, "'Interpret the Bible Like Any Other Book'? Requiem for an Axiom," *Journal of Theological Interpretation* 4.1 (2010): 91–110; James Barr, "Jowett and the 'Original Meaning' of Scripture," *Religious Studies* 18.4 (1982): 433–37.

17. This allegory apparently comes from Origen, *Letter to Gregory* 2.

18. Reno, *Genesis*, 10.

19. Reno quotes from *On Christian Doctrine* 1.35.

and Bishop Bossuet, and on to more recent figures such as Karl
Barth and Hans Urs von Balthasar.[20]

Opposed to the claim of the modern interpreter stands the Tradition, running up to this day, in stark contrast, like a cloud of witnesses testifying to an
existential truth ostensibly denied by the critics. Reno is quick to name with
which community of witnesses he in the main identifies, and we are not sur-
prised: "This series of biblical commentaries was born out of the conviction that
dogma clarifies rather than obscures."[21] It seems that, while historical-critical
sensitivity *per se* is methodologically permitted, the particular take on the relationship between philology and biblical study characteristic of the critical paradigm as Reno understands it is opposed to the doctrinal tradition in which
Reno seeks to stand and vice versa. Although he does not use the term, we might
say that Jowett's stance represents something heresy-like to Reno. We might
even guess as to that heresy's essence: it denies the integral relationship of the
living Christian doctrinal tradition and Holy Scripture while claiming for itself
full sufficiency for the interpreter—intriguingly a feature of Protestant thought
under a certain construal.[22] Reno's words that "as a tradition of scholarship,
historical-critical [sic] cannot provide us with all the resources necessary to interpret the Bible as the living source for Christian faith"[23] mean, in the light of
his total polemic, that the claims of the modern critic are overblown and in an
important sense deceptive. It is hard to imagine a categorization more pejora-
tive which yet retains nuance.

Thus far, we have reviewed Reno's understanding of what a theological
commentary for today ought to be, and we have briefly introduced some specifics of his stance towards Gen. 1–4. In the process, we have discerned partial answers to questions regarding how Reno might re-contextualize ruled reading
for a postmodern setting. Already helpful is the way in which his treatment of
theological commentary fleshes out ruled reading's contextual sensitivity in
terms of a living tradition and his explicitly defining the Rule of Faith as the
animating culture of that tradition. However, not all looks positive. The overall
coherence of his stance with the tradition of ruled reading, together with its

---

20. Reno, *Genesis*, 11.

21. Ibid.

22. As an evaluation of Jowett this construal does seems suggestive of a position to
which Jowett likely was at least sympathetic and which to a certain degree represents
Protestantism in a certain mode; however, it is worth noting, in all fairness to Jowett and
that Protestant mode, that to deny an integral relationship between doctrine and scripture is not to deny any and all possible constructive relationship between them. To me it
seems likely that Jowett favored readers being informed by the Tradition's "applications"
of scripture so that they might develop the "faculty divine" without which, he says, it is
impossible to "interpret" scripture, however distinct "application" and "interpretation"
are as activities in themselves, cf. Jowett, "On the Interpretation of Scripture," 337, 377,
404–5.

23. Reno, *Genesis*, 26.

promise for fleshing out ruled reading in today's context, is fairly clear but involves one or perhaps two points of as-yet unresolved dissonance: we have not yet seen whether and how the scriptures might lead its readers to *metanoia* wherein their prior questions and interpretive priorities are challenged. So far, the relationship of the Christian doctrinal tradition and scripture as he has articulated it encourages the reader to set the agenda by looking primarily to the Tradition construed as an aggrieved opponent of modernity, whose concern for a philologically discerned scriptural text is engaged in a sharp counter-polemic. Effectively, this threatens to strain the relationship between scripture and traditions of interpretation intuitively key to ruled reading.

Reno on Genesis 1-4

As noted earlier, Reno splits up our target passage of 2:4–4:26, treating 2:4–25 together with 1–2:3 as two complementary accounts of the Creation, then treating 3:1–4:26 as one passage covering the fall of humanity into a condition of sin and concupiscence, the inauguration of a "false covenant with the lie."[24] Central to what one sees is how one sees it, and, so, we will begin where Reno does, with 1:1. Joining him there is additionally advantageous because of the volume of pages spent on 1:1–2 relative to the rest of his discussion. Fully seventeen of the forty-seven pages he commits to 1:1–2:25 —roughly thirty-five percent of his chapter, double the space he commits to discussing the creation of humanity and five pages longer than his discussion of all of 2:4–25—is dedicated entirely to chapter 1's first two verses. The proportion of the commentary devoted to the first two verses of chapter 1, it turns out, is directly in the service of his aforementioned polemical agenda. In this way, Reno's controversy with modern criticism, and not simply his own constructive proposals, substantially informs his interpretation.

Genesis 1:1–2 raises for Reno precisely the controversy between interpretation in the Christian doctrinal tradition and the modern higher critic. To begin, he acknowledges a translation detail that, for him, evokes the controversy. The reference to "the beginning" (MT: *re'shiyth*, LXX: *archē*) in which God creates is semantically ambiguous. It can be taken temporally, naming the occasion that God created the world and relating it in a time-sequence to other events,[25] or it can be taken in an absolute sense, which, in Reno's view, is the sense hinted at by early, Greek translations of Genesis:

> We might say, for example, "The train began its trip at 7:25 p.m.," and following this usage, the preference of contemporary translators for a more temporal and restricted sense of

---

24. Ibid., 97.

25. Reno seems to have in mind one possible temporal sense versus the alternatives, and he sees opting for that temporal sense as necessarily rejecting theological interpretation in favor of the modern, critical approach for which he has strong antipathy. As we will see, this is a questionable interpretation, as multiple temporal senses actually seem possible and not all of them are objectionable given his theological desiderata.

"beginning" is certainly plausible.[26] Yet a point of departure or beginning can also refer to a basis or a rationale, a purpose, or a reason. A scientist can say, "The second law of thermodynamics is the basis-the beginning-of cosmology." Or, "Professor Smith's class was the basis-the beginning-of my love of science." This sense of "beginning" as source and origin is associated with the Greek term *archē*, the word used to translate Gen. 1:1 in the Septuagint and repeated in John 1:1.[27]

A reader might complain that, concerns for the doctrinal tradition aside, the Hebrew text should be privileged above Greek translations as more original, and, in any event, semantic preference for an absolute beginning, as opposed to the more humble temporal one, smacks of the influence of later Greek thought not germane to the interpretation of an originally non-Greek text. Not so fast, says Reno, citing two separate concerns, one historical, the other literary. For honesty with history, it should be recognized that Greek translation of what now is known as the Old Testament was widespread and produced by the same extended Jewish community that would *eventually* produce the MT or the version of the Hebrew often thought to prefer a temporal sense; while the original texts were Hebrew, the Greek witnesses to that original are at least as old as the MT.[28] Additionally, the Psalms show that the Hebrew word used by the MT for *beginning*, *re'shiyth*, can also connote a source or absolute origin, as in Ps. 111:10, "The fear of the LORD is the beginning of wisdom."[29]

Reno concludes, then, that the ambiguity between his temporal and absolute sense is real, and other heuristics besides privileging Hebrew over Greek must be brought to bear. One heuristic is raised, at least to this reader's eye, tacitly by the way in which Reno juxtaposes these two possible interpretations as mutually incompatible antitheses by way of the doctrine of God. If the absolute interpretation holds, Gen. 1:1 teaches that God is transcendent, "the power that brings the cosmos into existence," but if the temporal sense prevails then God is not: "At a certain point in time and in a particular place in a preexisting cosmos, a deity set about to form this particular world. God is a power within the cosmos."[30] If Reno's reader is an informed and committed Christian, accepting the critic's judgment should now, he thinks, be theologically problematic, for the orthodox doctrine of God unambiguously celebrates divine transcendence. In this way Reno draws thick battle lines between the modern critic, who now finds himself threatened with charges of heresy, and the traditional interpreter.

---

26. Here, Reno apparently refers to the decisions made for the New Revised Standard Version and the New Jewish Publication Society Bible, see Reno, *Genesis*, 29.
27. Ibid., 30.
28. Ibid., 29.
29. Ibid., 30.
30. Ibid.

Not surprisingly, then, the first heuristic that Reno *explicitly* deploys is a premodern author, yet, perhaps surprisingly, that author is a student of the synagogue, not the Christian Rule of Faith. Reno turns to Rashi, who, in summary, embraces the theological judgment that the Torah "should have begun with Exod. 12:2 and not Gen. 1:1," where Exod. 12:2 is, in terms of the narrative, the first commandment given to Israel through Moses: "This month [i.e., the month in which the Feast of the Passover is commemorated] shall be for you the beginning of months; it shall be the first month of the year for you."[31] Reno observes the occurrence of the word *beginning* in the verse and takes it as an echo of Gen. 1, adding as an important side observation that in the context of Exod. 12 it cannot carry a temporal sense. Thus, he concludes:

> We can now see, therefore, that Rashi cites the ancient rabbinic opinion that the Bible should have begun with Exod. 12:2 because he wants to reinforce that larger theological judgment about Gen. 1 as a whole: God's plan for the people of Israel is the most elementary, most fundamental aspect of creation. As another ancient interpretation glosses Gen. 1:1, "God looked into the Torah . . . and created the world."[32] The deliverance and sanctification of Israel, the Passover project so to speak, is that in which and for which God creates.[33]

This theological judgment, or something rather like it, Reno observes, is also apparently in play in the Gospel of John 1:1, namely "God creates out of his word or purpose,"[34] nearly a thousand years before Rashi. Together, especially with other examples adduced from Jewish tradition,[35] they indicate for Reno a strong tradition, persistent across otherwise significant parting of ways, of affirming the absolute, nontemporal interpretation of "beginning" in Gen. 1:1 as a commitment to "a basic theological principle. The divine plan or project, however spelled out, is the beginning out of which and for which God creates."[36]

---

31. Ibid.

32. Reno cites James Kugel's quote of Genesis Rabbah 1.1 in *Traditions of the Bible: A Guide to the Bible as It Was at the Start of the Common Era* (Cambridge: Harvard University Press, 1998), 45.

33. Reno, *Genesis*, 31.

34. Ibid., 32.

35. Besides Genesis Rabbah 1.1, Reno also cites *Targum Neofiti* 3.24 in Martin McNamara, trans., *Targum Neofiti 1: Genesis*, Aramaic Bible 1A (Collegeville, MN: Liturgical Press, 1992), 63–64.

36. Reno, *Genesis*, 32. For more detailed treatment of the ways in which Christians and Jews have explored this exegetical possibility, possibly in dialectical engagement with each other, see Philip Alexander, "'In the Beginning': Rabbinic and Patristic Exegesis of Gen. 1:1," in *The Exegetical Encounter of Christians and Jews in Late Antiquity*, ed. E. Grypeou and H. Spurling (Leiden: Brill, 2009), 1–29. An older and yet more seminal study of which Alexander is aware traces the same theme with regard to Col. 1:15, showing that as early as St. Paul in the first century C.E., "the beginning" of Gen. 1:1 (also Prov. 8:22) was interpreted nontemporally as Christ, see C.F. Burney, "Christ as the ΑΡΧΗ of Creation," *Journal*

With this traditional interpretation in view, the expected antagonist, the modern critic, is brought forward, at first somewhat generously given the earlier implied accusation of heresy:

> At this point contemporary scholars are likely to raise objections. . . . Historians worry that later doctrinal commitments exercise an extrinsic and anachronistic control over our interpretive imaginations. The danger is that we end up simply finding what we are looking for: confirmation of our dogmatic prejudices. In the meantime, the real meaning of the biblical text is lost. After all, as biblical scholars point out, the very next verse of Genesis evokes a standard ancient Near Eastern myth of primeval combat between the power for order and the power of chaos.[37]

This objection Reno acknowledges as potentially legitimate, but (in this case and too many others for comfort) premature, for "the modern tradition of biblical interpretation tends to be blind to the wealth of reasons in favor of traditional readings."[38] He then adduces several such reasons, in the process, and for argument's sake, even adding one that is not a traditional reading: the by now time-worn but still modern observation that Genesis is a redacted text, and the scribal hand responsible for 1:1–2:3 was apparently motivated to " . . . place temple and sacrifice at the center of our perceptions of the deepest logic and purpose of reality. The Priestly theology of temple and sacrifice is the *archē* or beginning of the . . . account of creation."[39] Between all these reasons, many deployed in such a way as to compel the acknowledgment of even the modern critic, the traditional reading stands rehabilitated, at the least—but Reno is not yet done. He has a point to make about biblical hermeneutics. After several pages in which he first lists and then explores in detail several theological desiderata, he states that point:

> . . . the traditional translation is part of a fully developed and well-considered theological outlook. A decision in favor of a substantive beginning rather than a temporal sequence sets the interpretive agenda for the Bible as a whole. Creation is for the sake of something prior and more fundamental: the divine project or plan. In the beginning, God subjected all things to his final purpose, just as an archer strings a bow in order to pull it back and load it with a force that strains forward toward its target (Rom. 8:20–21). Thus, the very first verse of the Bible encourages us to read forward, plotting the trajectory of the

---

of Theological Studies 27.106 (1926): 160–77. (Tangentially, I note that Alexander's treatment also states, however, that the majority witness of both the Christian and Jewish traditions is to a temporal sense for *re'shith / archē*.)

37. Reno, *Genesis*, 32.
38. Ibid.
39. Ibid., 34.

text in all its extraordinarily rich diversity as it aims toward the fulfillment of the Word that is eternally spoken by the Father "in the beginning," out of which and for the sake of which all things were created.[40]

If Reno's polemic were an onion, with this quote we have exposed something like its core. *Biblical* exegesis must open out onto the horizon of the whole Bible, and not only that whole, but that whole understood as witness to the purposes of God. If the allusion to Col. 1:16 ("all things have been created through him [Jesus Christ] and for him") at the end of the quote is intentional, and possibly even if it is not, that purpose in Reno's mind is not simply the universe of delight described in Genesis's opening pages but the ascended and returning Lord Jesus Christ, and so the reference to "the Bible as a whole," here, refers not to a bare record of past events, stories, and states of mind but to a living context for discerning God's character and design of salvation in Christ.

This understanding of biblical hermeneutics closely follows and supports Reno's earlier stated commitment to read Genesis so as to ask anew and answer the questions of the Christian doctrinal tradition and can be shown to lie near Reno's thought's core by recourse to other quotes scattered throughout the commentary. For one example, we may turn to his author's introduction:

> It should be obvious, therefore, that this diverse and eclectic approach [i.e., Reno's approach to Genesis] interpolates all sorts of issues and questions into Genesis, and readers who wish for a self-contained commentary that approaches Genesis on its own terms will be disappointed. I can't see any other way to proceed. It is precisely a feature of any view of scripture as the word of God that, when read on its own terms, the seemingly narrow particularity of the texts opens out onto the world. The first chapters of Genesis are obvious examples. They raise fundamental questions about metaphysics, the nature of evil, and the relation of God to the world and humanity. The same holds for the promise that through Abraham all the nations will be blessed. As a result, it is hard to see how anything is irrelevant to reading Genesis on its own terms.[41]

Genesis as a constituent part of Christian scripture is not an artifact of a past existentially separate from our present moment. Its early chapters do not serve either primarily or solely to answer questions about, say, ancient Semitic religions and worldviews of the Levant, however useful they might be to addressing such questions. They serve to tell us out of which beginning (or Beginning?) the rest of the history of God's people flows—seminally that history described in the totality of Holy Scripture, which encompasses our own as we abide with scripture's witness. This is a view of Genesis that contextualizes the same sorts of intuitions expressed by the likes of Irenaeus of Lyon in his debates

---

40. Ibid., 38.
41. Ibid., 21–22.

with the gnostics. For him, all scripture describes a united economy of creation and salvation, an economy that encompasses his own ministry as a Christian teacher and the encounter with the Spirit occurring in the Catholic churches. Reno's categories are somewhat different, as are his questions, but the core intuition is cognate, if not derivative of the pattern I have been calling ruled reading as it persisted in the early centuries. Furthermore, in the process of recontextualizing that pattern through debate with the modern critic, Reno has drawn out and set in relief a key motif from it. His interpretive paradigm is committed to asking questions developed by and out of a perspective of trust in the text, an understanding that the text is not about some original but now long obsolete mythology and past set of events, but rather is, in a sublime way, about the reader, whose existence is caught up in the same mystery that inspired the text to begin with.

When we observed this motif in ruled reading, we did so with respect to its then premodern context by way of Mary Carruthers and her treatment of the arts of memory in the Middle Ages and the ancient world. Reno has brought this motif forward into the postmodern environment and so illustrated its abiding promise. Further, the illumination is mutual. A contemporary of Reno's might, per his postmodern context, initially think that his pattern of theological interpretation straightforwardly expresses our general openness to reader-response hermeneutics. Whatever texts mean to their "original" audiences and in their "author's intentions,"[42] they come to mean new things to new audiences. However, that is not the argument being made here, either by Reno or by the doctrinal tradition in which he aims to stand, as the text of Genesis, for him, should be seen to cohere not simply with the whimsy of whoever is currently reading it but with the biblical whole, including the identity and experience of its reader seen within its witness. Elsewhere, Reno says this quite bluntly, with respect to Gen. 3:1, "At the very minimum, Jewish and Christian readers expect this verse to cohere with other parts of the Bible."[43] Since premodern ruled readers, who were not motivated by postmodernism, share Reno's stance in their own distinct cultural forms and contexts, our attention is drawn to those places where he calls for bounds that discipline the interpreter's imagination even as they empower it.

So far, Reno's exegesis of Gen. 1:1 promises a profound recontextualization of the ancient discipline of ruled reading for a modern and postmodern setting, with one observation, made in passing earlier, sitting somewhat uncomfortably. His discussion of 1:1's exegetical horizon and its openness to the total biblical witness began with a strikingly sharp dichotomy that tacitly accused the paradigmatic modern critic not only of insensitivity to hermeneutical nuances (such as relevance to the reader) but of heresy with regard to the doctrine of God. If the modern critic was right that "the beginning" referred to in 1:1 was temporal,

---

42. I put these terms, "original" and "author's intentions," in scare quotes because I stand among those who regard these concepts as problematic, particularly the latter.

43. Reno, *Genesis*, 77.

then God was a this-worldly deity and not the ultimately transcendent Mystery beyond all things. What strikes me about this judgment on Reno's part is not simply the sharpness of its tacit claim. After all, one can commit heresy in faithful ignorance, and so the charge need not be as stark as it seems. Rather, Reno's dichotomization seems something of an unnecessary and possibly even counter-productive leap of logic.

A host of theological and general hermeneutical observations underscore this point, and it might, perhaps, prove productive to contemplate a few of them. First, surely the transcendent God can self-manifest in a moment in time—say at the beginning of our story, our world existentially speaking—without compromising divine transcendence according to Christian faith. Indeed, that God has definitively done so is the claim of the doctrine of the Incarnation celebrated liturgically every time a Christian recites the Nicene Creed. Along these same lines, the force of Reno's theological argument is, to my eye, ironically blunted when viewed against the backdrop of the Great Tradition, particularly the mystical stream among some early Fathers for whom even God's relating to the world *as divine* was already a gracious condescension, and, so, an act of standing within, as it were, a creaturely frame of reference. In the fathomless depths of God's own being, if *being* we may call it, the Holy One is actually more than divine, as in, for example, the contemplations of "Denys" the Areopagite.[44] Once this theological desideratum comes into view, another temporal sense of "the beginning" than the one that offends Reno seems at least plausible, i.e., the same sort of temporal sense characteristic of the beginning of any story: *To start with . . . , It all began like so . . . , In the beginning . . .* , etcetera. Such a temporal sense serves not so much as a statement about what God is ("a power within the cosmos") as about what the (presumably transcendent) God has done *economically* with respect to our history. If this is the case, so far from being offensive to orthodoxy the temporal sense might actually be preferred by it because it preserves epistemological humility regarding God's nature and the scope of his purposes—a huge desideratum for Christian theology expressed repeatedly and emphatically in the tradition.

Second, let us assume for the sake of argument that Gen. 1:1–2:3 does anthropomorphically envisage God as "a power within the cosmos."[45] It does not

---

44. For one dramatic exposition of this observation, see Pseudo-Dionysius, *The Divine Names*, and, indeed, the entire *Corpus Dionysiacum*.

45. To this reader, it seems intriguingly possible that Gen. 1 does not so much depict God anthropomorphically as deimorphically—in the form of gods, where divinity per se can legitimately be seen as only obliquely referring to the Holy One, who remains nameless. Along these lines, many of the verses beginning from 1:1 are (technically) ungrammatical in Hebrew, the term *elohim*, which is masculine plural, rendered repeatedly such that it is forced to function as the presumed subject of the main verbs, all of which are masculine singular. If translated painfully literally, the Creator subject of each sentence is left tacit while annoyingly repetitive and syntactically illegal mention of "gods" keeps popping up. In this way, the reader is, if she is careful and attentive, confronted by the

follow that God cannot also be known to the reader as the Holy One beyond our world. In fact, that Christian (*mutatis mutandis*, Jewish) reading of scripture is robust to the ways in which sacred texts ground doctrine without straitjacketing it is one of its most intriguing features to scholars of hermeneutics. Famously, and with regard to Gen. 1:1–2:3, the first creation narrative rather poetically depicts our universe as consisting of layers, two of which (our earth / sea on the one hand and the celestial heavens on the other) are separated by a sort of impervious surface (MT: *raqiya'*, LXX: *stereōma*)—as my old Hebrew professor put it in a lecture one day, "like a giant terrarium where the people can live."[46] Even in the context of the passage this *sensus literalis* becomes hard to maintain, as when birds move in this surface in a manner parallel to how the sea-beasts cavort in the oceans, an impossible-to-imagine scene. Unquestionably by the time the Great Tradition gets a hold of it, the narrative's cosmology and even its seven day temporal sequence has been interpreted, to use a problematic but in our context unavoidable category, nonliterally.[47] Given this trajectory of interpretation, by the time modern Christian readers pick up Genesis, most feel no compulsion to find the text's cosmological and temporal descriptions as theologically problematic. Since this is the case, why should the Christian reader take a temporal reading of 1:1a to deny divine transcendence, especially once fully Christian and robust doctrines of creation and incarnation, of the sorts we discussed above, come into view?

The point behind this discussion is not that Reno's theological desiderata and accompanying interest in the absolute, substantive interpretation of *bere'shiyth* / *en archē* / "in the beginning" are wrong. Rather, his discussion of these points seems a valuable exercise for the exegetical imagination indeed. They open the soul's eyes and ears, so to speak, to ways in which the Genesis text presents opportunities for contemplating the divine plan as it comes to unfold in Christ and in Torah, possibilities dear to the Church and the Synagogue respectively. Also, along those lines, his hermeneutical point that modern, ostensibly critical, readings have too often for comfort dismissed traditional and canonical readings, and thereby posed a disservice by disabling the witness of

---

grammar itself with a metaphor-generating paradox. Of course, humans can process metaphors psycholinguistically in a manner that elides their character as metaphor if they are familiar and comfortable with whatever expression is being used, liturgy has a way of producing familiarity with scripture through memorization, and so actual perception of the grammatical paradox might not occur—yet, on the other hand, in the recognized dynamics of prayer as meditation, familiarity can become unfamiliarity and the commonplace become occasion for renewed, childlike delight—a second naïveté, wherein readers experience exactly the sort of affect I describe. That Gen. 1 and other scriptural passages do this can be seen easily in the way in which Christian tradition has frequently discovered the meaning of its Trinitarian confession, as scripture-mediated mystical experience, in such exegetical details.

46. Thanks is due here to Jerome Creach of Pittsburgh Seminary.

47. E.g., see Origen, *On First Principles* 4.3.1, where the early father protests the impossibility of interpreting Gen. 1 as having a somatic ("bodily") sense.

the scriptures taken as a *gestalt*, is well-taken. However, and as I intend my subsequent discussion to show, when Reno significantly relinquishes responsibility for close reading of the text's grammatical possibilities to the biblical critic, whom he then rebukes and partly dismisses, Reno (probably unintentionally) opposes doctrine and sacred text in a competitive economy of meaning. Heavy traffic from the side of doctrine seems to be creating a proverbial jam through which reverse influences from the text in the dialectic are unable to flow. The result has been, in this instance and to my ear, a flattening of the richness and resonance of doctrine itself, in this case the doctrine of God. Where I have resisted his reading and considered positively the temporal sense of *bere'shiyth*, possibilities for fleshing out the doctrine of divine transcendence and for deeply engaging traditional, canonical interpretations actually emerged.

With this observation, we should move to Reno's exposition of 1:2. Here his constructive engagement temporarily drops into the background and the polemic against modern higher criticism moves to the fore. To begin, he acknowledges a historical detail relevant to hearing an echo of how the text likely sounded to ancient audiences: namely, that creation myths cognate to that reflected in the early chapters of Genesis come down to us from the ancient world and that these myths depict the event of creation as a cosmic battle between a creator god and primordial chaos[48]—that is, the creator must deal with a preexistent substance, one that resists the creator. With regard to the same verse (1:2), Reno even observes that the plain sense paints a picture of a formless deep—some kind of preexistent substance?—upon which God acts in creating the world. For him, these sorts of observations threaten his preference to read the whole as teaching that God created all things from nothing.[49] At this point, Reno takes several pages to reiterate and spell out the hermeneutical point, visited in the paragraphs above, that truly *biblical* exegesis should engage, not derange, the total biblical witness, even while respecting its internal diversity. In this case, the doctrine that God created all things from nothing helps us understand in a deep way the pervasive motif cutting across both Old and New Testaments (*mutatis mutandis* the Tanakh) that condemns idolatry and singles out the uniqueness of the LORD God. It helps us to understand that idolatry is not simply or even primarily the act of worshiping statues but the irrational preoccupation with vanity and nothingness that dogs and defiles so much human life.[50] As a related second point, affirming creation from nothing allows us to see God's transcendence as a matter of God's uniqueness rather than a metaphysical quality. This, in turn, allows us to see God with us in the quotidian realities of life as

---

48. Reno, *Genesis*, 39.

49. Although Reno does not note this, I might note that it is one thing for a text not to teach a doctrine and quite another for it to teach that said doctrine is untrue. Genesis 1 could very well not signify to its readers and hearers an event of creation from nothing and yet cohere with a total biblical witness that does. Reno, perhaps because of his polemical agenda, does not comment on this possibility.

50. Reno, *Genesis*, 40–44.

the universal Lord who deals with us particularly in the mystery of election and supremely in the Incarnation of God as the man, Jesus. Reno's extensive discussion of these points—on the implications of the doctrine of Creation—is intuitively profound and, both in its homiletic cast and vast reach, seems a likely helpful resource for Christian teachers, besides illustrating the importance of his earlier-made, hermeneutical argument.

However, little of Reno's discussion surrounding 1:2 actually deals with the text and, to the degree it does, actually sees the text's plain sense as running counter to Reno's preferred interpretation:

> As traditional readers have long realized, the classical doctrine of *creatio ex nihilo* guides us toward a reading of the ambiguous words and phrases in Genesis that downplays the obvious, literal sense. But it does so for the sake of preserving our ability to give very straightforward and intellectually cogent readings of countless other biblical verses. If we set aside *creatio ex nihilo*, then I suppose we can become more intimate with a scholarly construct called "ancient Israelite religion." But this concept is a thin historical construct and can do little to guide our reflection toward the larger biblical vision of God and creation. If we are overly preoccupied with determining the dim outlines of ancient Israelite religion from the various sources of the Old Testament, then we fail to notice that our present approach to the Bible as a whole has become incoherent, and our talk about God vaguely metaphorical and metaphysically sloppy. It was precisely to avoid both this incoherence and intellectual flabbiness that the classical doctrine of *creatio ex nihilo* was developed—and developed with a clear awareness that the literal sense of Gen. 1:2 presents a problem.[51]

This seems a stunning admission, possibly even one infected with a touch of cynicism that goes beyond the merely polemical. Let us grant as a fact that Augustine,[52] Basil,[53] and other ancient readers who corporately constitute "traditional readers" were concerned with teaching *creatio ex nihilo*, that they were opposed by another party in their own context, and that that other party found

---

51. Ibid., 44–45.

52. Interestingly, Reno notes that Augustine grants the plain sense of the text at this point, even while the father affirms the doctrine of creation from nothing. Augustine apparently notes the weakness of an argument from silence, pointing out that the text teaches only that God shaped the universe using an unformed substance, and not that that unformed substance was co-eternal with God; that God could have created the unformed substance remains entirely possible in the narrative. See Reno, *Genesis*, 39.

53. Reno footnotes him at this point: "See, for example, the exegetical work that Basil does in order to turn readers away from the conclusion that the literal sense of this verse requires an affirmation of preexistent matter (*Hexaemeron* 1.9–2.1 in NPNF2 8.57–59)."

support for their position in Gen. 1:1–2. Does it follow from these assumptions that the ancient ruled reader "downplays the obvious . . . sense" in order to achieve coherence and a rationally appealing metaphysics? As we have already seen, this is a seriously questionable point. The early patristic commitments to believe so that we might understand and to seek only those textual senses that are worthy of God entailed not so much the domestication and downplay of the literal as prayerful attention to paradoxes and other textual conundrums. Normative practice assumed that human reason was limited and even fallen and that only God's revelation could raise reason above its own limits to participate in the divine nature. In that engagement, the plain sense of words was, at least ideally, taken very seriously, for it was in the rub of those details that the Spirit waited to transform mortal reason, and even to make it partake of the divine. By contrast, Reno admits that the "obvious" sense runs counter to what he needs to make the scriptures cohere for him and, therefore, must be downplayed.

That much sounds as if it takes some of its cues from ancient ruled reading but not others. The point is not that the doctrine of *creatio ex nihilo* is false, nor that it cannot, in actual fact and on a close reading, be found in the exegetical horizon of Genesis. Rather, it is that Reno seems here to overplay his hand as his polemical agenda takes over and actual reflection on the text fades to the background. His comments, ostensibly on 1:2, instead resolve almost entirely into an *apologia* for a traditional Christian conviction—and a general conviction at that, rather than a reading of the text in question. Further, Reno's move seems unnecessary and even somewhat counterproductive for defending his preferred interpretation. For example, Reno could have begun by pointing out how Genesis notably does not repeat the *Enuma Elish*, the Babylonian myth which likely represents a pattern in ancient Near Eastern thought. The reader expects a powerful Chaos Monster to be bested in cosmic battle by a heavenly Ba'al. Instead, God merely speaks. The expectations of the reader are shattered, and her imagination is left to imagine the relationship between God and the Chaos of the Formless Deeps very differently, for here, The Formless Deeps simply obey. This striking divergence from the *Enuma Elish*, further, resonates powerfully with the larger canonical and theological witness. For example, in Jonah God appoints and commands a great fish (a type of Chaos Monster?) and drives the Mediterranean storm (a Ba'al like activity, but with important differences), and, when these have served their purpose, God commands again and the fish obeys by vomiting up its human meal against its own interests. This reverberating echo grows yet louder in the New Testament as Jesus promises that the sign of Jonah will be the only one he offers to an adulterous generation (Mt. 12:39–41), which promise is then fulfilled by the way in which death is caught at its own game on the cross by the incarnate Word of God and bested in a total surprise—life snatched from nothing. By the time this echo reaches its crescendo in the developing tradition, celebrants of the divine liturgy are chanting jubilantly that Christ has trampled down death by death and naming him, in a way that now does evoke the old myths of the chaos-conquering Creator, the Death-slayer.[54] My ears strain for, yet miss, these reverberations and resonances, these tradition-spanning echoes, in Reno's treatment, apparently because, in his allergic reaction to the modern critic, he felt it necessary to downplay those possibilities within the text that troubled him. We have again encountered a place where his polemical agenda, in opposition to modern criticism and in defense of canonical readings, ironically flattens the latter, this time not simply by disengaging but by explicitly disabling the text's plain sense.

Reno on Genesis 3–4

When we move ahead to survey Reno's treatment of the fall in chapters 3–4, the features discussed in the previous section continue to greet the reader's eye. Much as his treatment of 1:1 revolves around the controversy with the modern historical critic on whether *creatio ex nihilo* can legitimately be found in 1:1–2, his discussion of chapter 3 opens by asking whether the serpent of chapter 3 is merely a talking snake or is rather the avatar of Satan. Following Gerhard von Rad, Reno concludes that it must be one or the other:

> Just who or what is the subtle serpent? The voice of the tradition is unequivocal: it is a worldly form of Satan, the fallen angel. The modern historical-critical tradition rejects this reading; von Rad is typical: "The serpent which now enters the narrative is marked as one of God's created animals. . . . In the narrator's mind, therefore, it is not a symbol of a 'demonic' power and certainly not Satan. What distinguishes it a little from the rest of the animals is exclusively its greater cleverness" (1972: 87).[55] So which shall it be: demonic power personified or the animal trickster of folklore?[56]

Either the modern historical critic is right and the snake is just a snake, albeit a loquacious one, or the traditional interpreter is right and the serpent is the Devil. Reno's extensive discussion of the question takes off from there, setting forth various desiderata for why the serpent must be Satan, and, therefore, why the historical critic must be wrong. The reasons he adduces are each in their own way interesting, and various readers might find them to varying degrees convincing. More importantly for my purposes here, they illustrate a way of imaginatively straining to attend to the text's silences and the possibilities that those silences create for interpretation.

In the meantime, what first strikes me about his overall reading is Reno's total stance towards the text, driven by his black-and-white dichotomies. Why the absolute dichotomization? And, why the need to domesticate the plain sense

---

54. Also, cf. the old medieval Christian fable *St. George and the Dragon*.

55. Reno quotes from Gerhard von Rad, *Genesis: A Commentary*, translated by John H. Marks, rev. ed., Old Testament Library (Philadelphia: Westminster, 1972; reprint, 1974), 87.

56. Reno, *Genesis*, 77.

to resolve that dichotomy? After all, intuitively, the animal trickster of folklore is never *just* an animal. The animal trickster is a god—one whose mischief ensures considerable madness and mayhem for the humans ensnared by it, as here, in the Genesis account. Further, as the motif of temptation, testing, idolatry, and sin comes to be revisited again and again in the scriptures, readers begin to discern patterns wherein the fundamental conflicts deepen, the stakes are raised to the point of life and death seriousness on a terrifying scale, catastrophe threatens, and prophesied-yet-unexpected reversal averts (and more than averts) the moral disaster. It is perhaps precisely the observation of this pattern that constitutes the spirit of apocalyptic, and, in this way, it is profoundly important that the serpent *is* the animal trickster of folklore and not *yet* the Dragon of the Apocalypse (cf. Apoc. 12) in the Genesis account—just as it is vitally important in a mystery novel that the murderer be just another innocent bystander until the crisis point.[57] Genesis invites the reader to sit tensed, on the edge of her chair, precisely because the serpent appears to be just that, yet in such a way and in such a total context that more must be going on than seems to be going on. Surrender to that experience, it seems to me, is the essence of conversion and initiation into the Christian doctrinal tradition that Reno otherwise calls for so aggressively and that such luminaries of the tradition as Origen saw as a crucial part of the Spirit's pedagogy.

Although Reno's resultant interpretation is, to my eye, strained and his discussion disappointingly disengages from the text to comment on philosophical and theological desiderata in the abstract, one feature of his hermeneutics, named earlier in passing, stands out as especially deserving of notice in his treatment of chapters 3–4: he tries to listen for where the text goes silent and then imaginatively fill in those silences in fitting ways. There are several places where he does this, some more persuasively than others. One striking example occurs where he takes a line from a homily of John Chrysostom's about the loquaciousness of the woman as she responds to the serpent's guile:

> Perhaps the serpent arrives on the scene more ignorant than wise, and he opens with a clever question designed to provoke the woman to betray crucial information. "I've heard that all these trees are off limits. Is it true?" he asks. "No," says the woman, "with God as my witness, I was told to refrain from eating the fruit of the one tree in the middle of the garden." "Oh, I see," he responds. Now, with this missing piece of information, the lawyer can proceed, knowing just where to focus his attention. "You foolish woman," he says to himself, "you have given me what I wanted to know, because you could not restrict yourself to a simple 'yes' or 'no'" (Matt. 5:37). Eve is

---

57. For one stimulating discussion of this dynamic to Christian readings of the Old and New Testaments, see David Steinmetz, "Uncovering a Second Narrative: Detective Fiction and the Construction of Historical Method," in *The Art of Reading Scripture*, ed. Ellen F. Davis and Richard B. Hays (Grand Rapids, MI: Eerdmans, 2003), 54–68.

too eager, too chatty, too forthcoming. She allows herself to be lured into a discussion with the evil one about the substance of God's commandment. "Do not throw your pearls before swine," warns Jesus (7:6), and that seems to be exactly what Eve does. "Such is the evil of idly and casually exposing to all and sundry the divine mysteries," John Chrysostom observes in his extraordinarily rich reading of Eve's transgression.[58]

The text is silent as to the serpent's motives, outside of perhaps oblique reference in its largely neutral, although perhaps vaguely ominous, description of it as crafty. Likewise, it spends no time developing a window into the personality and motivations of the woman. Yet, there is something about the text that fascinates and draws out precisely those questions. One dimension of that something that Reno immediately highlights is the canon-spanning motif of the dangers of having a "careless tongue."[59] Readers approaching Genesis as Holy Scripture operate from within a context that trembles before the subtly destructive power of words maliciously or even carelessly spoken. Reno identifies this, in the process letting his reading guide him to profound reflection on the nature of human moral failure:

> This larger biblical concern about the tongue and its dangers forms the background for Chrysostom's portrayal of Eve as the original gossipy housewife, whose wandering, undisciplined tongue leads to the original human sin. It is not prideful self-assertion that is the source. For Chrysostom, the root sin is negligence, expressed most clearly in the easy familiarity of neighborhood gossip. For in gossip we treat other people's lives as occasions for entertainment and titillation, as opportunities to express complacent superiority or to express a burning envy. With Chrysostom's interpretation, therefore, we see an important aspect of our sinful selves. We are not hyperalert seekers after advantage, men and women who puff ourselves up with arrogant self-importance. More often than not we are somnolent, lazy, and complacent folks who drift along with the crowd. We don't rush off to join the devil's party. Instead, we wake up one day and find that, after an unthinking, offhanded career as a fellow traveler, we have signed a loyalty oath as full members.[60]

Reno's observation promises a hamartiological gem. More significantly for discussion here, he was empowered to make it by a methodological openness to heeding voices from ages past and those silences in the text that are tensed,

---

58. Reno, *Genesis*, 87, citing John Chrysostom, *Homilies on Genesis* 16.6 in *The Fathers of the Church* 74.211 (Washington, DC: Catholic University of America Press, 1986).

59. Reno, *Genesis*, 87.

60. Ibid.

pregnant with possibility. Elsewhere, he makes explicit this commitment to listen for evocative silences, this time by way of celebrating the Synagogue's tradition of midrash and showing its consonance with Christian reading strategies:

> Midrash is a traditional Jewish style of reading. It involves a supplemented retelling that interprets by way of added emphasis, color, and dramatization, as I have done above. The skeleton of the biblical story is retained, but flesh is added. Midrash, however, is not unique to Judaism. These few verses depicting the original transgression provide the basis for an extensive tradition of Christian midrash. Milton's *Paradise Lost* provides one of the most famous examples. But there is nothing uniquely poetic or premodern about the tendency to fill out the story of the fall. Modern biblical critic Gerhard von Rad produces exegesis in this genre, and he does so with a panache for inventing motives and emotional responses that shed light on the psychology of sin (1972: 88–90). These examples of creative retelling are not surprising. This short portion of biblical text combines narrative realism with economy of expression, a combination that positively invites the reader to fill out the story with more detail. Here, then, the literary form matches the ambition of Genesis. The suggestive brevity of the verses invites us to interweave our many and diverse thoughts about the nature of sin into our reading. In the silences of the text we find a place for our own knowledge of the concrete form of human wickedness, and in so doing we vindicate the traditional view that this story tells us about the original sin.[61]

Intuitively, these words describe a real dimension of the text between 3–4. The text's economy of words, particularly when heard in the context of teaching or worship, leaves us on the edge of our seats, drawn to imagine details and connections not explicitly named therein. For preachers such as Chrysostom, cultivating attention to such potentiality is a vital part of the art not only of homily but, also, of discernment-in-context—of hearing the Word of God.

Here, Reno's observations on the silences of the text actually proceed as close reading of the text itself and, at least in principle and to a reader in the context of Church or Synagogue, illuminates compellingly. However, the move does not always strike as equally successful. The text also seems, to many a modern reader, to be silent in response to the exclamatory question, "A talking *snake?!*"—bringing us back to the striking dichotomy of von Rad that fascinates Reno for the bulk of his comments on Gen. 3. Reno's response is, as we have already seen, to read imaginatively into the silences. However, this time he reads not a canon-spanning motif but, rather, a popular, speculative Christian protology on the origin of the Devil and his angels and an equally speculative, comparative psychology of incorporeal spirits versus embodied beings, both for

---

61. Ibid., 86.

the sake of theodicy. The results are, to me, unpersuasive, much as his dichotomies seem unnecessary. Some consideration as to why seems important for
bringing this section to a close with some final observations regarding where,
to re-express allusion to the patristic allegory of doctrine's keys, Reno's hands
seem to fumble at the lock.

As just stated, Reno spends this section of his commentary occupied with
theodicy. He tries to excuse God from responsibility for evil by reading a popular, speculative tale of the fall of the angels into Genesis. This Christian protology is sufficiently public record that it hardly needs description here: before
time began, a prominent member of the heavenly choirs came to envy God's
sublime deity and so defected to become the arch-rebel, Satan. This story is accepted widely and bears a family resemblance to similar patterns expressed
elsewhere in the tradition.[62] Thus, the success or failure of Reno's theodicy
aside, the move does not immediately strike as unusual—one would be more
likely to find it simply conventional. Yet, because of the way in which it departs
not only from this text but from the total canonical witness, it rings a flatter,
hollower note or, perhaps, the scraping jingle of keys not quite fitting. The keys
of doctrine in the patristic adage were themselves *texts of Holy Scripture*; the early
Christian move would be to scan the total scriptural witness for words or motifs
that suggested intracanonical resonances or *types*. To a certain degree, and before he commences with his favorite point, his theodicy, Reno does just that,
and when he does he is persuasive, as when he points to the *Book of Job*.[63] When
he digresses at length to justify God's creative genius in spite of the human and
serpentine (Satanic?) moral failure (or catastrophe?), that attention to the text
in its canonical context drops away, as he strains after a silence that in retrospect feels, in fact, only apparent, not real—the pseudo-dichotomy between the
serpent really being a serpent and the serpent being Satan's worldly avatar.
Page after page of ink is spent arguing an extra-biblical psychology of incorporeal beings and the implications of this for human moral culpability until, to this
reader, the train of diabolical figures of the Bible drops into the periphery—from
the serpent of the garden, through the mysterious kings of Tyre (Ezk. 28:12–19)
and Babylon (Isa. 14:12–15), all the way to the New Testament's shadowy
tempter and, finally, the horrible, infanticidal Dragon of the Apocalypse. The
forward, eschatological thrust of the Christian form of the canon is eclipsed in
a way that seems to cut against the grain of Reno's primary aim. The result is
that the commentary lapses into silence on the text, even moving to disable
those dimensions of its sense most attended to by the targets of Reno's polemics,
even as it expands voluminously on matters external to Genesis. I feel myself
getting a good look at the outside of the door, with a frustratingly delayed entry
to peer inside.

However, given its homiletic productivity, Reno's perhaps overzealous pursuit of his polemical agenda and consequent marginalization of Genesis's plain

---

62. One passage famously read in this regard is Isa. 14:12–15.
63. Reno, *Genesis*, 79.

sense cannot be seen as a failure. First, depending somewhat on his reader's patience and memory for details, Reno's commentary may be seen to recover, at least to some degree, from his polemical over-corrections. Elsewhere in it he acknowledges the hermeneutical significance of the diversity internal to the Bible's witness,[64] and the Christian authenticity of devotion to the text's native priorities and shape over later systematic doctrinal reflection.[65] At several points, his exploration of the literal sense results in rich, although to my eye often delayed, gains. His treatment of 1:4 (the account of the creation of day and night) coordinates the darkness of night in that verse with the formless void of 1:2 in a rich reflection on the nature of evil and particularly idolatry, a reflection that then forms a thread that he follows throughout his commentary. In these ways he recognizes that "the literal sense of Gen. 1:2 presents a problem,"[66] that it is a "mysterious, evocative passage,"[67] and that the eventual proper response to the mystery is to wrestle with and explain it, rather than explain it away. These reverse corrections, together with his frequently illuminating attention to the power of economy or silence in the text and his bringing to the reader's attention the richness of interpreters of the past, do indeed fulfill the promise "to provide [readers] with experiments in postcritical doctrinal interpretation."[68] They indicate Reno's in-principle acknowledgment of the hermeneutical significance of the plain sense. Even the way in which Reno's embrace of theology's polemical mode (against the modern critic) is itself sometimes productive, albeit distracting in a commentary that ostensibly has the text itself as its primary object: it highlights the applied, existentially invested nature of interpretation.

Perhaps most importantly, and as regards the just mentioned existential investment, one feature of Reno's reading, to this point but tacitly dealt with in my summary, stands out in a way deserving of note, particularly given the way in which Reno will turn out to contrast somewhat with Moberly. While Reno's big-picture perspective seems insufficiently integrated with the dialectical dimension of ruled reading, with far too much one-way traffic from tradition to text for comfort, he nonetheless has a big-picture—his vision of creation arching towards Sabbath. This kind of wider view was crucial to the function of the Rule for Irenaeus. Given the strained nature of Reno's engagement with the text

---

64. E.g., this comment on ibid., 38: "Thus, the very first verse of the Bible encourages us to read forward, plotting the trajectory of the text in all its extraordinarily rich diversity as it aims toward the fulfillment of the Word that is eternally spoken by the Father 'in the beginning,' out of which and for the sake of which all things were created."

65. In Reno's own words, "Who can object to the impulse to defend scripture against simpleminded absorption into a preconceived doctrinal system? Any reading of scripture that ignores or distorts the text makes a mockery of the fundamental Christian commitment to the Bible as the word of God." See ibid., 40.

66. Ibid., 44.

67. Ibid., 45.

68. Ibid., 14.

itself, it is unclear if his picture functions in the same way and for the same purposes as Irenaeus's description of the Rule; however its presence seems, nonetheless, significant and worthy of note.

Observing Context(s): A Detailed Glance at R.W.L. Moberly

As with Reno, I will engage one of Moberly's expeditions into concrete, theological interpretation, his *Theology of Genesis*. My focus will be on critically engaging this one instance of his practice, particularly his treatment of 1:1–4:26,[69] for the sake of seeing how it illuminates and / or obscures how ruled reading might occur today. Along those lines, and also as with Reno, my reading of Moberly will examine two dimensions of his contribution. First, I will read for his big picture, particularly looking at his first chapter, suggestively titled "What is a 'Theology of Genesis'?" Second, I will look for his substantive readings of Gen 1–3.

The first thing we learn as we open *Theology of Genesis* is that *theology*, and particularly *theology-of-X* (where X is a biblical text), is a problematic category that begs redefinition. Theology relates to typically religious questions such as the question of God, and, in Moberly's words, "the more one looks at the material [of Genesis], the less it fits typical notions of what 'God' and 'religion' are all about."[70] That turn-of-phrase ("typical notions") is here all-important. Our notions are tied to our context, influencing the connotation of the phrase *theology-of-X* in at least two ways. To start, we have inherited the word *theology* from medieval and ultimately patristic sources and those sources are "post-biblical," [71] their understanding of theology involving and requiring "nuance and sensitivity."[72] Then again, we have tweaked that inheritance in ways that can lose that nuance:

> The term "theology" has a long and complex history from the Fathers to the present day, which makes it far from straightforward to use. Not least there has been a tendency from the early Enlightenment in the seventeenth century onward to use theology as a counterpart of religion, both of which are used in distinctively modern and contracted senses. "Religion" in the modern West is often used to denote a generic kind of thought, piety, and practices, quite distinct from those of politics, economics, and the natural sciences; it designates what happens primarily in an inward, subjective, and largely

---

69. Although Moberly gives substantial treatment to chapter 4 (Cain and Abel), for the sake of space I will stop with his treatment of chapter 3, noting only that, for him, 2–3 is one pericope and 4 is another. As with Reno, this strikes me as somewhat significant in its own right.

70. Moberly, *Theology*, 3.

71. Ibid., 4.

72. Ibid., 3–4.

private realm, distinct from what happens in public—so that
religious people who transgress these distinctions tend to encounter strong opposition. Theology is then sometimes conceived as an attempt to talk about religious experiences,
which risks being a kind of psychobabble with religious jargon; alternatively, theology may be a kind of metaphysical
speculation about invisible and intangible entities—an activity that bears no relation to, and certainly makes no difference
to, the realities of everyday life.[73]

Thus, it is problematic to turn to Genesis theologically starting *from our con-*
text and with our categorization of theology and religion. When we speak of theology,
the term comes preloaded with unhelpful expectations. The thing to do is to re-
initiate our context's readers to theology's classical nuance, as Moberly puts it:
"Only if one can recover a more classic sense of theology, as an attempt to understand everything in the world in relation to God, will one be better placed to
start to make sense of the theology of Genesis."[74]

The rest of his book can be read productively as an attempt at contributing
to such a re-initiation, starting from his first content-bearing chapter—a précis
describing the reorientation he feels is necessary. Critical *self*-perspective on
where one stands now is a crucial element to that process, and so Moberly begins there. Our modern world is one that became fascinated with the capacity
of critical philology to illuminate texts:

One common scholarly approach, which tries to deal with the
problem of possibly distorting preconceptions, is to understand theology in relation to the Bible as a primarily philological and historical discipline, a descriptive and analytic account of religious thought and practice. In this sense, to give
an account of the theology of Genesis is to characterize its
content in the categories of religious history: to show what
certain terms and ideas and practices mean in their originating context, in the tenth or sixth century BCE (or whenever),
and to map them in relation to each other and to other aspects
of ancient Israel's developing religious thought and practice,
and possibly those of Israel's neighbors also. Such a theology
of Genesis is not in principle different from giving an intelligent account of the content of any religious text, biblical or
otherwise—one would not in principle handle Augustine's
Confessions, the Qur'an, or the Bhagavad-Gita differently. The
task requires good philological and historical understanding,
so that one can appreciate the content of the text for what it
is, without prematurely assimilating it to the perspectives of
other texts, ideas, and practices from other periods of history

73. Ibid., 4–5.
74. Ibid., 5.

and different cultural contexts. Theology thus becomes, in essence, a history of Israelite religion in some form or other.[75]

Moberly adds, "There is obvious value in such an enterprise,"[76] a judgment
with which most readers will likely agree. Perhaps less obvious will be the growing cloud hanging over this project with its definition of theology, although as
post-modern readers some of us might feel the threat that Moberly is about to
name less or more. In his own words, "One does not, indeed almost cannot, come
to the text 'cold,' but only in the context of an enduring Jewish and Christian,
and consequent wider, cultural reception. This reception forms a kind of plausibility structure, a context for bothering with the text and for taking it seriously."[77] The point is not that the critical, philological task is a fool's errand and
impossible. After all, the value of that enterprise was and remains obvious. Rather, the point as Moberly sees it is that that value is entertained almost solely
because the Bible represents more than just texts haphazardly rescued from obscurity. We care about the Bible because of its enduring social and religious
function. The sociology of knowledge becomes an irreducible coefficient in our
interpretation of it.

The upshot of this is that the critical philologist in our context bothers with
the Bible by and large because the texts that are compiled and represented under this form are beloved and used to support catechesis, worship, and spiritual
discernment by the Christian church (and in related if somewhat dissimilar
ways are venerable to the Synagogue). This creates the possibility for, and possibly even demands, criticism of a second sort: ideological criticism, to an example of which Moberly will return in his reading of Gen. 4. To his eye these critics
somewhat unfairly, yet not in such a way as to deserve no empathy, often and
for rhetorical reasons describe theirs as an agenda rival to that of the modern
philologist, who they accuse of drawing readers' attentions to the Bible without
taking account of where its words act upon readers in potentially destructive
ways.[78]

For Moberly, raising the subject of ideological criticism is a transitional
point, bridging to one apparently much more central to him. The existence of
the ideological critic highlights where we have come from and indicates possibilities for where we might go. As to where we have been, the ideological critic's
imperative only makes sense in a situation where we actually care about the
Bible enough for it to inform our ethics. After all, no one really bothers with the
ideology of the *Enuma Elish* or any other text the god-talk of which we render
with the lowercase 'g', and why should they?[79] As to where we might go,

75. Ibid., 5–6.

76. Ibid., 6.

77. Ibid., 6–7.

78. Ibid., 8.

79. Although, in a post-Christendom context this situation might become increasingly changed, a possibility to which Moberly seems sensitive. In the act of flagging as
worthy of chastening some readings of Genesis that celebrate its contrasts to cognate

Moberly observes in passing, "In certain ways, ideological criticism often represents a secularized version of a *religious rule of faith*,"[80] indicating a path he intends to explore. We are arriving in the neighborhood of his concern for ruled reading. In Moberly's taking us through the desiderata of modern philology into and then out of the rhetoric of the ideological critics, we have now come three hundred sixty degrees along a spiral into terminological ground familiar to ancient interpreters. He does not spell out the comparison, but we can see his point from examples from the patristic era, particularly Origen. For that early theologian, the grubby details of scripture's literal sense were always divine yet frequently in a quasi-Socratic way. Scandalous textual features provoked the intellect to seek God *beneath* the letter and to wrestle with the text. In important ways, then, the ideological critic brings us back to an observation basic to the ancients' total stance and is therefore suggestive of ways in which that stance, or some appropriate relative of it, should be taken seriously, again.

All this leads to Moberly's core thesis:

> Whatever the complexities and ramifications of the debates about the relationship between scripture and tradition that have characterized both Jews and Christians down the ages . . . the fact remains that Genesis is received within the context of continuing traditions of faith, life, and thought, however variously these may be conceived. Although there can be an undoubted heuristic value in imaginatively bracketing these contexts of reception, so that the meaning of the Genesis text as an ancient text can better be appreciated, the appropriate stance for a theology of Genesis is *not only to bracket but also to incorporate*. The task will certainly have dimensions of what might be included in a history of Israelite thought and practice, but it will also engage with the reception of the text as a resource for probing its significance and exploring its possible appropriation.[81]

Incorporation is a subtle, demanding task in various ways, likely to make "some scholars nervous"[82] yet is necessary for the existentially invested interpreter—the interpreter who cares about what he is reading—for the very rea-

---

ancient literature, he writes: "It is all too easy for comparative discussions of the Old Testament in relation to ancient Near Eastern parallels to acquire a tacit dimension either of complacent superiority or of apologetic. Jews and Christians inherit ancient and still-living traditions of life and thought of which the biblical texts remain constitutive. . . . [W]here the stance is not shared, as increasingly it is not in the contemporary Western world, it is important to recognize that what may feel to the 'insider' like an objective and dispassionate comparison may look rather different to those whose frame of reference differs and so do not take the same things for granted." (*Theology*, 53–54.)

80. Ibid., 11, emphasis mine.
81. Ibid., 12–13, emphasis mine.
82. Ibid., 13.

sons that underlie the two paradigms of criticism, modern philological and ideological, just outlined. In short, no one seriously committed to engaging the biblical text, particularly not Christians and Jews, want simply to "lay it down on
the table as the ace of trumps."[83] For a paradigmatic modern, philologically
armed critic,[84] that involves respecting historical and cultural difference; for
the ideological critic such as Clines that means additionally granting something
like magisterial primacy to the proclivities of our own culture and time.
Moberly, without disregarding these, wants to take seriously what the aforementioned serious, typical Christian (and, *mutatis mutandis*, Jew) do in "long-
term living with the biblical text."[85]

This involves two—activities? Artifacts? An overarching category for the
two factors involved in "long-term living with the biblical text" Moberly names
is hard to find. The first is—explicitly—"recontextualization."[86] The second is
"some kind of rule of faith."[87] Recontextualization could connote many different properties of the Bible and, indeed for me, anticipates Moberly's arguments
about how the questions and perspectives of the reader affect the interpretation
of Gen. 1–2:4, which I will discuss further on in this chapter. However, here
Moberly has in mind the way that individual texts in the Bible are juxtaposed
with others which are in important ways different. Genesis is not Deuteronomy,
Paul's Letter to the Ephesians, the Gospel of John, or the Book of Ecclesiastes, all
of which differ, also, from each other.[88] When these are commended to the
reader as, in some sense, one *gestalt*—as they clearly are for Christians, whether
in the dynamics of catechesis, the liturgy or when published together as the Bible—important consequences follow:

> Ecclesial reflection on Genesis, and *mutatis mutandis* that of the
> synagogue, is generally characterized neither by harmonizing
> nor by distancing but by a range of highly complex synthetic
> moves, many of which are fluid and open to varying kinds of
> reformulation; and questions of practical appropriation are
> always mediated by questions of the wider life of the commu-
> nity in relation to scripture as a whole.[89]

Moberly does not elaborate with more detailed examples, perhaps because
some are almost trivial to name, nor does he take space for what synthetic
moves he has in mind. More important to where he is going is that negotiating
these moves requires some intellectual tool for "relating the parts to the tenor

---

83. Ibid., 14.
84. Moberly names Krister Stendahl, see ibid., 12–14.
85. ibid., 14.
86. Ibid.
87. Ibid., 15.
88. Ibid.
89. Ibid.

of the whole."[90] Moberly notes that "some kind of rule of faith"[91] will do the trick. As I have already mentioned, in important ways this brings us three hundred sixty degrees along a spiral, back to categories familiar to our exploration of theology and hermeneutics from the patristic period.

However, I am immediately, if subtly, struck by Moberly's terminology. It differs from the early fathers in ways that seem significant. For him *rule of faith* names a class of related hermeneutical assumptions; for them, there was *the* Rule of Faith / Truth, and it was one particular, concrete (if somewhat fuzzily defined) factor in reading Holy Scripture and in Christian life. This difference is highlighted further by the way in which Moberly describes rules of faith as characterizing not only Christian hermeneutics but also the hermeneutics of the Synagogue, whereas the Fathers' trajectory is towards distinguishing their perspectives from the (at that time, likewise emerging) perspective of Judaism.[92] In this way, Moberly categorizes the interpretive task in a way that functions on a higher level of abstraction than Irenaeus or Origen, seeking overlap and similarity between groups not only different from each other but also internally heterogeneous across both space and time. These differences are not inexplicable but do merit close examination, although doing so will temporarily take us some distance from examining his practice. Central to Moberly's efforts to re-initiate his reader to theology's classical stance is his locating ancient ruled reading on a larger map of religious practice to some of which the postmodern reader is likely to be familiar. By indicating not just the early Fathers' point of view but a set of analogous forms, he increases the likelihood that his reader will get what he is saying with imaginative empathy. However, the differences between what he refers to from his context as "some kind of rule," recognizable as one species of a larger genus of rules, and the Fathers' commendation from their setting of *the* Rule are striking.

Another difference between the ancient categorization and Moberly's is the way in which *rule* and *canon* relate but no longer connote one entity in Moberly's frame of reference, while they did so connote in the early centuries. *Rule* in Greek is *kanōn*, and literally connotes a "straight bar" or "measuring-rod," the Latin being *regula*. Since at least the time Irenaeus had engaged the so-called

---

90. Ibid.

91. Ibid.

92. However, it is important to note Moberly's qualification of the sense in which his categorization applies to the synagogue with the Latin *mutatis mutandis*, i.e., "by changing those things that need to be changed." My point here is not that Moberly has misconstrued the Rule but that his recontextualization of ruled reading inclines him towards importantly different patterns of relating to Judaism and its practitioners, and possibly other religious communities, than was characteristic of, e.g., Irenaeus and other early writers. Whether and how his change of stance might be authentic to ruled reading is a separate matter towards which I will at most be able but to gesture in the pages that follow.

gnostics in the second century,[93] these terms had functioned as a metaphor for the apostolic communion to which the Church initiated the faithful through processes that normally culminated in baptism. They identified as constituent of a Christian's epistemological stance her relationships to those God in Christ had sent in the Spirit's power, and the total sense of history and destiny that defined the Church's identity and mission. Thus, *canon* originally evoked at once an ecclesial location and a big-picture worldview, understood by those who embraced it to be an organic fellowship stretching back through the Church to the apostles and through them to the Ground of all spiritual authority whatsoever. The term only came to refer over time and metonymically to the scriptures collected and published under one *gestalt*. By contrast, in our context the metonym generating event is far past-tense. For Moberly as for other modern Christians, and particularly for him as a biblical scholar writing after Brevard Childs, the canon is the Bible understood as a theologically authoritative collection to be read in a way that dialectically applies its various parts to each other and to the totality of Christian life and witness. Clearly, these definitions are interrelated, the second being a logical development of the former given the sequence of conditions in which Christians have found themselves over the past two thousand years. However, while these definitions are related, they are not the same. Under the former, canon and Rule are the same thing—even, if you are speaking ancient Greek, the same word—while under the latter, they designate separately reified modes of apostolic communion, the interrelatedness of which is a puzzle of disputed solution.[94] Potentially at risk here is not simply historical curiosity but a critical awareness of the sort that Moberly earlier and with respect to the scriptures themselves observed was obviously valuable. The ancient ethos of the Rule / canon as I have described it might clarify how (post)modern readers might need to be re-initiated with regard to theology. In this sense, recognizing what sort of thing the Rule was for ancient Christians, and how they categorized it, opens doors for expanding upon Moberly's thesis.

On a different note, explicitly re-relating canon and Rule after they have been separated introduces possibilities for misconstruing what the Rule is when re-initiating postmodern readers to its use. That threat is one that is particularly concerning to Moberly in his wider writing. Particularly, I observe that Moberly

---

93. Since Irenaeus, functioning as an apologist, can already rely upon the descriptions he gives to persuade his readers, the probability is that his categorization had already accumulated some authority and was therefore not novel.

94. I am thinking particularly of the debates persisting between Protestants, Roman Catholics, and Eastern Orthodox on the relationship between scripture and tradition in theological method. For two distinct proposals regarding the importance of and possibilities for relating these factors anew in our context see Robert W. Jenson, *Canon and Creed* (Louisville: Westminster John Knox Press, 2010), and also John Webster, *Holy Scripture: A Dogmatic Sketch* (Cambridge: Cambridge University Press, 2003).

is also sensitive to that against which Reno's frustrations were directed, although in a way visibly more empathetic to the critics. One particular paragraph of his *The Bible, Theology and Faith* locates that empathy:

> The notion of a rule of faith, of course, regularly excites suspicion and hostility among professional biblical scholars, as being a tool for prejudgment, manipulation or coercion, and just plain bad scholarship—to say what texts 'must' mean on the grounds of post-biblical dogmas, and to attempt to marginalize or silence those who have the courage to show that biblical texts do not necessarily mean what later tradition has thought them to mean. There are, sadly, so many examples of a rule of faith being used thus that an attempt to gain a fresh hearing for it is not an easy task.[95]

To obtain that fresh hearing is one of Moberly's goals, so the critic's objection is one to which he is sensitive. To meet it will require that rules of faith be carefully re-understood so that they function heuristically,[96] as "guide" and not "inquisitor":

> How then might a rule of faith be understood? It sets the biblical text within the context of the continuing life of the Christian Church where the one God and humanity are definitively understood in relation to Jesus Christ. In this context there is a constant interplay between the biblical text and those doctrinal, ethical, and spiritual formulations which seek to spell out its implications. The concerns in this are at least twofold. On the one hand, the initial concern is not so much to explain the Bible at all (in senses familiar to philologist or historian) as to preserve its reality as authoritative and canonical for subsequent generations, so that engagement with the God of whom it speaks, and the transformations of human life which it envisages, remain enduring possibilities; that is to say 'God is here'. On the other hand, the interest is not so much the history of ideas and religious practices (though this remains an important critical control) as the necessities of hermeneutics and theology proper, that is, the question of what is necessary to enable succeeding generations of faithful, or would-be faithful, readers to penetrate and grasp the meaning and significance of the biblical text; that is, to say 'God is here' in such a way that the words can be rightly understood without

---

95. Moberly, *Bible, Theology and Faith: A Study of Abraham and Jesus* (Cambridge University Press, 2000), 43.

96. Moberly does not use the term heuristic in the paragraphs I cite, but does use it to flesh out and defend these paragraphs from John Barton in "Biblical Criticism and Religious Belief," *Journal of Theological Interpretation* 2.1 (2008): 85, where he describes reading with a rule of faith as a "heuristic and dialectical task" as opposed to "control and prior determination."

lapse into idolatry, literalism, bad history, manipulation, or the numerous other pitfalls into which faith may stumble. It is when the Christian community fails sufficiently to grasp the implications of its own foundational text that a rule of faith changes role from guide to inquisitor.[97]

This is a dense, complex, and important statement and ought to be unpacked. Rules of faith serve not so much to offer a competing explanation of the Bible philologically or historically, as to recognize the Bible *given such explanation* "within the context of the continuing life of the Christian Church where the one God and humanity are definitively understood in relation to Jesus Christ." Thus, the layered texts of scripture are, in their complex and multifarious history and philological potential, open, as one dimension of that potential,[98] to being used to discern Christ's person, nature, and will in the rub of the day-to-day—but not having ignored the critical controls of language's historical and grammatical coefficients. One still has to know how to read and read critically. The theological task is explicitly dialectical; the Christian's self-understanding, understanding of the Church, and understanding of God in Christ is open to transformation through live encounter with the text, taken in its givenness, in the context of daily community life and the exercise of mission. Because the text is foundational, having a rule serves to commend the scriptures as something existentially live—something with which the present and the hoped-for future are understood to be continuous and yet changing from the past in which the text in itself was originally constituted. Therefore, having a rule highlights as necessary "hermeneutics and theology proper," on the one hand, and philological care, on the other. The total effect is to constrain the application of the text within the aforementioned discernment so as to prevent the litany of pitfalls with which Moberly penultimately closes his paragraph (idolatry, literalism, etcetera).

This framework, including his closing commendation of a rule as guide, should sound by now familiar, having already considered the ethos of the patristic period as it was represented, variously, by Irenaeus, Origen, Augustine, and Hilary. None of these were concerned with silencing some putative original meaning of the text or substituting some other sense for it, and each was, in his own way, critical and even profoundly disciplined in his own setting. However, they were concerned with preserving a pattern of theological engagement with the scriptures in which their abiding authority was continually commended regardless of the changing seasons in which the Church found itself, with seeking a transformed existence, and with guarding the faithful against the same sorts

---

97. Moberly, *Bible, Theology and Faith*, 43.

98. Moberly elsewhere rebuts an attack that he and other theological interpreters believe the Bible to be exclusively useful for addressing questions of God. Rather, answering the question of God is, to him, one among many legitimate uses to which the Bible may be put, albeit the question he seems most interested in, see Moberly, "Biblical Criticism and Religious Belief," 84.

of pitfalls Moberly names. One way in which this was the case shines through particularly if we view Augustine's ontology of signs as a development of the same instincts present in Irenaeus's quest for types. When Augustine says that the wood thrown into the waters to make them sweet is a sign,[99] he is not denying the potential of the story to connote one of ancient Israel's wilderness adventures—actually, the power of his hermeneutical move depends on its having such potential—and neither is he committing his reader to a particular historical reconstruction of the Exodus. He is saying that, however this story came to be, Christian teachers should recognize the text's description of Moses's act as *significant*. In this case he does not clarify how it is significant; however it seems likely, given similar writings of the period such as Ambrose of Milan's *On the Mysteries*, that the bishop would say the story has implications for orienting catechumens and those recently baptized, e.g., by saying that the transformation of the waters by wonderfully mundane means challenges the faithful to take seriously Baptism and the Eucharist, however plain and humble water, wine and bread may be.[100] The world of the text, however much rooted in a past real, fictive, or somehow-or-other in-between, is relevant to the Church's present and future in a way that acknowledges, at least in principle, the dynamic conditions of history.

That analogy between Moberly's definition and the stance of the early Fathers noted, I also possibly detect a short but important transposition in Moberly's description of rules of faith from the early Fathers. His main point is that rules of faith, at their best, orient us to the sacred page. However, there also seems to be a second point to Moberly's terminology and argument: namely, as we already observed, to obtain a fresh hearing for (some species of) ruled reading in the academic guild. Their objection to it is that rules such as those Moberly is trying to describe have been used in the past to foreclose on the results of reading—to say in advance what the text cannot mean and what it must mean in a way that generates one-way-traffic from reader's expectations to the text. Moberly wishes to acknowledge this legitimate concern and so limit the rule and prevent it from becoming malignant, in his own words to change from a "guide" into an "inquisitor."

Legitimate and helpful as this is, Moberly's solution raises a question or perhaps rather a cluster of related questions. To put it baldly (although shortly I will have to back up and consider possibilities ignored by this form of the question): can whatever rule of faith is being used be challenged and changed in the course of encounter with the text? It seems likely that those from whom Moberly wishes to obtain a fresh hearing, (from what we have seen) particularly his occasional opponent John Barton, would say the answer must be no, by definition and, therefore, that ruled reading is necessarily a distinct activity from critical reading. Opposite that, and perhaps somewhat confirming John Barton's suspicions, it seems even more clear that the spirit of early Christianity along

---

99. See Augustine of Hippo, *On Christian Teaching* 1.2, where he refers to Exod. 15:25.
100. See Ambrose of Milan, *On the Mysteries* 9.51.

the trajectory today termed orthodox would find it unthinkable, even nonsensical, to say that the Rule could be challenged. In terms of the spectrum running from *adiaphora* through *bene esse* to *esse*, adherence to the Rule was, for Irenaeus and his successors in the Mediterranean world, *esse*. We see that the shift in context makes it somewhat difficult even to capture what sort of thing the Rule was for ancient ruled readers. Moberly's approximation, in terms of rules of faith, promises to describe the dialectics of their theological method; however, it notably does not yet describe the incorrigibility of their devotion, at least in a straightforward way.

So far, Moberly's method as described raises this question for us or draws out a way in which ruled reading, at least under a certain construal, sounds a dissonant chord in late modernity. To be fair to Moberly, he has not, to this reader's ear, created the dissonance for us so much as he has amplified it in the process of seeking creative resolution.[101] How, precisely, he will accomplish that resolution remains at best partly heard, leaving us expectantly vigilant as we turn to explore his actual practice. That said, I will immediately note one place where he hints at a strategy. Not all rules of faith are created equal, it turns out. Tacitly he observes, or appears to observe, that something that at least looks like the Rule, albeit the Rule obliquely identified and fuzzily described, can trump its lesser analogues—in his own words describing the role of biblical interpretation in the nineteenth century's debates over slavery:

---

101. One particular way in which this dissonance exists for modernity quite apart from Moberly's proposals is the way in which Christianity has developed over the centuries, and especially in the modern period, into a family of different branches, many of which regard each other as rivals and, therefore, of qualified legitimacy. Given that situation, it is impossible for a Christian in our day to discern the Rule of Faith (in Irenaeus's sense) apart from rules of faith (in Moberly's sense), and the latter often not only disagree with one another but are even differently construed by the respective communities in terms of their authority (e.g., a Presbyterian will regard creeds quite differently from a Roman Catholic, on the one hand, and a Baptist, on the other). However, and as a perhaps not unimportant aside, how qualitatively different is this from the ways in which ancient Christians were dependent on the guidance of their nearest bishop, who could differ within his college from other bishops by not insignificant nuances, and from the ways in which medieval Christians often found spiritual formation in distinct orders—all while still being recognized as standing in real communion within the catholic œcumene? If the analogy, in our increasingly post-denominational situation, between world Christianity in postmodernity and ancient/medieval Christianity works, then the dissonance Moberly here highlights for us might also find creative resolution in how the relationship between rules and the Rule is articulated. For one present-day proposal calculated with such features in play see Robert Wall, "The Rule of Faith in Theological Hermeneutics" and "Canonical Context and Canonical Conversations," in *Between Two Horizons: Spanning New Testament Studies and Systematic Theology*, ed. Joel B. Green and Max Turner (Grand Rapids: Eerdmans, 1999): 88–107, 165–82.

How this all [using rules of faith to relate the parts to the whole] may work is unpredictable. The fact that Genesis countenances, for example, polygamy . . . has not generally moved interpreters to suppose that they should adopt such practices. However, Noah's curse of Ham/Canaan did lead some Christians, most notoriously in North America and South Africa, to suppose that those who could be identified as Ham's descendants should be induced to serve those who identified themselves as descendants of Shem—*though this has been abandoned . . . because it has also been seen to compromise the fundamental Christian understanding of God and humanity.*[102]

The Rule of Faith under a certain construal ("the fundamental Christian understanding of God and humanity") has vetoed lesser rules, in this case a Western European Christian tradition that numbered Europeans among nations blessed in Genesis's ontology of the peoples and Africa's children as those accursed in that catalog.[103] This raises the possibility of distinguishing between the Rule and rules, where the latter function heuristically and the former, while also functional within the dialectic, is somehow more than heuristic. As we scan Moberly's treatment of Gen. 1–4 we should be particularly attentive to ways in which this possibility is either acknowledged and fleshed-out, left inchoate, or denied.

R.W.L. Moberly on Genesis 1–4

Moberly devotes four chapters to subject matter relevant to my focus on chapters 1–4. Interestingly, and similarly to my observations about Reno's divisions, while Moberly remarks occasionally on how literary cues signal pericope boundaries, three of Moberly's four chapters are themed around the medieval chapter divisions and the theological motifs traditionally assigned to them: "Genesis 1: Picturing the World" (on creation), "Genesis 2–3: Adam and Eve and 'The Fall,'" and "Genesis 4: Cain and Abel." Of these, for the sake of space and maintaining focus on our extended passage's core, we will constrain our discussion to his chapters on Gen. 1 and 2–3.

Before any of those chapters, however, comes a prolegomenon that sets all chapters in a larger context, and, here, Moberly's focus is decidedly on the rub of literary details: "On Reading Genesis 1–11." That literary focus goes beyond the hint supplied by his title. Recalling for us John Barton's desiderata for authentic biblical criticism, Moberly's interests immediately turn to questions of genre. Perhaps because of the long shadow of fundamentalism's dance of death with modernism, the tendency, Moberly observes, is immediately to designate

---

102. Moberly, *Theology*, 16–17, emphasis mine.

103. I find it personally intriguing that this Genesis pericope was also crucial in Irenaeus's description of the Rule of Faith in his *Demonstration of the Apostolic Preaching*, although he interpreted it quite differently than this American's pro-slavery antebellum forebears, see *Demonstration of the Apostolic Preaching* 19–20.

sections such as 1–11, with its at points fantastic content, as some species of myth. This temptation, Moberly feels, should be resisted. His reasons are illuminating of his argument, including the concerns we have already seen:

> All the common terms—myth, folktale, legend, saga—tend to be used in a wide variety of ways. Especially with usage of "myth," there is something of a chasm between scholarly understandings and popular pejorative uses. Thus, unless any term is carefully defined, it is unlikely to be helpful. Moreover, argument about the appropriateness of particular terms can easily displace attention to those features of the text that give rise to the use of the term in the first place.[104]

Thus, in our context it is better to challenge the frame of reference. We find ourselves being caught up in the dialectic Moberly commends. The text is going to be used to shake us out of our comfortable, but unhelpful, distinctions—in Moberly's words, "I propose, therefore, to eschew the use of any particular classificatory label and to focus rather on an inductive study of indicative features within selected texts."[105]

To which features should we attend? As before, when he was arguing for re-initiating our context's readers to theology, Moberly starts from a beachhead in our conscious experience and formation. However, now, rather than beginning from modernity, he begins with seminal interpreters in the Great Tradition. Origen is his first interlocutor, where, as we have already seen at length in our discussions of him, the early father had a flair for describing where referring scriptures' language to the world as we (tend to) experience it is problematic.[106] Augustine of Hippo follows, where the ancient bishop considers whence Cain

---

104. Moberly, *Theology*, 21.

105. Ibid., 21–22.

106. A quotation Moberly gives at length translates Origen's term as literal / literally. As Moberly observes in a note on the passage (see ibid. 23 n. 3), this is an instance of problematic translation. Origen's preferred term is *sōmatikos*, the connotation of which is roughly the same as that of the English bodily or of the body. In his larger argument in book 4 of *De Principiis / Peri Archon*, the early father will apply Prov. 22:20–21 (LXX) to the interpretation of scripture, saying that the interpreter should so attend to scripture as to be affected in all three of the components of a human person in a tripartite anthropology, namely the body, the soul and the spirit. He will then flesh out this thought further by way of *The Shepherd of Hermas* chapter 4, where Hermas is told to write two books for two different teachers who, in turn, will have two different audiences with Hermas himself having a third audience. These audiences Origen interprets allegorically as "children in soul"—to my eye catechumens are intended—mature Christians and, finally, the presbyters. The bodily sense of scripture, Origen says, is particularly accessible and apropos to the first audience. His thought, here, is apparently that some people best understand and are most benefited by the potential of scripture to speak to the concerns of everyday experience and the interpretation of mundane history, to use an example he actually deploys, the politics of historical nations in their ethno-cultural divisions as opposed to distinctions of a spiritual or intellectual sort between Israel, Egypt, Babylon, etc.

got a wife. The problem Augustine names is but one facet, Moberly observes, of a larger anxiety that Genesis's early chapters have provoked in readers—namely, how can the activities described in their pages be seriously imagined given the low population densities one might anticipate when we have only been told of the creation of two people, those two people have (apparently) only had two children, and one of those will be murdered in short order? Augustine proposes in answer that Gen. 1–11 simply does not say everything that can be said about Adam and Eve's family. Cain must have had sisters, and he must have married at least one of them.[107] Moberly's terms for Augustine's hypothesis is "omission," "selection," and "compression,"[108] and he traces the application of this hypothesis into the early modern period. However, there is a problem with this hypothesis, says Moberly: "its narrowly conceived view of how to handle problems does justice neither to the Bible nor to other forms of knowledge."[109] In its place, he begins to advance a different hypothesis:

> This hypothesis is that the story itself has a history, and in the course of that history, it has changed location, moving from an original context within the regular parameters of human history—presumably the world of ancient Israel, familiar to the narrator—to its present context at the very outset of human history. Such movement of stories is in fact a common phenomenon within the history of literature.[110]

Moberly follows this short thesis with several other examples of literary cues internal to Gen. 1–11 that this hypothesis explains nicely. Eventually, he brings in an architectural analogy to flesh it out, in the process setting forth a facet of this explanation he had previously passed over:

> In certain ways the early chapters of Genesis are rather like many pre-Victorian churches and cathedrals in the United Kingdom. Although each building is a unity as it now stands, careful inspection (and a helpful guidebook) reveals an internal history—differing kinds of stone, and differing architectural styles, from differing periods of history. Sometimes the additions are obvious as additions—most obviously graves in the floor and monuments on the walls; the textual equivalent to these is the note or gloss that has been incorporated into the text. However, one is sometimes confronted by marked differences within the fabric of the building. Almost always the correct way of understanding a marked difference of architectural style is not to hypothesize one architect who

---

107. See Gen. 5:4.
108. Moberly, *Theology*, 25.
109. Ibid., 27.
110. Ibid.

changed his mind and his materials, but rather to recognize
that the building is composite and has a history.[111]

Thus, we see that he has in mind a touchstone of modern pentateuchal criticism, in his own words, "individual narratives having a history of their own, in
the course of which they have been transposed from their original context and
relocated in their present context."[112] Observing this, particularly by also being
clued into the insight of modern historians that ancient authorial attributions
(such as the ascription of the Pentateuch to Moses) often do not designate what
moderns would mean by such ascriptions in our culture, "frees one up to work
inductively with the evidence that the text itself provides."[113] An important
gain is that "this approach does enable us to make sense of what otherwise is
either inexplicable or *can lead to rather forced harmonized readings* of the text that
look like special pleading."[114] At first, his reader might be tempted to think that
Moberly's goal is, in the best sense of the word, apologetic, much as Augustine's
likely was in part.[115] However, the part of the quote I have just italicized is important for understanding Moberly's larger point of view, particularly with regard to using rules of faith. For him, a major desideratum is that the Bible, while
a *gestalt*, should not be homogenized or systematized in a way that achieves a
pseudo-rational coherence at the expense of the realities of the text. I recall my
critique of Reno from earlier that, although the keys of doctrine unlock the
scriptures, not every key goes to every lock. Texts must be allowed to resist the
questions, concerns, and expectations we bring to them if they are authentically
to function as scripture. Jumping significantly forward in his argument,[116] this
leads to a succinct statement of Moberly's approach to 1–4:

> The Genesis parts are to be read in relation to a canonical
> whole—where what is canonical is not just the biblical corpus

---

111. Ibid., 33.

112. Ibid., 32–33.

113. Ibid., 34.

114. Ibid., emphasis mine.

115. As a recovering Manichean and one who long had been estranged from his
mother's Christian faith due to its seemingly intractable intellectual defects, the bishop
ever had in view presenting the scriptures in such a light as to win them a genuine hearing by a potentially prejudiced audience. Thus, when applied to the strategies diversely
characteristic of Augustine and, possibly, of Moberly, my use of the term apologetic is
nonpejorative, the justifiably negative connotation of apologetics in some modern Christianity aside.

116. Moberly himself takes his reader through a slightly digressive yet important
discussion of the divine-and-human nature of the scriptures as a theologoumenon, his
core point being that the processes that produced the text in its given, canonical form
are no more incompatible with their mediating divine revelation than putative author-
ship by a single inspired subject, e.g., Moses. The views of inspiration he relates fit easily
within orthodoxy and, indeed, look not unlike the synergistic outlook that characterized
Irenaeus and Origen. I skip over his discussion for the sake of space.

but also the continuing frames of reference within which its meaning is probed and appropriated. Such a trust is intrinsically related to a sense of the past and present fruitfulness of those traditions in their various Christian and/or Jewish forms. Within such contexts there is a commitment to think with the biblical text and its historic appropriations. Searching and critical questions are put to both text and tradition as a corollary of allowing text and tradition, received as mediators of a divine reality, to put searching and critical questions to the reader.[117]

Two things stand out from this paragraph. The first is his redefinition of "canonical whole" so that it encompasses "the continuing frames of reference within which its meaning is probed and appropriated." While there has been a slight shift of category from *canon* to *canonical whole*, the effect, to my eye, is nonetheless to situate the reader in a setting where the interpreter has the communion of the Church in view and not simply a list of scriptures. As we have already seen, this is how Irenaeus and other early fathers tacitly defined the Rule of Faith. The second is where Moberly locates the transforming tension in the dialectic. Earlier, I asked whether his construal of rules of faith set them, as a mode of tradition, opposite the text as a heuristic that posed questions to the text and, in turn, could be questioned and challenged by the text. We saw that that understanding was quite unlike how the early Fathers understood the Rule, which was above challenge. However, here text and tradition stand linked together as one object (the "canonical whole"?) opposite the reader and the reader's frame of reference. This, too, begins to sound more similar to how the Rule functioned in the early period. Whatever challenge tradition might be subject to, it has been anchored to the text which, presumably, is simply given in the dialectic and so in a profound sense stable in the face of challenge. While this categorization of the interpretive task is not identical to the ancient one, it begins to look not just influenced by, but actually isomorphic to ruled reading, perhaps as a species of it.

We can now move from treatment of his prolegomenon to reading Gen. 1–11 to his treatment specifically of 1:1–2:4.[118] Moberly opens his chapter by indicating in advance the sort of outline he intends for it—a serial treatment of dif-

---

117. Moberly, *Theology*, 41.

118. As an important aside, Moberly's actual chapter title, "Genesis 1: Picturing the World" does not seem to encompass 2:1–4. However, within the chapter he makes it clear that he has the whole account concluding at 2:4 in view, including, importantly, the hallowing of the Sabbath. The break for him is the natural, literary break separating off the seven day creation account from what follows it. As another aside, I note that this distinguishes Moberly from Reno, for whom 1–2 is one unit describing Creation and 3–4 is another describing Fall, giving the questions and concerns of a Western Christian systematic theology such priority that they effectively ignore, at this point, the text's literary shape.

ferent interpretations of the seven-day creation account—because mental pictures, of the sort we raised in our last paragraph, are precisely what is at issue in Gen. 1:

> In order to try to maintain a focus on Genesis 1 as a whole, I propose to offer several different readings of the text—the difference each time being the context envisaged—in part because differing contexts, for both text and interpreter, bring different readings. My primary concern is to argue that the theological significance of this biblical text is inseparable from the varying ways in which it impacts on the imagination; *how one pictures the world is the issue at stake.* However, the way in which one pictures the world relates to the varying contexts within which that picturing is done.[119]

What follows is a sequence of juxtaposed readings (and corresponding pictures of the world) of the creation account, one set after another in such a way as to effect a sort of argument in the mind of the reader. These readings are, in order, one of the text "in itself," two paradigmatically modern critical readings, a reading from one of the Synagogue's theological interpreters (Jon Levenson), and a reading that converses with a vigorous agnostic and opponent to Christianity (Richard Dawkins). After guiding the reader through this journey, Moberly offers a synthetic conclusion. I will treat these readings in summary with an attempt in view to highlight what I believe to be the sequence's design.

However much reading the text "in itself" may seem simple, it is, instead "less straightforward than it sounds" in Moberly's words, and the scare-quotes around "in itself" are his own.[120] To see some of the difficulties, we might note how other sections of his chapter will cover various pictures of the world generated from different starting points or angles. By "in itself" Moberly apparently has in view the picture generated by reading Gen. 1 from its own frame of reference or angle, as if the reader could sit inside Genesis's narrative flow as an observer, bracketing views from outside as much as possible. That picture in focus, Moberly leaves us explicitly with three impressions left by the picture of Gen. 1. First, "God is the archetypal craftsman in the archetypal week. This is a God who is active with and in the world he makes, a world that owes its existence to him."[121] Moberly has not used the word, but a biblically or liturgically literate reader can hardly keep from hearing the name *Immanuel* whispered in the background—a term taken from the prophet Isaiah, with wide resonance within the Old Testament, and applied in Christian interpretation to the person of Jesus. We therefore find ourselves standing inside Gen. 1 as a vantage point from which we might view everything else, centrally the rest of the Old Testament. Second:

---

119. Ibid., 42, emphasis mine.
120. See ibid., 43 n. 2.
121. Ibid., 47.

This is a picture of the world as the writer knew it. This is not a picture of a world that ceased in the next couple of chapters, when humans sinned, but a picture of the world familiar to the writer and his intended audience. As such, it incorporates the writer's understanding of the way the world is. . . . [T]he purpose of all this is to focus on portraying the world, the known world with life in it, as the result of God's work and the object of his delight.[122]

Because we are viewing the canonical whole from the standpoint of Gen. 1, which portrays God as a craftsman delighting in his handiwork and which reaches its climax, depending on how one reads the chapter break, either in the creation of humanity in God's image or in God's bringing all creation, with himself, into his Sabbath rest,[123] our picture of the world is, to use Moberly's words from elsewhere in the section, one where "darkness is not abolished, but is intrinsically less significant than the light."[124] This is a world where humanity and all creation exults in the glory of God. Finally, and following from that point:

There is . . . a natural sense in which Genesis 1 can function to evoke worship. This is, of course, strengthened by the text's use in liturgical contexts from ancient times through to the present. For its focus on the majestic nature of the God who makes the world, who gives such dignity and responsibility to humans, and who purposes ultimate rest, can readily evoke the response of Psalm 8:1, 9 (Heb. vv. 2,10), "O LORD, our sovereign, how majestic is your name in all the earth."[125]

We are left with a bright picture of the world, joined with God's people in an act of celebration and worship. With that picture still in our memory, Moberly changes the angle and the object of view to Gen. 1:1–2:4 as seen from historians' attempts to locate it, either within a reconstructed sociology of ancient Israel or against the contrasting backdrop of other ancient Near Eastern societies with their cosmogonic stories. Moberly's treatment of these angles is extensive, his appreciation for and critique of the approaches and conclusions involved multifarious. However, the cumulative effect of his analyses can be summed up by the word *contrast*. Genesis 1 depicts Israel's God as sovereign and his works as well-ordered and perfect while Israel's world, as she experienced it, was one ever threatened by loss of sovereignty, disorder, and the possibility of cultural dissolution before the competing claims of other gods. The starkness of the contrast is the flash now fading from our retinas, in Moberly's words:

---

122. Ibid., 47–48.

123. Moberly devotes some attention to the interpretive issues raised by the chapter break, see ibid., 47.

124. Ibid., 45.

125. Ibid., 48.

Although the considerations arising from these two examples
can be angled primarily toward a history of ancient religious
thought (e.g., Judahite ideological resistance to Mesopota-
mian hegemony), they can equally be valuable for a renewed
imaginative appreciation of Genesis 1 in itself, whose perspective on the world, when seen to have a strong implicit "this
and not that" dimension, can have deeper intrinsic resonance.[126]

Next, Moberly enlists the angle of his Jewish counterpart in theological interpretation, Jon Levenson. Somewhat at the risk of oversimplifying Moberly's
appreciative summary of Levenson, in succinct description that summary depicts before our eyes the inverse operation of Moberly's reading of the text in
itself. Like the historical critics, Levenson views Gen. 1:1–2:4 as his object, but
unlike them, his view is from the angle of his analogue to the canonical whole,
in this case Tanakh and rabbinical commentary.[127] The tools of philological and
historical method are not cast aside, but they are used to locate Genesis's account of the seven days from a kind of canonical viewpoint. Gen. 1:1–2:4 occurs
alongside other scriptural descriptions of God as creator, and those texts bear
striking resemblance to the aforementioned myths of Israel's neighbors. Those
myths related creation as a kind of divine conquest, a warrior god combating
monstrous primordial evils. Furthermore, ancient Israel's appropriation of that
vision of God-in-conflict with hostile powers occurred precisely at historical
moments where Israel was under threat and God's promises seemed to have
failed. When we stand in that textually mediated location, viewing Gen. 1:1–2:4
from there, the formless void, chaotic waters, and uncreated darkness that occupy the text's opening verses are striking. With the horror of the formless
deeps so dramatically in our vision, Levenson finds himself calling God "the potentially omnipotent"[128] rather than simply all powerful. Finally, this canonically formed perception operates with priestly, liturgical instincts—for Jews,
the use of Torah to discern *halakha* and distinguish between clean and unclean,
unholy and holy. When the Creator's ordering of the universe as described in
Genesis is viewed with such eyes, they can hardly fail to notice God performing
priestly works: separating light from darkness, blessing the creation, and even

---

126. Ibid., 53.

127. It should be kept in mind that Levenson's canon is significantly different from
Moberly's, and that not simply in terms of the texts included, but in terms of the frames
of reference considered authoritative. In a sense, even to refer to Levenson's "canon" is
to view him using an analogy to the hermeneutics of the Church rather than from his
own social and religious location in the interface of the Synagogue with the Academy.
This should be kept in view in any engagement with him, lest he be significantly misconstrued or his readings be re-deployed in a way he would not own for himself, however
legitimate the re-deployment may be in its own right.

128. The phrase is taken from a quote of Levenson occurring on *Theology of Genesis*,
56. The quote itself is from Levenson, *Creation and the Persistence of Evil: The Jewish Drama
of Divine Omnipotence* (Princeton: Princeton University Press, 1988), 41.

hallowing the Sabbath. Therefore the seven days of creation invite the faithful not simply to adore the Creator but, understanding themselves as a priestly community, to participate in the actualization of God's creative purpose and Sabbath reign.

Thus, the darkness that opposes God has been enlarged in our sights, even though it remains clearly subordinate to and coordinate within a larger and il-luminated vision. Having drawn out this interpretive possibility, Moberly now turns to a bleak, even nihilistic outlook that most any educated person in the Western world is likely to feel in her soul, even if she should try to hold it at bay. To do so, he calls up the anti-theist interpreter Richard Dawkins. Dawkins's post-Darwinian worldview is sufficiently commonplace that summary of it here is hardly necessary. Much more of interest is how Moberly accomplishes that summary and the aesthetic affect thereby achieved in the shadow of the other pictures of the world he has just depicted.

On the surface of things, Dawkins's picture (as Moberly summarizes it) is merely of a world without God, Dawkins's conviction being that the world that exists most likely has none. What makes Dawkins's view of the world interesting is that he is also viewing Gen. 1, this time ostensibly from the angle of modern biology. Initially this is indicated by the title of the book Moberly summarizes, *River Out of Eden*.[129] More important yet than this is how he argues against the-ism. He does so, Moberly points out, by way of William Paley's argument from design for the existence of God, an argument Dawkins admires and recognizes as significant in the intellectual development of Charles Darwin.[130] For Paley, the seemingly well-ordered, benevolent character of so much of the world is an insurmountable apologetic for the existence of God. In the process of articulat-ing this apologetic, the Church's doctrine of creation, Moberly observes, is transmuted into an argument from design.[131] Thus, Dawkins's ostensible angle on Gen. 1 (modern biology) turns out actually to be a prior concept of God, one philosophically dominant in the eighteenth and nineteenth centuries and influ-ential in some circles even today. This concept of God sees the Deity as a cosmic engineer, to use Dawkins's term.[132] This concept is read back into the text of Genesis, such that the reader now sees something like a mechanic or a watch-maker when she reads "In the beginning God . . . " This picture of God and the world, however, rapidly turns out to be inadequate, principally because of the chaotic opacity of biology's "pitiless indifference" to moral concerns, to use Dawkins's terms.[133] Its utter amorality is intuitively incompatible with a benev-olent and omniscient engineer yet quite easily explained should the creative

---

129. Richard Dawkins, *River out of Eden: A Darwinian View of Life* (London: Weidenfeld and Nicholson, 1995).

130. Moberly, *Theology*, 59.

131. Ibid., 62.

132. Ibid., 60. Moberly is quoting from Dawkins, *River Out of Eden*, 104–5.

133. It is important to note that the problem Dawkins raises cannot rightly be called the problem of evil, for, as he points out, the dimension of nature he is here examining

principle turn out to be something like survival of the fittest. Genesis 1 thus interpreted falls before the sword of theodicy.

Or, does it? By seriously grappling with Dawkins's arguments, Moberly is guiding his reader deeper along the hermeneutical spiral of the dialectic. His goal, it turns out, is to challenge not primarily Dawkins's nihilistic view of the world, but Dawkins's and Paley's reading of the seven days of creation, in the process leading the reader to a *metanoia* regarding God and re-initiation to the art of theology. Theology in the ancient sense does not define *God* by way of too-easy analogies to human designers as an explanation for whatever science has not yet explained.[134] Indeed, true theology doesn't try to define God at all, who, in God's relating to us, is *mystery*. Moberly's sentiments here deserve to be quoted at length:

> Unless one is willing to abandon the whole frame of reference in which God functions as an explanation analogous to the explanations of science, one will be sucked down steadily and inescapably into a theological bog. It is a matter of the two entirely different senses in which the word "mystery" can be used. There is the common use of mystery as a puzzle, where a situation is only mysterious because insufficiently little is known about it, and the mystery disappears when enough is known. . . .
>
> Yet the proper theological sense of mystery is to express an inherently deep reality, the grasp and understanding of which intrinsically becomes ever more demanding the more fully one engages with it—in the convenient tag, "the more you know, the more you know you don't know." God is not demystified by accurate knowledge: quite the opposite; and to appeal to God as the cause of the world is not to offer the kind of cause for which scientists look.[135]

But, if God is not a cause in the sense to which I am accustomed to speak of causes, in what sense is God the creator? Determined to join those who live long with the text, Moberly first redefines theology as a species of wisdom celebrated in the Old Testament.[136] Having done so, he proceeds to make an observation about how that wisdom is formed, with respect to the statement "God made the world," in those who live with the Genesis text:

> A characteristic Christian (or Jewish or Muslim) affirmation that complements "God made the world" is "God has made

---

is merely neutral, neither good nor evil. See Moberly, *Theology*, 62, where Moberly quotes Dawkins, *River Out of Eden*, 131–33.

134. The reference to analogies is an attack on an abuse, not right use. The problem is with the attempt to define, delimit, and explain by way of what properly speaking is an analogy and, therefore, not a definition.

135. Moberly, *Theology*, 63–64.

136. Ibid., 64.

me." What does, and does not, such an affirmation mean? Negatively, it does not mean that one's presence in the world is the result of something like a magician's trick, a sudden appearance without obvious explanation ("one moment I wasn't there, next moment I was"). . . . Positively, the affirmation entails an understanding of both origin and destiny, in terms of coming from God and going to God. Its primary significance is in terms of what it means for a present existential understanding in the here and now. The affirmation seeks to express such existential realities as trust, accountability, dependence, contingency, the sense of oneself as a creature in relation to a creator.[137]

Those who live long with Gen. 1:1–2:3 approach it respecting the mystery of God, and that, in turn, means that whatever processes operate in the natural world, God is in the details. An application begins to emerge for the series of pictures through which Moberly has guided us. Gen. 1:1–2:3, with its bright contours and festal climax, is not an invitation (much less a compulsion) to deny the dark side of nature seen as real by old paganism and triumphant by modern anti-theism, and thus to commit intellectual suicide by leaping into a Pollyannaesque phantasy. Rather, it is a challenge not to deny in the darkness what we have beheld in the light—not to lose the sense of trust, in Moberly's words. His conclusion is forthcoming and, again, deserves to be quoted somewhat at length:

> The problem of suffering is a well-known existential issue within theology and philosophy. Dawkins seeks to make it into a decisive argument against God, within theological as well as scientific categories, by simultaneously emphasizing its ubiquity, its necessity, and its amorality. The imaginative picture of a God who in sovereign goodness makes a world that is "very good," and who wondrously brings good even out of evil, is displaced by the imaginative picture of a world of overwhelming amounts of suffering whose only explanation is the maximizing of the survival of DNA in its "blind, pitiless indifference." But why should one accept an either-or dichotomy, when both-and may be nearer to the truth? Most people simultaneously hold a number of imaginative pictures of the world. Which comes to the fore depends to some extent on context. A walk in a green and sunny countryside or in the mountains encourages one kind of picture; looking at photographs of what the Allies found when they arrived in Nazi death camps or reading accounts of the Holocaust/Shoah encourages a different kind of picture. But both pictures must be held.[138]

---

137. Ibid., 64–65.
138. Ibid., 66.

Genesis understood canonically, Moberly considers, helps cultivate this sensibility in dwelling with mystery, this appreciation for paradox. Thus, he writes, "Genesis 1 is by no means the only picture of the world in the Bible,"[139] as Levenson's reading demonstrates and brief digression into the Psalms reinforces.[140] Finally, by analogy to those Psalms:

> . . . theological use of Genesis 1 must surely hold its picture of the world as an object of delight in tension with other pictures, those elsewhere in the Bible and those of modern science, which in various ways highlight evil, suffering, and randomness within the world. The positive understanding of the world remains more fundamental than any negative understanding—that is, good is somehow more basic than suffering and evil, for otherwise the vision of God is deformed, hope fades, and the personality becomes liable to disintegration. Even so, any mature understanding of the world as God's world—any affirmation of the enduring truth and value of Genesis 1—must embrace complexity and conflict whose only good resolution will lie in hard-won existential ability to live with deeper trust in God whose ways are mysterious, in the proper theological sense of that term.[141]

With these words, Moberly climactically concludes his chapter, awaiting his reader to turn the page and begin to question and be questioned by Gen. 2–3. Before we join him, a few points in turning from observation and summary to analysis, synthesis, and evaluation seem apropos.

First, although the effect seems likely unintentional and possibly illusory, Moberly's approach to and conclusions regarding Gen. 1:1–2:4 continue to evoke the spirit of some ancient Fathers, most potently Origen and more distantly Augustine. Although Moberly is not, at least to my eye in any clear way, allegorizing Genesis—the move for which Origen is, whether justly or unjustly, most (in)famous—he is treating in a serious way the text as a source of *provocation*, not only intellectual but existential. For him, scripture comforts precisely in how it names the paradoxes of human life and challenges us to take them seriously, with wisdom as the consequence. Similarly, for Origen the reading of scripture was pregnant with the possibility of a quasi-Socratic encounter with the Holy Spirit, the end of which was union with Christ in his capacity as the wisdom of God. For both our ancient apologist and (post)modern theological reader of scripture, this life-transforming wisdom, the capacity to live faithfully

---

139. Ibid.

140. Moberly guides his reader through Pss. 44 and 89, both of which pose, in distinct ways, the crisis to which the seeming failure of God's promises brings Israel, see ibid., 66–68.

141. Ibid., 68–69.

and well with a commanding integrity, is a penultimate goal in the reading of scripture, if not, as for Augustine, actually the end-goal.[142]

Second, the role Moberly sees for the dialectic of reading with rules of faith is demonstrated concretely with the way in which his pictures progress until his reader discovers, in her own culture's collective subconscious, an intellectually toxic and likely idolatrous concept of God in the polemics of Dawkins and apologetics of Paley. That God is unmasked and its golden-calf cast down in the process of taking Genesis seriously. In this sense, again, Moberly's dialectic evokes dynamics of ancient ruled reading, in this case the commitment to seek *metanoia*—repentance, utter change of mindset.

However, precisely that line leads me to a third point, this one a hanging question. Intuitively speaking, there is more to rightly responding to mystery, although not less, than the capacity to sit with paradox, to be still, when the early chapters of Genesis are in view. In the specific case of Gen. 1:1–2:3 in its relation to the narratives of Gen. 1–11, the Pentateuch, and even the Bible as a whole, the paradox we are about to find ourselves forced to acknowledge and sit with is that the first creation account ends in a glorified humanity ushered by God into Sabbath rest, but the second creation account will end in toil and prophesied, ignominious death.[143] Here, we are not dealing simply with another picture of the world somewhere else in the canonical whole or the scientific record or the human experience but with the very next picture of the world we encounter *in Genesis itself*. In the history of ruled reading—again, speaking intuitively—this paradox has proven especially significant, indeed crucial, for it names the problem of evil not from a general, philosophical, or existential frame of reference, but specifically in the frame of what Moberly has called the canonical whole as the problem of sin, fallenness, or paradise lost, the resolution to which is the eschatological, Sabbath hope. Given Moberly's concern for the canonical whole, for long term living with the text, and for the Christian Church as a particular community that has lived long with it, we find ourselves wondering whether Moberly will leave us simply sitting with the paradox in its general form or instead coordinate 2:4–3:24 with 1:1–2:3 so as to name the paradox in

---

142. Although it is important to note that, explicitly for both Augustine in *On Christian Teaching* and Moberly in all his writings, the definitive demonstration of wisdom is in Christ, who is the wisdom of God. See ibid., 15, where Moberly writes "For Christians, this canon includes the New Testament, in which God becomes definitively understood in the light of the incarnation—the life, death, and resurrection of Jesus." A significant consequence of this is that wisdom itself is not understood entirely *a priori* but dialectically through obedience to the Gospel.

143. Actually, it strikes me as worthy of serious examination whether the medieval / liturgical chapter boundary at the end of Gen. 3 is a hard or a soft literary break—or whether it even is a break at all, the really significant seam occurring at the beginning of Gen. 5. If that is the case, then the section typically designated the second creation account is actually a constituent of a larger literary unit, the end of which seems ambiguously positive on balance, with the advent of Shem and humanity calling on the name of the LORD.

terms of the text in itself. Of course, and heeding his own protest that limited space of necessity prevents every question from being addressed,[144] he might do this more or less; however, with the re-contextualization of ruled reading in view, we should pay special attention to whether and how he relates these two texts within the canonical whole.

Indeed, Moberly's opening observations in his chapter, "Genesis 2–3: Adam and Eve and 'the Fall'" amount to a defense of the passage's classical significance in terms of relating what the early Fathers called the Rule of Faith. Countering an objection that allusions to the story of the fall within the Old Testament are impossible to find, and, therefore, that the story is actually not as important as the Tradition has taken it, Moberly notes that "the location of Gen. 2–3 at the very outset of the Old Testament, with the first interactions between God and humanity, gives a contextual weight to the narrative that is as great as could be."[145] This is a note he strikes repeatedly throughout his chapter; for example, he notes that the narrative of Adam's and Eve's creation occurs not merely in the Bible's opening pages as a literary accident, but rather that it stands preserved there "in a structurally crucial position at the beginning of Israel's account of the world."[146] Although he does not use the categories either of "rules of faith" or "Rule of Faith" or "ruled reading" or any other of the terms he might have used to evoke the idea directly, we are left with the distinct impression that here, perhaps more even than elsewhere in his book, Moberly has in view what it means to comment not simply on one or another pericope but on the canonical whole. This should be kept in mind as we examine what he has to say about Gen. 2:4–3:24.

His chapter title notwithstanding, he deals but minimally with the balance of chapter 2. Of primary interest to him, rather, is responding to James Barr's revisionist account of the fall, or, rather, Barr's *rejection* of that reading as inauthentic to the text.[147] To Barr's eyes, Gen. 3 has been distorted by the Tradition as a story of a demonically manipulated Adamic fall reversed by the new Adam, Jesus Christ. Moberly summarizes Barr's critique as one that counters this view of Gen. 3. Instead of narrating a moral catastrophe in which humanity's relationship to God is fundamentally and negatively altered, Barr says it is a simple and probably somewhat comedic tale in which a human pair almost obtains immortality, but fails to so. In view of this, God's prohibition (of the Tree of the knowledge of good and bad) is morally arbitrary, the Serpent's assessment of the fruit's real potency is correct, and the divine threat of punishment is turned into an empty threat when the forbidden activity is engaged anyway and God

---

144. Moberly, *Theology*, xxii.

145. Ibid., 71.

146. See ibid., 78 n. 10.

147. In the sentences that follow, I will be referring to Moberly's summary of Barr to be found in ibid., 71–75. Moberly, in turn, refers to Barr's *The Garden of Eden and the Hope of Immortality* (Minneapolis: Fortress, 1993).

fails to carry out, in any clear or straightforward fashion, the promised execution.

It is at this point that Moberly demurs. He grants Barr's observation that the Serpent's words seem to be confirmed and God's are called into question but adds that this "portrayal of God that emerges" "is one aspect of Barr's account of Gen. 2–3 that seems not to bother him at all but that perhaps should bother him more than it does."[148] The reason why is substantially the defining point Moberly has already raised: that the narrative occurs at a structurally crucial location. The entire balance of the scriptural witness enjoins trusting God, taking him at his word in every season and regardless of appearances. Moberly's previous chapter on Gen. 1:1–2:4 substantially dealt with this as a matter of theological interpretation, concluding, as we have seen, that the paradox into which that creation account invites the reader is one wherein trust with realism is cultivated. Yet, here, at the very outset of the scriptural witness, precisely where we would expect the authorizing communities of the canonical whole to be most careful and self-reflective, God's trustworthiness is assaulted wholesale. This problem is only exacerbated further if we take seriously that God's accuser in the story is the Serpent which, Moberly points out, is not *yet* an enemy from the standpoint of the narrative itself but which is already an enemy from the standpoint of any likely reader, especially a typical denizen of the ancient Near East.[149]

In the midst of preparing this counter, Moberly takes us again into territory familiar to us, namely an ancient pedigree for Barr's reading. The various schools opposed by Irenaeus of Lyon in the second century C.E., today collectively called the gnostics, tended to read the Serpent's words positively and God's negatively. However, unlike Barr and like Moberly, they thought this enormously significant. It indicated nothing less than that the god of the Old Testament was a lesser and corrupt divinity, from whose tyranny gnostic enlightenment would deliver those capable of attaining it. Moberly's point in raising this uncanny correspondence between Barr and the ancient gnostics is actually not a tacit charge of heresy as a kind of nuclear option against Barr's reading,[150] which would be an inappropriate move for a biblical scholar operating in a secular context. Rather, he seeks to evoke the possibilities for and challenges to ruled reading in today's context. In his own words:

> My proposal . . . is not to use the Gnostic precedent for certain
> central aspects of Barr's reading as a way of dismissing it; ra-
> ther, I want to use it heuristically, to stimulate a rereading of
> the biblical text. For when a narrative is open to various read-
> ings and resists simple closure—as the history of interpreta-
> tion of Genesis 2–3 clearly shows—then it can hardly be open
> to objection to see whether there is an alternative reading

---

148. Moberly, *Theology*, 76.
149. Ibid., 79–80.
150. See Moberly's brief discussion of Barr's hermeneutics in ibid., 76–77.

that does justice to the specifics of the text while at the same time standing closer to classic Christian rather than Gnostic instincts. In effect, this is to remind ourselves that theological interpretation, while needing to attend carefully to textual specifics, depends for its overall plausibility on the larger frame of reference to which it appeals and within which it functions.[151]

Moberly has returned us to the arguments of his introductory, methodological chapters. *Frames of reference* and *heuristics* are in view, in this case the heuristic, interestingly, being a familial resemblance between Barr's reading and the gnostic one, and the "larger frame of reference" to which Moberly points his reader is the Christian orthodoxy to which he wishes to address the heuristic as a probe, essentially asking the text, "Is your God really trustworthy?" The searching question he seems to hear in turn from the canonical whole is "What do you see reflected in Genesis 3 when you *choose* to trust?"

Adopting this new question as his revised heuristic assumption, he now tries to do as he has just suggested in the paragraph quoted above—see if the new question enables him to do "justice to the specifics of the text while . . . standing closer to classic Christian . . . instincts."[152] His re-reading from the starting point of this heuristic swiftly notes two properties of the text. The first is the relationship of Gen. 3 to the Pentateuch and Old Testament, wherein the language of death and life when expressed as an oracle from God is frequently metaphorical.[153] The second is a property we have seen before—the effect of *scriptural, canonical* paradoxes upon a reader. When these two properties come together, Moberly observes that the disorientation produced by the apparent confirmation of the Serpent's words over against God's has prepared the reader to come to a deeper sense of what death and life might mean—that death is possibly more than simply cessation of physical life, and that one can experience the horrors of death keenly apart from the sleep of the grave. He writes:

> If one applies this [i.e., the observation that "death" can function metaphorically] heuristically to the Eden narrative, after the surprising initial denouement in Genesis 3:7, one finds that the continuing narrative is readily open to a metaphorical construal of death. Although previously God and the man had worked together (2:19, 22), now the sound of God nearby inspires fear so that the man hides (3:8, 10). Although previously the man had delighted in the woman as "bone of my bone and flesh of my flesh" (2:23), now he refers to her as "the woman you gave me" and points the finger at her (3:12). That is, in the primary relationships between the man and God, and

---

151. Ibid., 77–78.

152. Ibid., 78.

153. Moberly specifically notes Deut. 30:15–20 viewed in its larger context, see ibid., 83–84.

between the man and the woman, elements of alienation and estrangement have come in and have, as it were, poisoned the well. Then, in the following divine pronouncements, in addition to hostility between humans and snakes, the primary roles of the woman and the man in their ancient context, as wife and mother and as farmer and food producer, respectively, will become burdensome. Or, to put it differently . . . these are to be seen as an outworking of death, understood as alienation within human life in its various primary forms.[154]

It is perhaps important to note that Moberly's proposed reading is one that he has immediately tested. Were he simply to have observed that metaphorical interpretation is possible and that readerly disorientation could occasion it, we would likely remain unpersuaded. What makes his reading click is that it makes sense of what follows Adam's disobedience in a way that Barr's reading does not. To Barr's eye, nothing really changes after the forbidden fruit is consumed, except that human trust of God has been called into question—which seems not to matter much. However, here Barr's reading is surely tin-eared, for the patterns of alienation Moberly makes much of were absent before. Furthermore, although Moberly does not note this, we might observe that Gen. 3 flows nigh seamlessly into Gen. 4, wherein the patterns of alienation crescendo in murder and exile, the latter being an experience that ancient Israel held close to her heart as an abiding and catastrophic consequence of her stubborn disobedience and symbol of alienation from YHWH. All this in view, Moberly concludes with a proposal regarding the text's genre and thrust, as a story designed, again, to inculcate wisdom:

> The context of puzzlement and disillusionment may also be the context of moral and spiritual maturing. For one may look again at those principles already held and dig deeper, as it were, so as to ask whether they may indeed be true even if such truth is no longer at a surface level in the kind of way that was initially supposed. This, I propose, is the strategy employed within Genesis 2–3—to lead the reader into deeper understanding of what is, and is not, meant by "death" as the consequence of disobedience to God. The felt liberation may be misleading, and the sense of impunity illusory, for death may be present metaphorically in a diminution of, and alienation within, the personal and the public life of humanity. If believers have not fully felt the force of the possibility that God's words may not be trustworthy and true—for so much in life seems to contradict them, and the cynic or the doubter is rarely short of evidence to which to appeal—they will not be

---

154. Ibid., 84–85.

led into a more searching understanding of the real significance of their beliefs; but such leading is vital to moral and
spiritual health.[155]

Lightning has struck the same spot twice. Genesis 1:1–2:3 brings the reader
to paradox which produces wisdom; Gen. 2:4–3:24 confronts her, again, with
paradox (albeit under another name), and wisdom is the design. As before and
in concluding summary of Moberly's chapter, a few points seem in order.

First, his reading again and for the same reason reminds us sharply of Origen—only now even more so than before. When only Gen. 1 was in view, the
paradox was between its apparent picture of the world and other pictures of the
world. Genesis 2–3, however, contains its own paradox, at least when read
within the frame of reference that is the canonical whole. It immediately provokes the reader, even is explicitly designed to do so. This is precisely the argument Origen makes regarding the design of scripture in *Peri Archōn*, albeit assigning agency in the design explicitly to the Holy Spirit and only tacitly to human authors, whereas here Moberly inverts that order, assigning the explicit
design to the mundane realm and the tacit one to divine inspiration.

Second, his reading intuitively fits within the ruled pattern. It is not simply,
to use his own phrase, closer to classic Christianity. To my eye, his reading is
orthodox not merely in the sense of adhering to certain dogmatic particulars
but in the deeper sense of expressing an attitude, an orientation to that which
the Faith bears witness, which Irenaeus termed "clinging unswervingly to the
Rule." I speak at least partly by way of conjecture, but it seems possible to me
that it is this characteristic that provokes Moberly's occasional opponent John
Barton to read him and other theological interpreters with a jaundiced eye. For
Barton (as a disciple of Barr?) the choice to hear searching questions from the
Tradition and reapply those heuristically likely looks altogether suspect when
the consequence is, again and again, coherent with even if distinct from read-
ings from the past.

However, this brings me to a third point, one I raised at the outset of reading Moberly. I observed then that the way in which he re-categorized and transposed ancient ruled reading into a mode of regarding rules of faith rather than
the Rule, and the way in which that regard promised to treat those rules heuristically, seemed strikingly distinct from the ancient pattern. The commitment to
rules as heuristics was particularly provocative in this respect, because, again,
to raise the allusion to Irenaeus I have so often made, the Rule was "clung to
unswervingly" in ancient ruled reading, and the connotation of *unswerving* is far
stronger than *heuristic*. Later, Moberly seemed to play a yet different note in his
transposition, one that promised some resolution to the dissonance between his
categorization and the ancient one. Specifically, in speaking of how to interpret
Gen. 1–11, he anchored the tradition to the text as a canonical whole, supplying
a stability to the tradition that more closely resembled Irenaeus's confidence in

---

155. Ibid., 86.

the Rule. Here, in Moberly's treatment of the fall, we see that tether uniting tradition and scripture brought to the surface. Moberly has returned to the language of heuristics, the classic Christian understanding brought to a conversation where, at least in principle, it is open to critique, revision, and even rejection. The tether, however, holds, showing that the text and the tradition can cohere in a way that does injustice to neither. Flatly terming *rules of faith* "heuristic" seems unhelpful for re-contextualizing ruled reading, at least where Irenaeus's convictions remain desiderata; however, if what Irenaeus referred to as the *kanōn* is by Moberly referred to as the canonical whole, Moberly's reading brings us to a perhaps useful sense of what it means to re-contextualize ruled reading. In our context, it becomes necessary to articulate, in some sense explicitly, that the Rule to which we cling unswervingly is neither some vision of the text in itself, nor some construal of tradition as something external to scripture, nor any other sundered parcel of the post-Reformation and post-Enlightenment minefield, but rather the tether that identifies the ancient texts to be scripture by anchoring them to the life of worship and the vocation of worship as truly life by anchoring it in a relation of accountability to the text.

Finally, and as a point possibly of criticism, if only mildly so, Moberly's treatment of 2:4–3:24 leaves us with our question from the end of 1:1–2:3 only partly answered. He has now coordinated the two creation accounts, but only tacitly, obliquely and on a high level of abstraction by way of identifying each as occasion to grow in wisdom, and specifically trust. The vision of wisdom he proposes and call to trust he gives is profound and echoes the patristic dictum *credo ut intellegam*. However, I feel more might be said concerning how Gen. 1:1–2:3 and 2:4–3:24 cohere, the death and toil with which the second one ends provoking in me the searching questions, "When is God's Sabbath rest?" "What has happened to the image of God?" No one book can answer all questions, and Moberly's treatments have already done much, but, for the Tradition, these questions, or ones cognate to them, are intuitively central to initiating readers to the Rule of Faith, apart from which ruled reading is impossible. For ruled reading to be recontextualized it seems probable we should answer them, at least tentatively and heuristically.

I close this section with one such proposal briefly stated. Gen. 1:1–2:3 is like a preface, a prolegomenon, or a promise. When one comes to Gen. 3 and later 4, that promise seems impossible to fulfill, for humanity has rejected its vocation to choose life, and instead death reigns. It is as if Gen. 1 might have said something that it did not say, something along the lines:

> *In the beginning . . . God said, "Let there be light!"*
>   *But, the formless void replied, "No!"*
> *And the shifting sands refused*
>   *to be conformed to the image of God.*
> *So, then God . . .*

But, Gen. 1 does not say this—does not even admit the sorts of lacunae or pregnant silences, interrogated by Reno, wherein our new expectations might fit. Instead, the Word leaves me with male and female made in God's image simply, and humanity with all creation ushered promptly into the Sabbath. If I take seriously Moberly's (and Origen's) strategy, then the expectation created in me when I read Gen. 1 becomes not simply an image I hold in tension with other images but a heuristic by which I question and find myself questioned by Gen. 2–4, the balance of the primordial history, the generations of the patriarchs, the rest of the Pentateuch, and on into the canonical whole.

The State of Ruled Reading in Theological Interpretation

We have now visited two post-modern theological interpreters, summarizing, analyzing, and venturing evaluations of two of their offerings for the promise each, respectively, shows for recontextualizing ruled reading on our present-day scene. The length and serial character of that analysis demands some closing recapitulation and targeted coordination, lest we lose the forest for the trees.

As a point of departure, it is worth noting ways in which Reno's and Moberly's contexts of operation and social location are similar but distinct. Both are academicians working in sub-fields of theological and religious studies, and each labors in the shadow of a growing discontent with at least a certain prevailing construal of biblical studies. Each scholar, likewise and interestingly, reprises (in distinct ways) premodern Christian categories, particularly Irenaeus's name for that which catechesis was designed to inculcate in the early centuries: the Rule of Faith. Their attention to that ancient category makes their respective contributions all the more interesting, for my purposes in this book, as it supplies corroborating evidence that post-modern theological interpretation is a context wherein ancient ruled reading might grow new roots below and fruits above.

Not all, though, is similar; there are several important points of difference, each perhaps related to their social locations. Reno is a systematic theologian publishing in an explicitly Christian context, and, at the time he was writing his *Genesis*, he was laboring in a Jesuit university. While this by no means guarantees or even constrains his interpretive efforts within confessional boundaries, it does open possibilities that secular contexts methodologically bracket, notably the option of appeal to religious authority, as Reno, to my eye, tacitly does in his discussion of the doctrine of creation from nothing in the context of Gen. 1:1–2. Moberly, as a biblical scholar writing for a secular publisher and working at a secular university, sets these possibilities to the side. To get more to the key point, these differences in location also seem to influence how the Rule of Faith is described. For Moberly, the Rule is one species of a genus of rules, and those, in turn, are understood abstractly in terms of plausibility structures. The Rule's application is thereby justified, so to speak, out of concern for the sociology of knowledge—a major epistemological desideratum of the post-modern scene. This positively correlates to ancient ruled reading in how it directly highlights the hermeneutical spiral characteristic of premodern interpretation, particularly with regard to Origen and Augustine. Again and again Moberly's actual interpretations of Genesis and not just his abstract specification of hermeneutical theory illustrate this when scripture becomes, for him, an occasion for being confronted by paradox and mystery, with unexpected *metanoia* of tacitly held convictions resultant as a consequence.

However, not all correlates positively, notably when Moberly describes rules of faith as heuristic. While his reasons for doing so are important,[156] indeed impossible to ignore, there is a problem: Moberly's description does not, at least explicitly and clearly, account for the ancient Christian's existential commitment to cling unswervingly to the Rule. On the contrary, it seems to require the interpreter to stipulate from the outset that the Rule, like all other rules, is subject to revision. Moberly does offer fascinating and important practical options for reprising the ancient devotion to the Rule under a new categorization when he focuses on the canonical whole, with likely important consequences for his debates with Barton. This praxis, however, I had to draw out of the tacit structures and background of Moberly's proposals; left to themselves, a strong accent remains on the heuristic character of various rules of faith rather than unswerving devotion to the Rule of Faith. Finally, Moberly's treatment of Genesis lacks—likely as a matter simply of lack of space, but possibly for more serious reasons—the sorts of big-picture coordination of distinct passages that was characteristic of early ruled reading, where the ancient paradigm viewed the scriptures as sources for discerning the whole identity-story, so to speak, of Immanuel and the people of God. In Moberly's (apologetic?) engagement with the modern critic, he does not revisit this ancient desideratum. Consistent with this, I might additionally highlight one, puzzling, lacuna that we have not already mentioned: Moberly does not engage at all themes that Reno has at least touched upon, including the doctrine of *creatio ex nihilo*, related Logos Christology, and a Sabbath eschatology. Given the strength at least of the Christological and eschatological motifs in the New Testament—and, therefore, in the canonical whole—this absence seems notable, even if it is due mostly to concerns for space.

Reno's definition, by contrast, comes closer to defining the Rule explicitly, in conceptually cognate ways to Irenaeus, as the intellectual culture or doctrinal

---

156. Personal correspondence with Moberly while drafting this chapter disclosed three such important motivations behind his categorization of rules as heuristic: 1) the concern of the modern biblical critic for the givenness of the text, 2) (related to [1]) the dialectical character of ruled reading, and, 3) the institutional speciation of Christianity through two thousand years of development into various denominations and cognate patterns of organization, a feature of Christianity dramatically characteristic of Protestantism in its various forms. I take these three concerns as obviously germane to recontextualizing ruled reading for our day, the criticisms I am about to state notwithstanding.

tradition of the Christian Church to which the Christian is finally committed, and he forges ahead unstintingly towards a big-picture perspective wherein *creatio ex nihilo* looms large, eschatology is explicit, and Christology receives at least a gesture. This objective is pursued along with a polemical agenda against the same modern critic Moberly attempts to engage more sympathetically. This proves to be the case especially wherever that modern critic seems to Reno to be putting up roadblocks in the way of developing the sorts of big-picture, story-telling potential which ruled reading traditionally discerned in its (proto)biblical engagements. The promise to re-engage premodern readings and reading strategies, as such, rings a clear, if indeed, not a resounding note. Perhaps significantly, this corresponds to an interpretive success when Reno is able to push relentlessly towards an interpretation of Genesis as creation arching towards Sabbath as a *telos* for God's works, and when Genesis becomes occasion for clarion reflection on the nature of sin, specifically idolatry. In this way, where Moberly identifies the genre of Genesis's early chapters as a kind of wisdom literature, Reno's interpretations frequently echo sublime wisdom on the human condition, and, somewhat tacitly, human destiny, drawn out homiletically through textually occasioned meditation.

Given these gains, it is perhaps somewhat surprising then—even, at points, disappointing—when Reno's approach to the text repeatedly and unnecessarily opposes what he himself acknowledges to be scripture's plain sense and ignores as hermeneutically irrelevant key literary features, notably the break at 2:4. In failing here, Reno's course diverges from the hermeneutical spiral intrinsic to ruled reading, his polemical agenda temporarily taking over while interpretation *of the text itself* drops to the background. Since his polemics are waged against the modern critics, who have taken the legacy of the Renaissance humanists and their concern for critical philology as their high ground, the consequence, it seems to me, is the marginalization of properly philological concerns, a move that seems quite counter to ruled reading at its core if Augustine or Origen or Hilary—or for that matter modern readers ranging from Calvin to Barth—are to be taken as serious, even seminal exponents. Put another way, Reno's construal of theology fosters significant one way traffic from his big-picture concerns (for Sabbath and the condemnation of idolatry) to the text, with the result that the Rule, although defined in like manner to the ancient practice, now functions in a somewhat un-ruled way, his interpretations sidestepping the scriptures in their religiously authoritative givenness. We find ourselves hearing the symphony of the Great Tradition, but with that voice that is the Book of Genesis become oddly muffled, with the consequence that the symphony is no longer as aesthetically compelling as it might otherwise have been.

Thus, I end this chapter with a conundrum. One proposal for theological interpretation reprises ruled reading out of a nonconfessional location with the impressive result that the hermeneutical spiral, concern for the text in itself, and even ascent towards wisdom characteristic of ruled reading play out compellingly. However, that same proposal, precisely because of its location, does not (cannot?) account (except, perhaps, in a cryptic or oblique way) for some things intrinsic to ruled reading—primarily the reader's unflinching devotion to the Rule, and less clearly the big-picture concerns of early ruled readers. Complementing this, Reno's alternative proposal, in defining ruled reading from a confessional location, accounts for devotion to past readings, including to some form of the big picture arrived at by ancient ruled readers and so, in that way, accounts for devotion to the Rule under the mode of communion or at least engagement with great readers of the past—intriguingly not only Christians but, also, rabbis. However, Reno does so by way of substantially sidestepping, even occasionally muting, the text that was ostensibly the source of those ancient readings, short-circuiting the process of interpretation in aesthetically jarring ways. Yet, ignoring the negative and heeding the positively correlating aspects of Moberly's and Reno's offerings, each looks as if he gives a compelling account of aspects of the ancient pattern.

Ruled Reading in the Unfolding Epic: Concluding Reflections on the Arts of Homily and Devotional Criticism

What I have been calling ruled reading may likely seem, by this point in my larger argument, something of a paradox in its own right: both a relic of a lost, classic Christian culture and yet, in a hidden fashion, very much alive. On the one hand, we have an on-balance negative assessment of the ancient discipline in the modern context, to the point that even some sympathetic to premodern approaches, such as Henri de Lubac, who appeared in cameo in my introduction, regarded those approaches as incompatible with biblical exegesis on the modern scene. On the other hand, classical Christian convictions and practices have persisted into the modern and postmodern worlds even in circles that utilize biblical criticism, motivating readers to relate the biblical text to questions of doctrine, worship, and the life of faith. To this day seminaries instruct students in biblical studies as part of background research for homilies, and Bible studies, even when designed to observe and thereby bridge social and cultural distance between us and the premodern world, do so out of the conviction that *devotion* actually benefits from that distance being observed. In my own pastoral experience while these practices may both (and, again, perhaps paradoxically) subvert modernity's preferred stance *and* challenge religious devotion as presently enacted, they are pervasively and usefully undertaken among the faithful. In this sense, though both Reno's and Moberly's proposals involve calls to do something different from modernity, their accounts of reading with (some form of) the classic Rule of Faith in mind look existentially engaged with currents that endured the crisis the modern world represented and which cross it towards the ancient and premodern horizon. Moberly and Reno each does what he does—and, in a way, so also does even John Barton—because of wider patterns of interest that suggest that Legaspi's scriptural Bible lives still, and not just as a shade. Ruled reading, it seems, is not dead but obscured in our context. It has become like an undertow in interpretation's vast sea. This supplies powerful motivation for remedying ruled reading's obscured condition—something that many writers at present, several of whom have been interviewed, here, seem in fact eager to do.

Might we venture an explanation for, or at least a more involved description of, the subaqueous condition under the assumption that it demands remedy? An observation of contrast between Reno and Moberly suggests a place to begin. Reno attempts explicitly unswerving devotion to the Rule and engages a polemical agenda against those who said that, for the text to be approached with fresh eyes, ruled reading's devotion must needs be suspended. The results are frequently interesting and beautiful, especially when they challenge readers to seek scripture's big-picture *gestalt*, but are also sometimes unpersuasive, as when they surrender the text's plain sense to doctrine's cultured despisers. By contrast, Moberly forswears, or seems to forswear, unswerving devotion to the Rule of Faith so that he might be committed to heuristic investigation. His readings then suggest the existential viability of doctrine's starting points (heuristically adopted) when they persuasively treat the text, received as a given, seriously and orient the reader to it in ways that feel fresh and new. However, once I have come to the end of Moberly's *Genesis*, I find that I have been brought, as it were, to a narrow, shrouded doorway over which is inscribed the classic dictum *credo ut intelligam*, but not formally bid enter.[1] Moreover, John Barton's antipathy towards the theological interpreters appears to come to focus near the point where Moberly and Reno diverge in approach: as Barton reads "theological interpretation," its call for *theological devotion* to be shown *objectively given* texts sounds incredible. Between Barton, Moberly, and Reno, I think I perceive an interpretive culture that considers *unswerving* devotion to the scriptures via patterns of *dialectical* discernment as, at best, paradoxical, if not perversely contradictory, and so implausible or impossible.

Yet, if the first half of this book argues along the right lines, ancient ruled reading was precisely such a pattern. The (even historically speaking, plausible) assumption of Christianity was that its life of discernment was continuous with that wherein the writings it regarded as sacred also had their origin; therefore, those writings seminally recorded the Church's own identity and vocation— they were, to use my concluding category from chapter 1, the Church's *identity story*. Those writings were holy, in turn, for the same reason the Church was holy: Christ, the word of God, to whom the Spirit had consecrated the writers and processes that thereby led to him. Therefore, those scriptures were, to use my concluding category from chapter 2, Immanuel's story. Thus, Christian communities heard scripture (has the paradigmatic mode of encounter with scripture ever not been public worship?) as both a literary artifact with an objective, stable, transcendent givenness, and also as a living occasion for discerning intersubjective, unfolding identity in the Spirit. As a given text, transcending the

---

1. Correspondence with Moberly indicates that this is intentional on his part, the academic guild being a place where a clarion credo would, more likely than not, be subject to misunderstanding and premature censure. My note that his paradigm stops just short of ruled reading with respect to this quality, while yet deriving inspiration from the ancient paradigm, is intended merely to draw out this feature of Moberly's thought, not to critique his method.

reader and conveying foundational witness to the truth of God and identity of God's people, philological and literary critical tools are useful to prevent readers from closing the angle of the dialectical spiral into a perverse circle. On the other hand, as an occasion for discerning continuing identity, typological and allegorizing stances, and conceptualization as prophesy and wisdom, are necessary to discern the unfolding significance of the text, because the text referred primarily not to a dead past but to Jesus Christ, in union with his Church, as this union unfolds *en route* to the *Eschaton*. What was it that coordinated critical tools with open-ended, doctrinal vision and discernment? There was a hermeneutical spiral tuned to perceive the objectively given scriptures' unfolding reference in a never-ending act of devotion.

While this book has not been an argument concerning the history that scholars call the canonization process, the arguments made here can perhaps be related to two classic questions drawn from that study: is the canon closed, and, if so, when did it close? If the observations made over the course of this book are along the right lines one answer to these questions is, from ruled reading's perspective, that the canon has, in a certain sense, always been closed, counterintuitive as that conclusion may seem. For early Christianity the canon, viewed from various angles over the centuries, was primarily the scriptures' true *hypothesis*—the salvation they disclosed and wherein their own patterns of sense and reference took their origin and coherence. Scripture's texts then became this canon in a sacrament or mystery in a manner coherent with the Church's Eucharist, by the Spirit's power at work in the Church, in the process coming to serve as indefeasible witness to the Reality with which the Church had to do. Only by standing within that indefeasible witness, heeding it, could the horizon for discerning canon in the primary sense—the salvation of the Lord—be discerned. Therefore scripture is also truly canon. What we call the canonization process was, from the theological starting point of early Christianity, this deepening perception of indefeasibly foundational apostolic and prophetic witness to the salvation of the Lord. Simply put, scripture was not just about past events and states of mind; it was about a still-ongoing encounter with an unchanging reality of inexhaustible significance, Christ-with-his-Church, in the words of the *Epistle to the Hebrews*, "the same yesterday, today and forever."[2]

When the outlook described in my previous paragraphs is encountered by interpreters in the modern world, its paradigm is experienced as interpretive values in painful tension. Straightforward description of that tension is hard to come by, so ruled readers' activities go underwater, with only some aspects of their practice visible on the surface. A reader such as Moberly can read in practical ways according to the Rule without explicitly accounting for what looks (to some, such as John Barton) like *de facto* unswerving devotion. A ruled-reader like him very well might treat one or more rules (e.g., doctrinal desiderata such as concern for God's character) as heuristics for dialectically approaching the

---

2. Heb. 13:8.

catholic *Rule*, which continues to command loyalty over and above the heuristic, small-r rules. By emphasizing the heuristic quality of these rules, the underlying devotion vanishes beneath the surface.

Might this subaqueous condition be remedied and ruled reading be re-contextualized in a postmodern setting? Again, observation of Moberly and Reno, with Legaspi and Barton, might prove helpful. Of these, Reno is the most extroverted in express devotion to the Rule. One consequence, partly due the polemical nature of his writing, is that his devotion sounds occasionally anti-critical. A Barton-esque scholar might simply refuse to respond, labeling Reno's reading as noncritical at best and so uninteresting to the critic except where assault on criticism's territory from its religious despisers demands a defense. A theological interpreter engaged with Moberly's method may, in turn, see Reno's relative lack of attention to the *sacra pagina*'s givenness and demur. He ceases to speak of the Rule and instead attends to rules, not simply to keep a stake in, to use Legaspi's terms, biblical criticism's hermeneutical territory but for properly Christian doctrinal reasons. At issue in both these interpreters is his understanding of what (sort of thing) the Rule is or might be.

But, here we have actually observed in passing, although I did not draw as much attention to this fact at the time, that early Christians' answers to the question "What sort of thing is your Rule?" changed with context. For Irenaeus, the Rule was, in terms drawn from the rhetorical schools in the ancient world, the true *hypothesis* of scripture. For Origen, it was more like what William Abraham and the canonical theists of today think it was: a list of plain doctrines starting from which exploration of scripture could commence.[3] For Hilary it was scripture's power to shake finite, mortal reason out of its rationalistic stupor to deepen in participation in the Divine Mind. For Augustine, it was the semiotic world of "things" to which scripture's "signs" referred, the paths of which, where properly mapped, led to the Love of God. Since these early fathers could recontextualize the Rule, using different categorizations to describe what sort of thing it was in different situations, might not we?

Let us start by being apophatic, to use an analogy from the discipline of spiritual theology: what is the Rule *not*? It is often assumed that the Rule of Faith / doctrine is a fixed-form reference to abstract conceptualities to be nigh identified with (or as) a creed or proto-creed. This outlook seems to me to stand behind the otherwise hard-to-explain commitment of William Abraham, my comments positively correlating the school of canonical theism with Origen notwithstanding, to define the word *canon* by the English word "list." What if the Rule were (only) that? How would ruled reading proceed? It would seem to entail saying that the encounter with scripture primarily has to confirm (or at least cohere with) doctrinal theories (e.g., of the atonement, or the Eucharist, or

---

3. The refrain that canon originally meant list echoes throughout W.J. Abraham et al., *Canonical Theism: A Proposal for Theology and the Church* (Grand Rapids, MI: Eerdmans, 2008).

election, etc.) whenever some element of the list is in play. Whenever some element of the prescribed doctrines is not in question the Rule becomes irrelevant. Interpretation would not need it in such cases.

However, the evidence I have adduced here is that the Rule has not always been identified so narrowly with a creed or proto-creed, however much it did entail forming creeds as intellectual artifacts for future use. Indeed, defining the Rule as a list of doctrines seems something of a stretch, not simply in our context but even in the ancient one. Even for Origen, the Rule committed the reader to seek the scriptures' actual reference and inner logic in a *neverending, dialectically executed, open* act of intellectual devotion, and the meaning of the ostensibly clear doctrines from the preface turns out to be dependent on that open, ever-ongoing act. This becomes even more clear in Hilary's commitment to "take away more than he brought" (*De Trinitate* 1.18) and in Augustine's ministerial use of neo-Platonism to describe an ascent of the mind to ever purer concepts of Wisdom (*De Doctrina*) and Love (*De Catechizandis Rudibus*). Does Irenaeus, perhaps, display something more like devotion to a fixed-form, given he says the Rule is handed on in baptism and calls for unswerving devotion to it? The answer, again seems no, for reasons Christopher Seitz states succinctly:

> The rule of faith in the period in question [i.e., the ante-Nicene] *is based upon* a proper identification of what the fathers called the "hypothesis" of Scripture, and an assumption of this, in the area of "order" (*taxis*) and "arrangement" or "connection" (*hiermas*). The rule does not take the same form when we see it articulated, because it is not a fixed formula and it does not point to an incipient creedal declaration or response, or externalized or externalizable statement. It is not an effort at a precise statement of the "hypothesis" of Scripture but rather *is based upon* a proper identification and apprehension of this, as over against alternatives; that is in fact the claim being made.[4]

Seitz evokes Reno's definition of *doctrine* for us, from my chapter 4:

> The great tradition of Christian doctrine was not transcribed, bound in folio, and issued in an official, critical edition. We have the Niceno-Constantinopolitan Creed, used for centuries in many traditions of Christian worship. We have ancient baptismal affirmations of faith. The Chalcedonian definition and the creeds and canons of other church councils have their places in official church documents. *Yet the rule of faith cannot*

---

4. Christopher Seitz, *The Character of Christian Scripture: The Significance of a Two-Testament Bible* (Grand Rapids, MI: Baker Academic, 2011), 195.

be limited to a specific set of words, sentences, and creeds. It is instead . . . the animating culture of the church in its intellectual aspect.[5]

The observant reader (of this book's chapter 1) may counter that the Rule was handed down or inculcated in catechumens approaching baptism, most plausibly using creedal or other liturgical elements. However, the observation that candidates for baptism were initiated to the Rule using some sort of tool from the Church's sacramental toolbox actually reinforces the conclusion that the Rule itself cannot be identified reductionistically or minimalistically. Early Christianity's liminal occasions, climactically baptismal and eucharistic, were understood to be encounters with the triune God.[6] The goal was introduction to a life of perceiving and being transformed in incomprehensible and deifying light. Any sense in which creedal or proto-creedal elements were the Rule of Faith in early Christianity was subordinate, then, to the sense in which the eucharistic bread was Christ's body and wine was his blood. My point here is not to advance a low view of the Eucharist but, rather, assuming (per Justin Martyr[7]) a high view of the mystic supper, to advance a high and properly sacramental view of the Rule and of the scriptures that were read in its light—and even as its written modality. Where creeds are the Rule of Faith, they are so by directing the confessor, to echo C.S. Lewis,[8] "further up and further in" to visions of glory that are evoked by, but cannot be reduced to, mortal words.

If fixed-form reference to abstract concepts is what the Rule is not, what, then, is it—or might it be in recontextualization or translation to a postmodern *ethos*? Reno's description of it as a "culture in its intellectual aspect" is helpful. Waxing poetic with late ancient Christian practices and commitments in view, the Rule turns out to be something more complex than conceptual abstraction, something that was caught up with the discovery and formation of identity and mission. Likewise observing the Rule's relationship to Christian identity (and inspired by recent research by N.T. Wright), Paul Blowers argues that "the Rule of Faith . . . served the primitive Christian hope of articulating and authenticating a world-encompassing story or metanarrative of creation, incarnation, redemption, and consumption."[9] While that sentence stops short of calling the Rule itself a narrative, Blowers adds a bare few lines down that:

---

5. Reno, *Genesis*, 12. Emphasis mine.

6. Thomas Finn extensively discusses how Christians went about this in his multivolume series on *Early Christian Baptism and the Catechumenate* (Collegeville, MN: Liturgical Press, 1992).

7. Justin Martyr, *First Apology* 66.

8. C.S. Lewis, "Further Up and Further In," in *The Last Battle* (New York: HarperCollins, 1956), 185–97.

9. Paul Blowers, "The Regula Fidei and the Narrative Character of Early Christian Faith," in *Pro Ecclesia* 6 (1997): 199–228, with the quote cited being from 202. Blowers is significantly inspired by the work of N.T. Wright from the latter's *New Testament and the*

> . . . the Rule, being a narrative construction, set forth the basic
> "dramatic" structure of a Christian vision of the world, posing
> as an hermeneutical frame of reference for the interpretation
> of Christian Scripture and Christian experience, and educing
> the first principles of Christian theological discourse and of a
> doctrinal substantiation of Christian faith.[10]

Nathan MacDonald raises cogent criticisms of an over-aggressive reliance on the category of narrative for penetrating early Christian theology, and, with him, we may demur on whether *narrative* entirely captures what the Rule was in itself, especially since so much of both scripture and creed is not clearly narrative in genre.[11] That acknowledged, the idea that the Bible refers to the world as it most truly is in God's saving designs or, per Augustine, a universe of *res*, the contours of which are disclosed by the scriptures used dialectically to discover that universe, seems intuitively promising.[12] The Rule, then, would be a worldview, an instinct about reality, a cultivated common sense, a disciplined stance and means of perception, and an aesthetic. The early modern John Calvin describes the Bible as a pair of spectacles through which all else might be seen,[13] and given what I am arguing here, if the Bible is, per its history, simultaneously the scriptures and the Rule those scriptures disclose in dialectical engagement with their *gestalt*, Calvin's description applies to the Rule and seems quite apt. Defining the Rule as a world and means of perceiving that world explains the apologetic utility of the Rule to Irenaeus—for it enables reality checks on the claims of purported religious teachers—even as it also explains the Rule's role in supporting speculative theological deduction in Origen's catechetical hermeneutic, deifying surrender to God's nature in Hilary, and ascent to wisdom in Augustine.

What might ruled reading look like if the Rule, especially in its lived, doctrinal modality is construed, as described above, organically: as teaching, as initiation, as an outlook, and as the world perceived by disciplined and sacramentally enlarged perceptiveness? It would demand attention to the scriptures received in their givenness *because they are scripture* and, therefore, with certain

---

People of God, vol. 1 of *Christian Origins and the Question of God* (Minneapolis: Fortress Press, 1992).

10. Ibid.

11. Nathan MacDonald, "Israel and the Old Testament Story in Irenaeus's Presentation of the Rule of Faith," in *Journal of Theological Interpretation* 3.2 (2009): 281–98.

12. And, in any event, Blowers's larger argument speaks of the Rule as involving narrative as one dimension even as he also speaks of the Rule as a narrative in some sense. For this reason, his argument seems to remain significantly robust to the concerns raised by MacDonald and heuristically useful for exploring postmodern recontextualization of ruled reading so long as objections such as MacDonald raises are taken into adequate consideration.

13. John Calvin, *Institutes of the Christian Religion* 1.6.1.

assumptions dialectically in play. Listing these assumptions will only ever be a tentative and incomplete enterprise precisely for the reasons described above, but, for the purposes of exemplification, consider these propositions: that the texts in question are holy, that they cohere with each other for the reader who lives long with them among God's people, that they disorient and reorient readers in salvific ways (i.e., they empower conversion), that they disclose a possibility of communion with God and his saints, that they enable ongoing *metanoia* in identity and vocation, and that honesty with them in their *gestalt* transforms the mind in the triad that is its conceptual (truth), aesthetic (beauty), and ethical (goodness) perception of existence. Honest, prayerful, disciplined, wonder-filled wrestling with the scriptures in their totality is the location wherein who we are in God's story might be perceived.

I might spell out some of these assumptions synthetically and in greater detail. Take recent debates, live for interlocutors for this book such as Craig Allert,[14] over the scriptures' inerrancy or infallibility, or, to use a categorization that seems to entail analogy to the old christological debates, a high view of scripture. Particularly in "conservative" circles, the scriptures are often spoken of confessionally as inerrant and/or infallible. *Contra* that conservatism, "liberals" see them characterized by the foibles and fallibility of their human tradents and, therefore, to require relativization and even deconstruction by present-day readers. However, what we have seen here is at once more complex and more simple than either of these proposals. The fathers praise the scriptures and that praise is a confessional act directed to the Word and Spirit of God, communion with whom (and with whose saints) the text is understood sacramentally to be. One can see easily enough how such praise could be repeated in a present day context by ascription of inerrancy or infallibility to the text, however, to cohere with the ancient understanding, that inerrancy could—probably would—turn out to be a surprisingly messy inerrancy: the guarantee of the scriptures' catechetical, Socratic application, their ability to disorient and provoke, and thereby to guide (or drive!) readers deeper into the life of God. Moberly's repeated lifting up of wisdom as an end in the purview of Genesis's opening chapters is exemplary in this regard.[15] Put another way, problems in the text, where real and whether of a textual, philosophical, or theological character, are important to recognize as resources for deepening, not negating, doctrine (conceived of, again, along the lines discussed earlier in this conclusion). The name of the game is not to foreclose on the results of reading but to insist that, whatever tentative closure eventually be obtained—and any closure must, actually, be tentative, lest the scriptures cease to be sacrament or icon of the living Word of God, who is incomprehensible—that closure must not be the closure of scripture's messy, quotidian details explained away.

---

14. See, for example, his "Inspiration and Inerrancy," in *A High View of Scripture? The Authority of the Bible and the Formation of the New Testament Canon* (Grand Rapids, MI: Baker Academic, 2007), 147–72.

15. See Moberly's *Theology of Genesis*, 64.

On a related note, biblical *authority*, like inerrancy and infallibility, is likewise become a shibboleth in our setting. "Conservatives" affirm it; "liberals," "progressives" or "revisionists" take offense at it; species of "moderates" who tire of the fundamentalist-modernist dance of death try to substitute alternative formulae (e.g., W. Abraham and the canonical theists' formula, "means of grace").[16] Intuitively speaking, the devotion shown Holy Scripture in late ancient Christian ruled reading, if recontextualized for our day or any other, likely would actually embrace diverse ascriptions of authority to scripture, for the strongest possible negative language is used to describe those whose devotion to scripture was found wanting in the seminal period. The resolution of the fourth-century christological debates are exemplary on this point, as we saw with Hilary of Poitiers in chapter two. The underlying logic for this high view of scripture can be seen easily enough from my first chapter. If the argument there, that the scriptures were understood as a prime mode of communion with the Word of God's human (and angelic?) emissaries, is along the right lines, the scriptures are, effectively, a kind of icon, even though their form is verbal rather than pictorial. They become a means not merely of formulating ideas but of loving (and being loved by?) the saints and angels and the One Who Sits on the Throne around which they ceaselessly worship. Once thus recognized, critique of bibliolatry sounds at cross ends with the native trajectories of any intuitively Christian theology, even for relatively iconoclastic traditions (such as Evangelicalism actually is); for verbal as with pictorial icons, the seventh ecumenical council's declarations will turn out to hold the day.

So ascription of authority to the Bible is, likely, simply a given. If the arguments explored here are correct, however, that authority, like inerrancy and infallibility, is *per* the Bible as sacrament of the incomprehensible Word and Spirit of God, and so the authority of a living witness to the Truth, received as a teacher whose principal concern is to help the student grow into the image of God. In epistemological terms the evangelical children's song "Jesus Loves Me" is exemplary and perhaps illustrates the possibilities for postmodern contextualization. "Jesus loves me // this I know // for the Bible tells me so," describes the Bible as epistemic warrant for that sort of knowledge that is personal, relational, and subjective. This is not to say that the Bible's constituent literary strata cannot be used to approach questions of a scientific or historical character once subjected to philological analysis. It is to say that, when the Bible seems not to speak definitively to what is constructed as a core concern in our context, that one natural reason may well be that the communion of which the Bible is a mode prioritizes other questions more highly, and its living voice is changing the subject. In this way, the angles of philology and devotion actually coordinate to tune the angle of the hermeneutical spiral to deconstruct and reorient the

---

16. See W.J. Abraham, *Canon and Criterion in Christian Theology: From the Fathers to Feminism* (Oxford: Oxford University Press, 1998), esp. his first chapter, "Orientation: Authority, Canon, and Criterion," 1–26.

reader's religious imagination according to the Holy Spirit's catechizing and converting aims.

Some will object that confession of the Bible's authority in this subjective sense, suggesting that it might not always speak to the matters currently preoccupying us, can function to excuse unbelief. ("I interpret the Bible differently than you do, therefore I can ignore your reading when you think the Bible means _____ in our present controversy.") Indeed, it seems intuitively right to point out that suggestions, such as the one I have made in the immediately preceding paragraph, can function rhetorically in empty, self-serving, and disingenuous ways. However, where taken seriously, the confession that the Bible possesses authority not simply to speak to our concerns *but to demand we re-prioritize them* is more demanding of readers, not less, for the attitude constitutive of such confession is love, the experience it anticipates is conversion, and the deepening practice envisioned as that conversion takes place is faithful obedience.[17] This is for two reasons. First, the recognition that the scriptures possess authority and function epistemically with regard to personal, relational, subjective knowledge does not silence debates on other concerns but creates the space wherein, to use an aphorism of the Orthodox devotional text, the *Philokalia*, I "apply everything to [my]self" before applying them to others.[18] Second—and perhaps even more importantly where, in our world, secular ideologies so often dominate conversations—when the Bible functions in this way, the agendas for debates are discerned in terms of the world disclosed in honest, repentant engagement with scripture and not merely in terms of what is currently a hot item politically. If I may immediately use a biblical allegory, it is as if the disciplined reader were the child Samuel awakening to the dread-yet-familiar voice of Israel's Holy One; the only proper answer for our ideal reader is first to say, "Speak, Lord, for your servant is listening!"—and then do just that.[19]

The just-stated methodological principle likely will, according to the plausibility structures of much polite, enlightened Western culture, border on the phantasamagoric. Dale Martin, who I interacted with in this book's introduction, provides one angle of access to the problem with his favorite aphorism: texts do not mean, people mean with texts.[20] To speak of the Bible having a living voice seems to confuse what sort of thing the Bible, as text, must actually be. However, here we might also recall, as a counter, the complaint of Brian Daley that much modern biblical criticism seems committed to methodological atheism. In much popular, postmodern discourse, Martin's aphorism seems loaded to consider texts in general, and the Bible particularly, as occasions

---

17. Along parallel lines J. Todd Billings challenges the tradition of evangelical topical preaching of turning the Bible into a proving ground for extra-biblical, effectively secular theories of morality and sociability, see *The Word of God for the People of God: An Entryway to the Theological Interpretation of Scripture* (Grand Rapids, MI: Eerdmans, 2010), 4–11.

18. Mark the Ascetic, "On the Spiritual Law: Two Hundred Texts," 6.

19. 1 Sam. 3

20. Martin, *Pedagogy of the Bible*, 31.

wherein human persons *as we are normally accustomed to encounter them* negotiate meaning in a time-bound present.[21] What if, however, we function as methodological theists—if we view the Bible as a text the prayerful, yet critically aware, reading of which opens graced access to those who have been made gods by grace, the communion of saints? If such a methodological commitment is cogent, then, perhaps, the scriptures can be said to have a kind of (sacramental) agency—namely, the agency of the saints and the Spirit who sanctified them to God's self-revelation. Such methodological theism will still concern itself with the scriptures in their givenness, which surely entails, in postmodern context, critical use of criticism's tools, for postmodern is not anti-modern. However, it will do so in order to participate in a larger life extending, through the history of interpretation, into the whole search for the Church's Bible that ruled reading presupposes was constitutive, in the Spirit's grace, not only of the text's canonization but of its production. Having done so, the goal will turn out to be not to perceive the text simply but to perceive the universe that that whole history of interpretation, with every tradent in it, indwells, a universe that that text, dialectically engaged as sacrament of the Word of God, authoritatively discloses. Typological and prophetic exegesis becomes natural, as the reference of the text turns out to be not primarily a past (either ideal or actual) I am trying to reconstruct, but the past, present, and future in which God is calling humanity to conversion.

Under such construal of infallibility, inerrancy, and authority the critic's disciplined, philological and literary critical attentiveness to the text seeks what I might term, on analogy to what traditionally has been termed scripture's "plain sense," its plain *impact*—an impact that may well turn out to be most easily expressed, in turn, in typological or allegorical terms spelled out through principles of analogy robustly held. Sometimes a reader claims a scripturally mediated experience that at best shallowly acknowledges the text's historical-cultural particularity, grammar, lexical semantics, and / or role in the yet-unfolding tradition of reading it alongside all the other sacred texts of Immanuel's worshippers. When this is the case, the critic does an invaluable service in the dialectics of ruled reading by alerting the reader that she should attend more deeply than she has, simply to be honest with what is there for eyes to see and ears to hear. The critic does not do so assuming an inert Bible with static meanings to be (also, rather statically) subscribed to or dismissed by the reader, rather like a patron of an all-you-can eat buffet. Rather, the assumption of the methodological theist is that God exists and rewards those who diligently seek, ask, and knock. Returning to my Samuel-in-allegory, such a reader, bringing every effort of reason and imagination before the presence of the Living God

---

21. Martin himself, to my eye, does not seem committed to such a reading of his proposals but does, on balance, emphasize the hermeneutical priority of presently living and responding human communities, e.g., liberationists, feminists, evangelicals, etc. His ideal readers seem to be, for lack of a better description, the sorts of persons who you could run into at the Society for Biblical Literature annual meeting.

through the holy tent that the Bible is, waits to hear what the Spirit says to the churches. She acknowledges with humble, joyful gratitude the messy, quotidian possibilities of the sacred letter, received in canonical *gestalt* (whether or not its presupposed, inner coherence and eschatological horizon is yet being perceived), precisely so as to meet the precondition for mortals seeking, through a dim glass darkly, vision of the dizzying space that is the divine liturgy celebrated by the Church triumphant before the Throne of God and of the Lamb. That precondition is that we be properly surrendered to the self-disclosing infinitude, as Saint Hilary put it, of The-One-Who-Is, the blessed and holy Trinity. In such reading-as-worship, the reader may well answer the question, "What did He tell you?" with a not-yet-satisfied "I do not yet understand well enough to say." However, she must not answer along with the fool, "What God?"[22]

What is the place of the doctrinal tradition in such critical engagement? Might I suggest, in the light of all the above, a procedure for measuring readings in the history, distant and recent, of interpretation? Take a doctrinal formulation or significant reading either from the history of interpretation or the rub of daily life as a small-r rule; then, search the scriptures in their givenness to see, as it were, where that reading came from. In the process, the goal is not solely to put these interpretations to the test (necessary as the task of discernment is) but actually to flesh them out in scriptural terms—to render them accountable to the Bible understood as the textual modality of the canonical *gestalt* that, as a matter of historically plausible presupposition, is the tradition in which the heuristic reading has its origin. If that fleshing out works, plausibly unlocking scriptures' locked doors, than it is shown truly to be a species of doctrine—a ruled reading—for the keys of doctrine unlock the scriptures. In this way, the tension between critical awareness of the text and doctrinal reception of it is held together by way of putting the latter in its best possible light, assuming that, whatever meaning doctrine has and whatever orientation it provides to the scriptures, that meaning and orientation has to be accountable to the Bible from reading of which it sprang. In this way traditional interpretations are neither discarded as irrelevant nor granted an authority over scripture and functional apart from fresh, scripturally occasioned and regulated bowing before Christ.

What, at the end of the day, might this look like? Here I must humbly risk my own heuristic suggestion of a small-r rule, in this case taken from my own attempts to live into the ontology of scripture explored in these pages, thereby to come full circle back to the ancient discipline considered in this book's opening chapters. One of my hats is as associate pastor of a Presbyterian congregation. In that context I am often assigned a Lord's Day to preach, complete with predetermined scriptural text, prayerfully selected by the head of staff pastor beforehand in consultation with his fellow pastors and elders. The task set me is to practice *devotional criticism* towards the text so as to be personally re-

---

22. Ps. 14:1

shaped into a surrendered voice for the designated Sunday.[23] I sit down with the text and a panoply of philological and other tools, some designed to flesh out its semantic possibilities, others to consider its history of reception, and yet others to regard the world as disclosed by the biblical *gestalt* with the immediate text as a focus for prayer. The goal is to produce a kind of personal commentary as an immediate artifact, and, utilizing that commentary in turn, a roughly twenty minute, live, liturgical exercise wherein the congregation reads the scripture together, expresses worship to Christ in his capacity as the Word of God (*"Hear the Word of God! . . . This is the Word of the Lord! Thanks be to God!"*), and then seeks to hear Him together with a mind to experience his love, to be renewed by his Spirit, and to obey God among our neighbors.

Because the goal of enacting this liturgy is already heuristically in play, the entire act of critical study is immediately undertaken as a form of prayer, and the primary object of my criticism becomes not the week's text—which nonetheless is being regarded critically—but myself and my people. Isaiah's lament often (although not always) becomes my own, whatever text be my immediate focus: *woe is me, for I am lost, for I am a man of unclean lips and I dwell amongst a people of unclean lips, for my eyes have seen the King, the LORD of hosts!*[24] The prayer of Samuel, "Speak, Lord, for your servant is listening!" becomes my own, fleshed out in terms that for me are existentially live. *Where has my life and that of my people come, through over-familiarity with* this *scripture, ironically to hold the Spirit whose voice it is in contempt? Where has our first love cooled and religion's sacred fires burned dim into sentimental clichés?* The exercise becomes one not of seeking to hear something novel (for novelty, too, can turn out to be the most clichéd thing of all),[25] but really to flesh out the doctrinal presupposition that, whether we have heard this Word before or not, we need really to *hear* it again, with our whole being become transfigured into a bondservant's ear-pierced-through.[26] Nor is the goal to experience only challenge without comfort, for also presupposed in the dialectic is that God is making covenant anew with his people (or else we would not together be seeking Christ),[27] and, in view of that divine fact, the word according to the prophet Isaiah (received as canonical text even if not necessarily as historical Jerusalemite) is live: *Comfort, comfort my people, says your God. Speak tenderly to Jerusalem, and cry to her that her warfare is ended, that her iniquity is pardoned, that she has received from the LORD's hand double for all her sins.*

---

23. John Chrysostom's admonition (from his eighty-sixth homily on the Gospel of John) that the priest lends tongue to God is ever on my mind here, as is the confessional guidance of my own tradition that the preached word is but one sacramental modality of the living Word of God, Jesus Christ

24. Isa. 6:5

25. Cf. Acts 17:21 with its surrounding context.

26. Deut. 15:12–17

27. Jn. 6:44–45

Thus engaged, the role of my critical imagination becomes sanctified to hear scripture afresh. I do not deny either my or my congregation's preunderstandings, but I come before God through scripture in the expectant hope that those preunderstandings will receive re-vivification and deeper initiation. The alien language, culture, and history both of the text and of its tradition of reception becomes, for me, opportunity for holy disorientation. The act of worship that emerges from that disorientation then is itself humbly understood to be a spoken form of God's Word and therefore of awesome sacramental authority derivative of the Bible's own sacramentality. This might seem a hubristic claim, all the more arrogant for my having claimed it actually is humble, but, consider: water does not rise above its own level, and here the level is that of the Bible received as functionally inerrant, infallible, and authoritative word of God for the people of God. The preacher prepares in holy awe, daring neither to manhandle the ark of God's covenant,[28] nor to offer the strange fire of *faux* holy teachings near its sacred place,[29] and the congregation, as bride of the Lamb, listens determined to love and to be loved by Jesus, looking to him as the Lord risen with healing in his wings, and not to perform cult to some idol in servile dread.[30]

I hope the observant reader can observe, in my attempt at describing my personal homiletic, a likeness to how patristic homilies, constructed as artifacts of ruled reading, actually proceed. That is, my description of the art of biblical study, undertaken in service to Christian worship, aims to stand within the Bible's own terminological world and semiotic universe. The preacher I aim to be is a Reformed divine, who in turn is admiring John Chrysostom, who in turn is standing with Samuel, and Isaiah, and the anonymous deuteronomistic historian, and the mysterious chronicler, and St. John the Theologian and gospel writer. The art of ruled reading thus constructed is not an attempt at abstract, conceptual understanding of the Bible, but rather an attempt to discern *and to enact* what it looks like to live inside the Bible's world as one responding to the sending-call of the God of which it speaks when heard in its canonical totality. In this way the Great Tradition of doctrine suggests starting categories and, even more importantly, the *imitatio Dei* by the saints to be undertaken with them as best I can. This sets up the hermeneutical spiral to converge upon meaning. Criticism—not only or even primarily of the text, but of my own self—in turn disciplines my vision by reminding me that my existing praxis is prophesy indeed, and yet still immature,[31] the Bible commending to my searching eye intelligible but incomprehensible mystery that can be discovered properly only

---

28. Taking due warning from 2 Sam. 6 and 13.

29. Taking warning from Lev. 10:1–3, cf. also 2 Chr. 26:16–21. For St. Irenaeus this act, especially as named in Lev. 10, supplied biblical, narrative definition for the Greek word transliterated into English as heresy (*Against the Heresies* 4.26.2).

30. Cf. Num. 21:6–9 and Mal. 4, taking warning and encouragement from 2 Kgs. 18:1–5.

31. 1 Cor. 13, esp. v. 9.

by moving from whole to part and from part back to the whole in never-ending discipleship to the Jesus-Immanuel whose story it tells. The preacher imitates the saints as they imitate Christ, discovering that, because the Bible is Immanuel's story it is also theirs, and so also the preacher's. I come full circle back to the definition of ruled reading with which I ended chapter 2.

Bibliography

Modern Sources

Abraham, William J. *Canon and Criterion in Christian Theology: From the Fathers to Feminism.* Oxford: Oxford University Press, 1998.

Abraham, William J., Jason E. Vickers, and Natalie B. Van Kirk. *Canonical Theism: A Proposal for Theology and the Church.* Grand Rapids, MI: Eerdmans, 2008.

Alexander, Philip. "'In the Beginning': Rabbinic and Patristic Exegesis of Gen. 1:1." Pages 1–29 in *The Exegetical Encounter of Christians and Jews in Late Antiquity.* Edited by E. Grypeou and H. Spurling. Leiden: Brill, 2009.

Allert, Craig D. *A High View of Scripture? The Authority of the Bible and the Formation of the New Testament Canon.* Grand Rapids, MI: Baker, 2007.

Adam, A.K.M. *What Is Postmodern Biblical Criticism.* Minneapolis: Fortress, 1995.

Agnew, Francis H. "The Origin of the NT Apostle-Concept: A Review of Research." *Journal of Biblical Literature* 105.1 (March 1986): 75–96.

Ayres, Lewis. *Nicaea and Its Legacy: An Approach to Fourth-Century Trinitarian Theology.* Oxford: Oxford University Press, 2004.

Balthasar, Hans Urs von. *Seeing the Form.* Vol. 1 of *The Glory of the Lord: A Theological Aesthetics.* Edinburgh: T&T Clark, 1982.

Banov, Georgian, and Mark Pendergrass. "Noah." Sparrow Song, 1980.

Barr, James. *The Garden of Eden and the Hope of Immortality.* Minneapolis: Fortress, 1993.

———. "Jowett and the 'Original Meaning' of Scripture." *Religious Studies* 18.4 (December 1982): 433–37.

Barth, Karl. *The Epistle to the Romans.* Translated by Edwin C. Hoskins. Oxford: Oxford University Press, 1968.

Barton, John. *The Nature of Biblical Criticism.* Louisville: Westminster John Knox Press, 2007.

Baukham, Richard J. *Jude, 2 Peter.* Word Biblical Commentary Series 50. Waco, TX: Word, 1983.

Beckwith, Carl. "The Condemnation and Exile of Hilary of Poitiers at the Synod of Bézier (356 C.E.)." *Journal of Early Christian Studies* 13.1 (2005): 21–38.

———. *Hilary of Poitiers on the Trinity: From De Fide to De Trinitate.* Oxford: Oxford University Press, 2008.

———. "A Theological Reading of Hilary's 'Autobiographical' Narrative in De Trinitate I.1–19." *Scottish Journal of Theology* 59.3 (2006): 249–62.

Behr, John. *The Way to Nicaea.* Crestwood, NY: St. Vladimir's, 2001.

Billings, J. Todd. *The Word of God for the People of God: An Entryway to the Theological Interpretation of Scripture.* Grand Rapids, MI: Eerdmans, 2010.

Blowers, Paul. "The Regula Fidei and the Narrative Character of Early Christian Faith."
    Pro Ecclesia 6 (1997): 199–228.
Bokedal, Tomas. "The Rule of Faith: Tracing Its Origins." *Journal of Theological Interpreta-
    tion* 7 (2007): 233–55.
Braaten, Carl and Robert W. Jenson. *Reclaiming the Bible for the Church*. Grand Rapids, MI:
    Eerdmans, 1995.
Brown, Raymond E. *The Gospel According to John, XII–XXI*. New Haven: Yale University
    Press, 1970.
Bruce, F.F. "Some Thoughts on the Beginning of the New Testament Canon." Pages 85–
    108 in *The Bible in the Early Church*. New York: Garland, 1993.
Bultmann, Rudolf. "New Testament and Mythology: The Problem of Demythologizing
    the New Testament Proclamation." Pages 1–44 in *New Testament and Mythology and
    Other Basic Writings*. Edited and translated by Schubert M. Ogden. Philadelphia: For-
    tress, 1984.
Burney, C.F. "Christ as the ARXH of Creation." *Journal of Theological Studies* 27.106 (1926):
    160–77.
Burtchaell, James Tunstead. *From Synagogue to Church*. Cambridge: Cambridge University
    Press, 1992.
Carruthers, Mary. *The Book of Memory: A Study of Memory in Medieval Culture*. Cambridge:
    Cambridge University Press, 1990.
Clark, Elizabeth. "Creating Foundations, Creating Authorities: Reading Practices and
    Christian Identities." Pages 553–72 in *Religious Identity and the Problem of Historical
    Foundation*. Boston: Brill, 2004.
———. "Origen, the Jews, and the Song of Songs: Allegory and Polemic in Christian An-
    tiquity." Pages 274–93 in *Perspectives on the Song of Songs*. Berlin: Walter de Gruyter,
    2005.
———. *Reading Renunciation: Asceticism and Scripture in Early Christianity*. Princeton:
    Princeton University Press, 1999.
———. "'Spiritual reading': The Profit and Peril of Figurative Exegesis in Early Christian
    Asceticism." Pages 251–74 in *Prayer and Spirituality in the Early Church*. Everton Park,
    Queensland, Australia: Australian Catholic University, 1998.
Childs, Brevard. *Biblical Theology of the Old and New Testaments: Theological Reflection on the
    Christian Bible*. Minneapolis: Fortress, 1992.
Clines, David A.J. "Why Is There a Song of Songs and What Does It Do To You If You
    Read It?" Pages 94–121 in *Interested Parties: The Ideology of Writers and Readers of the
    Hebrew Bible*. Sheffield, UK: Sheffield Academic Press, 1995.
Chapman, Stephen B. "The Canon Debate: What It Is and Why It Matters." *Journal of The-
    ological Interpretation* 4.2 (2010): 273–94.
Collins, John J. "Biblical Theology and the History of Israelite Religion." Pages 24–33 in
    Encounters with Biblical Theology. Minneapolis: Fortress, 2005.
———. *The Bible After Babel: Historical Criticism in a Postmodern Age*. Grand Rapids, MI: Eerd-
    mans, 2005.
Cosgrove, Charles H. "Toward a Postmodern Hermeneutica Sacra: Guiding Considera-
    tions in Choosing Between Competing Plausible Interpretations of Scripture."
    Pages 39–61 in *The Meanings We Choose: Hermeneutical Ethics, Indeterminacy and the
    Conflict of Interpretations*. London: T&T Clark, 2004.
Daley, Brian. "Is Patristic Exegesis Still Usable? Some Reflections on Early Christian In-
    terpretation of the Psalms." Pages 69–88 in *The Art of Reading Scripture*. Edited by
    Ellen Davis and Richard B. Hays. Grand Rapids, MI: Eerdmans, 2003.

Davies, W.D., Dale C. Allison. *A Critical and Exegetical Commentary on the Gospel According to Saint Matthew*. Edinburgh: T&T Clark, 1988.

Dawkins, Richard. *River out of Eden: A Darwinian View of Life*. London: Weidenfeld and Nicholson, 1995.

Dawson, David. "Allegorical Reading and the Embodiment of the Soul in Origen." Pages 26–44 in *Christian Origins: Theology, Rhetoric and Community*. Edited by Lewis Ayres and Gareth Jones. Abingdon, U.K.: Routledge, 1998.

Dawson, John David. *Christian Figural Reading and the Fashioning of Identity*. Berkeley: University of California Press.

Eden, Kathy. *Hermeneutics and the Rhetorical Tradition: Chapters in the Ancient Legacy and Its Humanist Reception*. New Haven: Yale University Press, 1997.

Emmenegger, Joseph. *The Functions of Faith and Reason in the Theology of Saint Hilary of Poitiers*. Washington, DC: Catholic University of America Press, 1947.

Farkasfalvy, Denis. "The Eucharistic Provenance of New Testament Texts." Pages 27–51 in *Rediscovering the Eucharist: Ecumenical Conversations*. Edited by Roch A. Kereszty. Mahwah, NJ: Paulist, 2003.

Farrar, F.W. *History of Interpretation*. London: Macmillan, 1886.

Fee, Gordon. *The First Epistle to the Corinthians*. Grand Rapids, MI: Eerdmans, 1987.

Finn, Leonard. "Reflections on the Rule of Faith." Pages 221–42 in *The Bible as Christian Scripture*. Edited by Christopher Seitz and Kent Harold Richards. Atlanta: Society for Biblical Literature, 2013.

Finn, Thomas M. *Early Christian Baptism and the Catechumenate*. Collegeville, MN: Liturgical Press, 1992.

Fowl, Stephen. *Theological Interpretation of Scripture*. Eugene, OR: Cascade, 2009.

Froehlich, Karlfried. *Biblical Interpretation in the Early Church*. Philadelphia: Fortress, 1984.

Gamble, Harry Y. *Books and Their Readers in the Early Church: A History of Early Christian Texts*. New Haven: Yale University Press, 1995.

———. "The Formation of the New Testament Canon and Its Significance for the History of Biblical Interpretation." Pages 409–29 in *The Ancient Period*, vol. 1 of *A History of Biblical Interpretation*. Edited by Alan J. Hauser and Duane F. Watson. Grand Rapids, MI: Eerdmans, 2003.

———. *The New Testament Canon: Its Making and Meaning*. Philadelphia: Fortress, 1985.

Grant, Robert M. *Irenaeus of Lyon*. London: Routledge, 1997.

Greene-McCreight, K.E. *Ad Litteram: How Augustine, Calvin and Barth read the "Plain Sense" of Genesis 1-3*. Issues in Systematic Theology 5. New York: Peter Lang, 1999.

Hanson, R.P.C. *Allegory and Event*. Louisville: Westminster John Knox Press, 2002.

Hays, Richard B. *Echoes of Scripture in the Letters of Paul*. New Haven: Yale University Press, 1989.

Humphrey, Edith M. *Scripture and Tradition: What the Bible Really Says*. Grand Rapids, MI: Baker Academic, 2013.

Jenson, Robert W. *Canon and Creed*. Louisville: Westminster John Knox Press, 2010.

———. *A Theology in Outline: Can These Bones Live*. Edited by Adam Eitel. New York: Oxford University Press, 2016.

———. *The Triune God*. Vol. 1 of *Systematic Theology*. New York: Oxford University Press, 1997.

Jowett, Benjamin. "On the Interpretation of Scripture." Pages 330–433 in *Essays and Reviews*. London: John W. Parker and Son, 1860.

King, J. Christopher. *Origen on the Song of Songs as the Spirit of Scripture: The Bridegroom's Perfect Marriage Song*. Oxford: Oxford University Press, 2005.

Kolp, A.L. "Partakers of the Divine Nature: The Use of II Peter 1:4 by Athanasius." *Studia Patristica* 17. Oxford: Pergamon Press, 1982.

Kugel, James. *How to Read the Bible: A Guide to Scripture, Then and Now*. New York: Free Press, 2007.

———. *Traditions of the Bible: A Guide to the Bible as It Was at the Start of the Common Era*. Cambridge: Harvard University Press, 1998.

Lambe, Patrick J. "Biblical Criticism and Censorship in Ancien Régime France: The Case of Richard Simon." *Harvard Theological Review* 78 (1985): 149–77.

Legaspi, Michael. *The Death of Scripture and the Rise of Biblical Studies*. Oxford: Oxford University Press, 2010.

Lessing, Gotthold Ephraim. "On the Proof of the Spirit and of Power." Pages 51–56 in *Lessing's Theological Writings*. Edited and translated by Henry Chadwick. Stanford: Stanford University Press, 1956.

Levenson, Jon. *Creation and the Persistence of Evil: The Jewish Drama of Divine Omnipotence*. Princeton: Princeton University Press, 1988.

———. *The Hebrew Bible, the Old Testament, and Historical Criticism*. Louisville: Westminster John Knox Press, 1993.

Levine, Amy-Jill. "Distinct Canons, Distinct Practices." Pages 191–214 in *The Misunderstood Jew: The Church and the Scandal of the Jewish Jesus*. New York: HarperCollins, 2006.

Logan, Alastair H.B. *The Gnostics: Identifying an Early Christian Cult*. London: T&T Clark, 2006.

Louth, Andrew. *Discerning the Mystery*. Oxford: Oxford University Press, 1990.

Lubac, Henri de. *History and Spirit: The Understanding of Scripture According to Origen*. Translated by Anne Englund Nash. San Francisco: Ignatius, 2007.

———. *Medieval Exegesis*, vol. 1. Grand Rapids, MI: Eerdmans, 1998.

———. *Scripture in the Tradition*. Translated by Luke O'Neill. New York: Crossroad, 2000.

Luz, Ulrich. *Matthew 8-20*. Translated by James E. Crouch. Minneapolis: Fortress, 2007.

MacDonald, Nathan. "Israel and the Old Testament Story in Irenaeus's Presentation of the Rule of Faith." *Journal of Theological Interpretation* 3.2 (2009): 281–98.

Margerie, Bertrand de. *An Introduction to the History of Exegesis*, vols. 1–3. Petersham, MA: St. Bede's, 1991–93.

Marshall, I. Howard. *The Pastoral Epistles*. International Critical Commentary Series. Edinburgh: T&T Clark, 1999.

Martens, Peter William. *Origen and Scripture: The Contours of the Exegetical Life*. Oxford: Oxford University Press, 2012.

Martin, Dale. *Pedagogy of the Bible*. Louisville: Westminster John Knox Press, 2008.

Meadowcroft, Tim. "Theological Commentary: A Diversifying Enterprise." *Journal of Theological Interpretation* 7.1 (2013): 133–51.

Metzger, Bruce M. *The Canon of the New Testament: Its Origin, Development, and Significance*. New York and Oxford: Oxford University Press, 1987.

Moberly, R.W.L. *The Bible, Theology, and Faith: A Study of Abraham and Jesus*. Cambridge: Cambridge University Press, 2000.

———. "Biblical Criticism and Religious Belief." *Journal of Theological Interpretation* 2.1 (2008): 71–100.

———. "Christ in All the Scriptures? The Challenge of Reading the Old Testament as Christian Scripture." *Journal of Theological Interpretation* 1.1 (2007): 79–100.

———. "'Interpret the Bible Like Any Other Book'? Requiem for an Axiom." *Journal of Theological Interpretation* 4.1 (2010): 91–110.

———. *Prophecy and Discernment*. Cambridge: Cambridge University Press, 2006.

———. *Theology of Genesis*. Cambridge: Cambridge University Press, 2009.

———. "What Is Theological Interpretation of Scripture?" *Journal of Theological Interpretation* 3.2 (2009): 161–78.

O'Keefe, John J., and R.R. Reno. *Sanctified Vision: An Introduction to Early Christian Interpretation of the Bible*. Baltimore: John Hopkins University Press, 2005.

Räisänen, Heikki, et al. *Reading the Bible in the Global Village: Helsinki*. Society for Biblical Literature: 2000.

Rad, Gerhard von. *Genesis: A Commentary*. Translated by John H. Marks. Revised edition. Old Testament Library. Philadelphia: Westminster, 1972; reprint, 1974.

Radner, Ephraim. *The End of the Church: A Pneumatology of Christian Division in the West*. Grand Rapids, MI: Eerdmans, 1998.

Reno, R.R. *Genesis*. Grand Rapids, MI: Brazos Press, 2010.

Ricoeur, Paul. *The Symbolism of Evil*. New York: Beacon, 1967.

Rombs, Ronnie J., and Alexander Y. Hwang, eds. *Tradition and the Rule of Faith in the Early Church*. Washington: Catholic University of America Press, 2010.

Schneiders, Sandra M. *The Revelatory Text: Interpreting the New Testament as Sacred Scripture*. New York: HarperCollins, 1991.

Seitz, Christopher R. *The Character of Christian Scripture: The Significance of a Two-Testament Bible*. Grand Rapids, MI: Baker Academic, 2011.

———. *World Without End: The Old Testament as Abiding Theological Witness*. Grand Rapids, MI: Eerdmans, 1998.

Shanks, Hershel. "Contrasting Insights of Biblical Giants: BAR Interviews Elie Wiesel and Frank Moore Cross." *Biblical Archaeology Review*, August, 2004.

Sugirtharajah, R.S. "Critics, Tools and the Global Arena." Pages 49–60 in *Reading the Bible in the Global Village: Helsinki*. Atlanta: Society for Biblical Literature, 2000.

Spinoza, Baruch. *Tractatus Theologico-Politicus*. Translated by Samuel Shirley. Leiden: Brill, 1989.

Steenberg, M.C. *Irenaeus on Creation: The Cosmic Christ and the Saga of Redemption*. Supplements to Vigiliae Christianae. Leiden: Brill, 2008.

———. "Linking Beginnings and Ends: Irenaeus of Lyon." Pages 16–54 in *Of God and Man: Theology as Anthropology from Irenaeus to Athanasius*. London: T&T Clark, 2009.

Steinmetz, David. "The Superiority of Pre-Critical Exegesis." *Theology Today* 37 (April 1980): 27–38.

———. "Uncovering a Second Narrative: Detective Fiction and the Construction of Historical Method." Pages 54–68 in *The Art of Reading Scripture*. Edited by Ellen F. Davis and Richard B. Hays. Grand Rapids, MI: Eerdmans, 2003.

Stendahl, Krister. "Biblical Theology, Contemporary." Pages 418–32 in vol. 1 of *Interpreter's Dictionary of the Bible*. Nashville, TN: Abingdon, 1962.

Sundberg, Albert C., Jr. "The Old Testament of the Early Church (A Study in Canon)." Pages 63–84 in *The Bible in the Early Church*. New York: Garland, 1993.

Torjesen, Karen Jo. "'Body', 'Soul', and 'Spirit' in Origen's Theory of Exegesis." Pages 287–301 in *The Bible in the Early Church*. New York: Garland, 1993.

———. *Hermeneutical Procedure and Theological Method in Origen's Exegesis*. Berlin: Walter de Gruyter, 1986.

Torrance, T.F. "Transition to the West: The Interpretation of Biblical and Theological Statements According to Hilary of Poitiers." Pages 392–427 in *Divine Meaning: Studies in Patristic Hermeneutics*. Edinburgh: T&T Clark, 1995.

Treier, Daniel. *Introducing Theological Interpretation of Scripture: Recovering a Christian Practice*. Grand Rapids, MI: Baker Academic, 2008.

Trigg, Joseph. *Origen*. London: Routledge, 1998.

Vessey, Mark. "Jerome and Rufinus." Pages 318–27 in *The Cambridge History of Early Christian Literature*. Edited by Frances Young et al. Cambridge: Cambridge University Press, 2004.

Wall, Robert. "Canonical Context and Canonical Conversations." Pages 165–82 in *Between Two Horizons: Spanning New Testament Studies and Systematic Theology*. Edited by Joel B. Green and Max Turner. Grand Rapids, MI: Eerdmans, 2000.

———. "Reading the Bible from within our Traditions: The 'Rule of Faith' in Theological Hermeneutics." Pages 88–107 in *Between Two Horizons: Spanning New Testament Studies and Systematic Theology*. Edited by Joel B. Green and Max Turner. Grand Rapids, MI: Eerdmans, 2000.

Watson, Francis. *Text, Church and World: Biblical Interpretation in Theological Perspective*. Grand Rapids, MI: Eerdmans, 1994.

———. *Text and Truth: Redefining Biblical Theology*. Grand Rapids, MI: Eerdmans, 1997.

Webster, John. *Holy Scripture: A Dogmatic Sketch*. Cambridge: Cambridge University Press, 2003.

Williams, Daniel. *Ambrose of Milan and the End of the Arian-Nicene Conflicts*. Oxford: Clarendon Press, 1995.

———. "A Reassessment of the Early Career and Exile of Hilary of Poitiers." *Journal of Ecclesiastical History* 42.2 (1991): 202–17.

Witherington, Ben, III. *Conflict and Community in Corinth*. Grand Rapids, MI: Eerdmans, 1995.

Young, Frances. "Alexandrian and Antiochene Exegesis." Pages 334–54 in *The Ancient Period*, vol. 1 of *A History of Biblical Interpretation*. Edited by Alen J. Hauser and Duane F. Watson. Grand Rapids, MI: Eerdmans, 2003.

———. *Biblical Exegesis and the Formation of Christian Culture*. Cambridge: Cambridge University Press, 1997.

———. *Virtuoso Theology: The Bible and Interpretation*. Cleveland, OH: Pilgrim, 1993.

Classic / Patristic Sources

"The Westminster Confession of Faith." *The Constitution of the Presbyterian Church (U.S.A.) Part 1: The Book of Confessions*. Louisville: Office of the General Assembly Presbyterian Church (U.S.A.), 2016.

Augustine of Hippo. *De doctrina Christiana*. Edited and translated by R.P.H. Green. Oxford: Clarendon, 1995.

———. *The Confessions*. Translated by Maria Boulding, O.S.B. and edited by John E. Rotelle, O.S.A. Hyde Park, NY: New City Press, 1997.

———. *Instructing Beginners in Faith*. Translated by Raymond Canning and edited by Boniface Ramsey. Hyde Park, NY: New City Press, 2006.

Hilary of Poitiers. "Letter to the Emperor Constantius." *Hilary of Poitiers: Conflicts of Conscience and Law in the Fourth Century Church*. Translated by Lionel Wickham. Liverpool: Liverpool University Press, 1997.

———. *On the Trinity*. Translated by Stephen McKenna, C.SS.R. Washington, DC: Catholic University of America Press, 1954.

Ignatius of Antioch. *The Epistle to the Ephesians*. Translated by Maxwell Staniforth. London: Penguin, 1968.

Irenaeus of Lyon. *Against the Heresies Book 1*. Translated by Dominic J. Unger, O.F.M. CAP. Ancient Christian Writers 55. New York: Paulist, 1992.

———. *Against the Heresies Book 2*. Translated by Dominic J. Unger, O.F.M. CAP. Ancient Christian Writers 65. New York: Paulist, 2012.

———. *Against the Heresies Book 3*. Translated by Dominic J. Unger, O.F.M. CAP. Ancient Christian Writers 64. New York: Paulist, 2012.

———. *Against the Heresies*. In *The Apostolic Fathers with Justin Martyr and Irenaeus*, vol. 1 of *The Ante-Nicene Fathers*. Edited and translated by Alexander Roberts and James Donaldson. Edinburgh, 1885.

———. *Demonstration of the Apostolic Preaching*. Edited by Iain M. MacKenzie and translated by J. Armitage Robinson. Aldershot, U.K.: Ashgate, 2002.

John Chrysostom, *Homilies on Genesis*. Translated by Robert C. Hill. Washington, DC: Catholic University of America Press, 1986.

Justin Martyr. *The First and Second Apologies*. Translated by Leslie William Barnard. Ancient Christian Writers 56. New York: Paulist, 1997.

Origen of Alexandria. *On First Principles: Being Koetschau's Text of the De Principiis*. Translated by G.W. Butterworth. Gloucester, Mass: Peter Smith, 1973.

———. *The Song of Songs Commentary and Homilies*. Translated by R.P. Lawson. Ancient Christian Writers 26. Westminster, MD: Newman Press and Longmans, 1957.

Pseudo-Dionysius the Areopagite. *The Complete Works*. Translated by Colm Luibheid. Mahwah, NJ: Paulist, 1987.

Index

CPSIA information can be obtained
at www.ICGtesting.com
Printed in the USA
BVHW072007041119
562896BV00001B/2/P

9 781575 069951